MOZART

His Music in his Life

MOZART
His Music in his Life

IVOR KEYS

PAUL ELEK
GRANADA PUBLISHING
London Toronto Sydney New York

To my wife Anne

Granada Publishing Limited
Frogmore, St Albans, Herts AL2 2NF
and
3 Upper James Street, London W1R 4BP
866 United Nations Plaza, New York, NY 10017, USA
117 York Street, Sydney, NSW 2000, Australia
100 Skyway Avenue, Rexdale, Ontario M9W 3A6, Canada
PO Box 84165, Greenside, 2034 Johannesburg, South Africa
CML Centre, Queen & Wyndham Streets, Auckland 1, New Zealand

Published by Granada Publishing in Paul Elek Ltd 1980

Copyright © 1980 Ivor Keys

A passage from *Mozart's Operas* by Edward Dent, © Oxford University Press 1960, is quoted on
page 215 by permission of Oxford University Press. The illustrations supplied by Bärenreiter-
Bildarchiv (see List of Illustrations) all appear in *Mozart und seine Welt in zeitgenössischen
Bildern/Mozart and his World in Contemporary Pictures* (bilingual edition), initiated by Maximilian
Zenger, presented by Otto Erich Deutsch, Bärenreiter, Kassel, Basel, London and New York, 1961.

ISBN 0 236 40056 8

Printed in Great Britain by
Unwin Brothers Limited,
The Gresham Press,
Old Woking, Surrey

Granada ®
Granada Publishing ®

Contents

Illustrations

Introduction

When the late Paul Elek suggested that I could and should write a book about Mozart he charmed me out of hesitations by implying that no-one could claim to love music and yet refuse such a paid labour of love. But the Mozart literature is comprehensive enough to make any part-time writer hesitate. The enquirer after Mozart's toothaches, for example, need look no further than the late Carl Bär's article in *Acta Mozartiana*, volume 3, 1962, starting at page 47, in German. In the circumstances it seemed imperative, if I were not to sink in a morass of preliminary reading or re-reading, to restrict myself almost exclusively to what was written by, to, or about the Mozarts in Wolfgang's lifetime. This was a long but not daunting task, thanks to the great works of documentation listed in the notes at the end of this book. So comprehensive are they that it is highly unlikely to be anyone's fault but mine if anything which purports to be a fact turns out not to be true. By the same token, to give a reference vouching for each fact would mean a morass of footnotes, or at least one numeral for every sentence were the notes banished to the end of the book. Verbal inelegance is an occupational hazard; to add such visual inelegance—in a book on Mozart of all people—seemed to me an unacceptable price for looking scholarly. Notes on sources are given, chapter by chapter, at the end.

Another thing which, with Paul's connivance, this book lacks is a single note of music notation. It is possible to be a music-lover without knowing—or at least wishing to see in a literary work—the symbols which represent an aural experience. Of course the enriching of aural experience is one of the aims of the book, and it is the fruit of reading—analysing if you will—every work which Mozart wrote. The index of works shows that the majority are mentioned. But the usual dual shape of 'life and works' is not used here. The life and the works, with Mozart, are inextricably mingled. The life is the grist of the works, which are for the most part as they are, when they are, and where they are because of the life. But I don't seek to explain the inexplicable wonders, nor to demythologise the miracles of creation.

Since the botanist and mineralogist Ludwig Ritter von Köchel's 'Chronological and thematic index of the complete musical works of Wolfgang Amadé Mozart' was published in Leipzig in 1862, more than a century of research has naturally altered not only some of the chronology but also many other details. But Köchel's original numbering of Mozart's works is used in this book, being sufficient for ordinary purposes.

I thank Antony Wood and Peter Dodd for patient reading and perceptive advice, none the less valuable for not always being taken. I also thank Elizabeth Elek for patience—again that word—and kind encouragement, and I hope she will feel that we have between us done something that Paul would have liked.

IVOR KEYS
Birmingham, January 1979

1

The Father's World

At eight in the evening of 27 January 1756 there arrived what many musicians regard as the greatest human gift so far bestowed on mankind—the boy at that time named by his father as Joannes Chrysostomus Wolfgang Gottlieb. 'John' was many a musician's respected name as well as the first name of the father and maternal grandfather. As for 'Chrysostomus', could anyone—except perhaps Schubert—vie with Mozart as a 'golden mouth'? 'Gottlieb' became the Greek 'Theophilus' and the Latin 'Amadeus', and whether held to be 'God-loving' or 'Beloved by God' the name was equally appropriate—its bearer certainly died young. The 'Wolfgang' remained in lifelong usage. It was the name of the baby's maternal grandfather and the Wolfgangsee was the name of the lake on which stands St Gilgen, in whose district the mother—Anna Maria *née* Pertl—was born.

But the father, Leopold Mozart, Vice-Kapellmeister (Assistant Director of Music) to the Prince-Archbishop of Salzburg, was impatiently awaiting another birth, the appearance in print of his *Versuch einer gründlichen Violinschule* ('Essay on the fundamentals of violin-playing') which Johann Jacob Lotter brought out in the summer of 1756 in Augsburg, Leopold's native city. Affectionate family-man that he was, Leopold must have been realistic enough to suppose that the *Violinschule* was far more likely to bring him immortality than the baby. The pitiless statistics of eighteenth-century childbirth saw to that. In eight and a half years of marriage Wolfgang was Anna Maria's seventh and last child. She was thirty-six years old when she bore him. The only other survivor was the fourth, Maria Anna Walburga Ignatia (or 'Nannerl'), born in 1751. On such a slim thread hangs so much human happiness.

When the prodigious genius of Wolfgang was borne in upon Leopold, his every thought and action was imbued with the necessity to nourish and protect it. We hardly need Leopold's own testimony: 'This matter is my responsibility to almighty God; otherwise I should be the most

ungrateful of his creatures'. If one of us were granted the parenthood of
such a son, which is presumably just as possible in the twentieth as in
the eighteenth century, what should we do about it? The question is
worth asking, because Leopold is often imagined and indeed described
as a bigoted and grasping tyrant, combining smallness of mind with
mediocrity of achievement. Father and son did indeed ultimately and
inevitably go their separate ways, the son to a final poverty that the
father's death spared him the sight of, but we cannot label a mind small
because it could not always grasp what Wolfgang was intuitively and
inexplicably doing. As for explanations on paper, there can be no doubt
with whom, by training, the logical discrimination and literacy in the
wide sense lay. The expert on the handwriting in music and words of
father and son, Wolfgang Plath, whilst acknowledging the places where
the son is copying the father's 'professional' hand, sees the clear contrast
in general between Leopold's persistent clarity, his Jesuit-School-cum-
University literacy of hand and thought, his capacity for calligraphy, and
Wolfgang's hand—more 'modern', imprecise, often large of gesture and
often inconsistent. What is more, there is no evidence of Wolfgang's
having any formal schooling at all. What we do know, and shall see in
this book, is that we have some precious insights into details of Wolfgang's
compositional methods because he reckoned Leopold to be a worthy
recipient of them, both as a professional musician of technical calibre
and as an intimate and loving father, both these capacities having been
proved over and over again. Leopold was indeed uniquely qualified, as
far as qualifications can be measured for a unique task. No other great
composer had a father who was a respectable composer in a wide variety
of genres, an executant and administrator of sufficient skill and authority
to become a Vice-Kapellmeister of a well-found musical establishment
of some hundred players and singers (for all that Wolfgang might
ultimately say of it in pique), and a writer who achieved a European
reputation, the *Violinschule* having been translated into Dutch in 1766
and into French c.1770—it ran to two editions in the original German
in Leopold's lifetime, and he may have seen the third which appeared
in the year of his death, 1787.

Leopold's forbears had lived in and near Augsburg for a century and
a half before he moved to Salzburg. They have been often referred to by
such terms as 'small craftsmen', the trades particularly mentioned being
stone-masons and book-binders, the latter being particularly associated
with Leopold's brothers, father and paternal grandfather. But in this
connection to dissociate 'craftsman' and 'artist' is an anachronistic
Romanticism which is often wide of the mark. Adolf Layer, in *Die
Augsburger Künstlerfamilie Mozart*, has indeed shown some of these

craftsmen to be architects and sculptors of a high order; see for example the three portrait sculptures by Leopold's uncle Franz (1681-1732), the first (c.1716) being the head of St John the Evangelist from a former high altar of the parish church of Deggensdorf, the second (c.1725) St Anna, and the third (c.1735) St Joachim, both from the church of the Sacred Blood at Neukirchen. The speaking beauty of their proportions prompts one to say: if this is mere craftsmanship, let us have more of it. Direct attribution in book-binding is more problematic, but Layer shows a leather book-cover belonging to the Augustiner-Chorherrenstift of St Georg in Augsburg which is very likely to be the work of, or at least representative of, Johann Georg Mozart (1679-1736), Leopold's father. The combination of workmanship, industry and tactful taste is carried on into Leopold's music, even the least serious, and contributes to the unmistakable contempt of both Leopold and Wolfgang for the incompetents and cynics who fall below this level—most often, and least surprisingly, Italian singers, though the French meet hearty chauvinism as well, doubtless reciprocated.

Leopold's education in Augsburg—a twelve-year one—was at the Jesuit school and high-school (Gymnasium and Lyceum) of St Salvator. The foreground subjects were Latin, Greek and Religion, but also taught were History, Geography, Mathematics and 'Physik'. The privilege was not wasted on him, and his leaving certificate from the Lyceum describes him as 'ornatum et eruditum' and, handwritten, as graduating 'magna cum laude'. The names of the classes, such as Rudimenta, Grammatica, Lesser Syntax, Greater Syntax, Humanity, show a progression up to the topmost class of Rhetoric. This was not a façade of an empty tradition. The stress laid on stage performances, usually with singing as well as speech, made clear the classical aim of a disciplined bodily demeanour allied to an incisive but balanced mind and crowned by a persuasive literacy, powerful because of the pinpointing of ample resources. These were the qualities for the service of church and state that the Jesuit Fathers foresaw and hoped for in their pupils. Leopold's stage debut for St Salvator was in 1724, two months before his fifth birthday, as the youngest in the cast of a tragedy called 'Paulinus'. It was doubtless this and subsequent stage experiences that not only gave him sympathetic insight into Wolfgang's operatic problems but encouraged him to let Wolfgang tread the boards, also at the age of five, in a school-drama 'Sigismund King of Hungary' by the then organist of Salzburg Cathedral, Johann Ernst Eberlin, who a decade before Leopold had also learnt his stagecraft at St Salvator. Leopold's farewell Augsburg performance was at the end of the school year (early September) of 1735. The piece was the tragedy 'Cussero', the story of the rebellious son of King Selymus.

From the title-page of the libretto can be seen that it was played to
separate audiences of men and women, and a list of the large cast of
actors and singers shows Leopold among the latter taking the conspicuous
part of Phaëton, the rebellious heaven-storming charioteer in the parallel
classical legend drawn from Ovid's *Metamorphoses* which served as sung
Prologue and Intermezzo to the spoken drama.

We have evidence that Leopold also sang as a boy in two principal
Augsburg churches, St Ulrich and Sacred Blood, both places of pilgrimage
with considerable music. In a letter to Wolfgang in 1777 he remembers
singing a cantata in St Ulrich at the wedding of Hofrat Öfele to 'the
beautiful Lepin, a merchant's daughter, who sang well, played the clavier
and had 30,000 florins' (how typical a remark!). Wolfgang two days
before had written of the admiring surprise with which he had just heard
of his father's dashing organ technique as a boy in Augsburg.

Leopold's classical education shows not only in quotations from Horace
and (in Greek) from Homer in the *Violinschule*, though this must be one
of the last instrumental 'tutors' to use them. An attitude of mind combined
with an attitude to life are enshrined in two Greek proverbs which
survive in the Oxford Dictionary of Quotations and, if I may be personal,
in the relics of even an English classical education, which must have
been the commonplaces of pedagogues throughout Europe—and which
resound in what Leopold and Wolfgang have to say to each other. In a
sense the classical style is built on them. One is γνῶθι σεαυτόν (know
thyself), an anonymous inscription from a temple in Delphi, quoted in
Juvenal's Satires, xi, 27. How one feels for both the frantic father and
the sublimely ingenuous son when Leopold writes (16 February 1778):
'It is your own good heart which makes you give your complete trust and
love to anyone who unreservedly praises you . . . whereas, as a boy, your
modesty was so extreme that you began at once to weep when you were
overpraised. The greatest art is to learn to know yourself, and then, my
dear son, do as I and study other people so as to know them well.'

The second maxim is the anonymous μηδὲν ἄγαν (nothing in excess),
quoted by Plato in Protagoras, 343b. Lovers of Handel will remember
how Jennens, his frequent librettist, dexterously arranged for him an
alternation and amalgam of Milton's *L'Allegro* and *Il Penseroso*, and
then in typical eighteenth-century fashion added a third part: *Il Moderato*,
a paean which Handel found rather hard going. But the underlying
wisdom of the maxim was vital, whether confined to matters of technique
or expression, or applied to the all-important balancing, and rendering
coherent, of the drama inherent in the new classical style, which both
Leopold and Wolfgang must have had in the back of their minds when
they discussed the matter of *il filo* (the thread). To take only two of

Leopold's remarks that could have been made by either of them: 'Performers there are who vibrate on every note as if afflicted with the palsy.' 'A Virtuoso of the imagination often takes half a bar over a semi-quaver in an *adagio cantabile* before recovering from his paroxysm of feeling; he cares nothing about the time; he plays in recitative.'

But perhaps the most typical and revealing quotation is that which Leopold chose to put beneath his portrait which served as a frontispiece to the *Violinschule*. It is a quotation from 'Cicero', from a treatise on Rhetoric addressed to Herennius (*Rhetorica ad Herennium*, 3 XV). It is not now accepted as a genuine work of Cicero, but was certainly accepted in the canon, and was doubtless required reading, when Leopold reached the class of Rhetoric in his last year at St Salvator. It may be translated: 'It is therefore fitting in the matter of gesture [posture for a violinist] not to show either conspicuous charm or slovenliness, lest we should look like either actors or workmen.' This middle line resounds again and again in Leopold's advice to Wolfgang. Looking at the attitude reflected down the long nose of Leopold in the frontispiece, one is tempted to think that a shade more 'conspicuous charm' and less disdain might have brought him something higher than a dead-end vice-kapellmeistership (and indeed to Wolfgang some other professional fate, for that matter).

As Leopold says in his preface to the *Violinschule*, it owes its impulse to the Berlin musical theorist F.W. Marpurg, who published a reference 'periodical' from 1754 onwards entitled *Historisch-kritische Beyträge zur Aufnahme der Musik* ('Historical-critical contributions to the advancement of music'). Marpurg there praises two recent German treatises, one dated 1752 on flute-playing by Quantz, Frederick the Great's flautist, and the other on keyboard-playing by Carl Philipp Emanuel Bach, the redoubtable second son of Johann Sebastian (1753). Marpurg then deplores the lack of a similar work for violinists. His periodical carried in 1757 the first, and very enthusiastic, review of the *Violinschule*. Like the other two treatises it is far more than a mere guide to instrumental mechanics; it is a precious key to the style of the day not only in such matters as the treatment of dotted notes and ornaments (with which, incidentally, there is no evidence that Wolfgang and his music disagreed) but also in the broader aspects of musicianship, in divining the emotional expression and the tempo (nothing in excess!), and with a passionate insistence, which Wolfgang echoes, on playing in time. It is both modernist and wry. A cursory description of old time-signatures ends with the sentence: 'As however it no longer serves any purpose to scribble down their poor obsolete stuff, amateurs are referred to the ancient writings themselves.' And in the same vein: 'If it be true that the Greek music healed diseases, then should our modern music call even the dead from their coffins.' Some exercises are introduced: 'Here are the pieces for practice. The more uncongenial they are the more am I pleased, for that is what I intended to make them.'

The pieces themselves, duets for pupil and teacher, are short and shapely, and the workmanship of their counterpoint is impeccable, but there is hardly a trace of the limpid melodiousness that we loosely call 'Mozartian'. But the latter style, basically of 'tune' and accompaniment, can only be rendered as an unaccompanied duet by a technical tour de force, as indeed Wolfgang achieved in the duets for violin and viola, K.423 and 424. Leopold could however adopt the new-fangled melodious style, especially in the soprano solos into which concerted religious music of the time was wont to relax, and it is significant that similarities of handwriting and other accidents caused works written by Leopold to be published as early works of Wolfgang in the original nineteenth-century collected edition. As a composer Leopold could well have referred the middle-line maxim of μηδὲν ἄγαν to himself as he steered a course between the dense workmanship of the dying baroque style and the dangerous simplifications of the new rococo charm—a course for which there were no charts, Haydn and Wolfgang not yet having made them.

Evidence that he took himself seriously as a composer can be seen in the autobiographical contribution to Marpurg's bulletin he made in the 'Account of the present conditions of the music of his Grace the Archbishop of Salzburg in 1757', where a lengthy paragraph enumerates 'Herr Mozart's compositions which have become known in manuscript, the most noteworthy being many contrapuntal and ecclesiastical works [N.B. the 'modern' implication that ecclesiastical music was not necessarily contrapuntal]; further a large number of symphonies ... over thirty grand Serenades ... many Concertos ... countless Trios and Divertimenti ... twelve Oratorios and a multitude of theatrical works ...' The list does not disdain to mention 'Turkish music' (pre-echoes of *Die Entführung*, the Violin Concerto in A, K.219, and the Piano Sonata in A, K.331?), 'music for a metal piano' (the keyed glockenspiel of *The Magic Flute?*), and finally 'a Sledge-Drive with five sledge-bells, not to speak of Marches ...'. For a pictorial supplement to this list we may look again at the frontispiece to the *Violinschule* bearing in mind that here was Leopold's one guaranteed opportunity of presenting himself seriously in print to the world at large, apart from such things as the *Peasant's Wedding* (also in the hands of the *Violinschule* publisher). Catching the eye on the left-hand side are: Sinfonia, Fuge, Missae, Offert[orium], Pastorell, Trio, and on the right: Divert[imento] and March[e]—the last could hardly be English at that date, and the spelling

Left: Portrait sculpture by Leopold's uncle, Franz Mozart: Saint Joachim, in the church of the Sacred Blood, Neukirchen (see page 15)

Right: Even if it cannot be proved that this example of bookbinding in leather preserved at Augsburg is by Leopold's father, it undoubtedly shows the expected standard of craftsmanship and artistry, well beyond the workaday implications of our word 'bookbinder' (see page 15)

St Salvator's College, Augsburg, scene of Leopold's twelve-year Jesuit education

The handsomely engraved frontispiece of Leopold's *Violinschule*. The author is supported by his quotation from 'Cicero' (see page 17) and surrounded by numerous categories of his music

Siegmund Christoph von Schrattenbach, Prince-Archbishop of Salzburg from 1753 to 1771

Melchior Küsell's engraving, dated about 1680, of the interior of Salzburg cathedral (see page 28)

2

The Salzburg Heritage

1756–63

In the mid-eighteenth-century, as indeed for a century before that, a musician, whether composer or director of music or rank-and-file performer, would be paid by authorities of church and state, and the kind of music demanded of him would vary accordingly. The freelance travelling virtuoso hardly existed outside the select ranks of international opera-stars. Public concerts, in the sense that all and sundry paid for tickets and sustained their cost irrespective of a lead and a subsidy from an aristocracy, were almost unknown; exceptionally in England a mercantile middle class had since Purcell's day been wealthy and independent enough to indulge its taste for listening to professional music outside the opera-house, and indeed a famous partnership in London concert-giving, that of J.C. Bach and C.F. Abel, began a few months before the Mozarts arrived there in 1764. The career of this English Bach's father, Johann Sebastian, shows the church/state alternative with drastic clarity; as Kapellmeister to the Calvinist Duke of Cöthen from 1717 to 1723 he was not called upon for concerted church music, but instead produced the central core of his instrumental works—concertos, chamber music, the first book of the '48'—whereas the moment he left Cöthen for St Thomas's, Leipzig he threw himself into a round of composition and direction which produced for a start both settings of the Passion and five cycles (mostly of new composition) of cantatas for the church's year.

Salzburg in Mozart's day never had an opera-house. How different his life might have been if it had! But this apart its numerous and skilled musical establishment was kept busy by the conflation of religious and secular duties caused by the Archbishop being at the same time a prince of the Church and a prince of the Empire. The Archbishops' political independence from Vienna varied inversely with the Imperial fortunes in war and finance, but it had been a recognised independence since Rudolf of Habsburg made them princes in 1278. This position obtained until the see was secularised in 1802. The principal venue for the church-

27

and-state ceremonies detailed in the Church and Court Calendar was the great seventeenth-century cathedral built after the style of St Peter's, Rome. An engraving of c.1680 by Melchior Küsell shows such an occasion, with musicians prominent in the galleries. For the Mozarts the traditional style of cathedral church music would be that of the restrained contrapuntal weaving of vocal strands in what the eighteenth century took to be sixteenth-century style. It was not only performed in church but was the staple preliminary discipline of any serious composer intent on a technique. Mozart acquired it from his father, and from painstaking observation of others' efforts in the strict style—indeed one of its names was *stile osservato*. Wolfgang never lost his respect for the required skills of contrapuntal manipulation—the deliberate re-use of an archaic subject in the Requiem's Kyrie and the *jeux d'esprit* in the finale of the 'Jupiter' symphony hardly need mentioning—and the mental juggling involved is paralleled by his fondness for the mathematical brain-teasers he asked his sister to send him during his first journey to Italy.

But the 'state' element required the enrichment of orchestral sound. This could be done at a fairly simple level by duplicating the upper voice parts, sometimes an octave higher, by the sheen of the violins, and by letting the orchestra play preludes and interludes. At the far end of this process such concerted church music could take on the guise of a symphony with voices thrown in. The classical symphony in the hands of Haydn and Mozart is essentially a quick-moving drama of contrasts, an antithesis to the uniform stereotype of seamless contrapuntal weaving. The search for an equilibrium between these forces was a preoccupation of the eighteenth-century Salzburg cathedral composers down to Mozart's day. A very respectable line they were, including Leopold, and all setting about their task with Teutonic workmanship and professional effectiveness. One way to this equilibrium was to make no bones about the reserving of some sections for the old-style contrapuntal treatment, making a 'set-piece', for instance 'Pignus futurae gloriae', the penultimate section of a Litany of the Blessed Sacrament. But an up-to-date seductively irresistible element was also at hand to reassert the primacy of the voice—the Italian opera style, with its mingling of the virtuosic and the sweet, coming into Teutonic music like a beaker full of the warm south. Had Salzburg possessed an opera-house it is very likely that its proximity to Italy would have helped ensure the appointment of an Italian to the Kapellmeister's position earlier than 1763, when Lolli succeeded Eberlin, a move which permitted Leopold's promotion to Vice-Kapellmeister.

A few church works of Carl Heinrich Biber (Kapellmeister 1743–49) and Johann Ernst Eberlin (1749–62) are in print (in the series *Denkmäler der Tonkunst in Österreich*, volume 80), and they show the transition between old and new styles. Biber was the son of the famous violinist-composer Heinrich Biber. His 'Missa Brevis sanctorum septem dolorum B.M.V.' (1731) contains contrapuntal choral movements whose sober rhetoric reminds us that Bach was his contemporary, but it also includes combinations of the four solo voices which are constantly and dexterously changing. As a 'Missa Brevis' it has to cover a lot of textual ground quickly, which inevitably means a more chordal, modern style, and here the music is held together by telling figures on the first and second violins—as in much Salzburg music, there is no written-out part for violas. It is interesting that the set of performance-material has on its cover 'Dura 12 minutte'; perhaps the brevity prized by Wolfgang's Archbishop Colloredo was already in demand.

Eberlin was a composer respected by both Leopold and Wolfgang, and in his motet 'Quae est ista' in the *DTÖ* volume referred to above we see the Italian opera making more obvious inroads. Most of it is a love-duet continuing the cross-fertilisation (established in the Middle Ages) of religious love—of the Blessed Virgin, or of Christ and the church as his bride—with the images and music of secular love. Here the soprano is the love-lorn believer and the alto the consoling Mary. The duet, mainly in thirds, is a most graceful halfway-house; more sheerly charming, perhaps, than Bach's religious love-duets, and having the sweetness but perhaps not the dash of Dorabella and Fiordiligi in *Così fan tutte*. The violins contribute charming runs and shakes, another pre-view of *Così*. The complementing or setting of the emotional scene by the orchestra is an obvious strong-point of Eberlin's, notable also in his oratorio settings. Another *DTÖ* volume, No. 55, contains extracts from the school-drama 'Sigismundus' which the five-year-old Wolfgang performed in, but also a complete oratorio whose literally-translated title is 'The blood-sweating Jesus'. The very title shows how far the personal religious reaction has supplanted the communal-traditional one, and indeed it fits with the use of oratorios as substitutes for operas in Lent. With Eberlin the spectacular and detailed comments of the orchestra do much to tighten the emotional screw, particularly in accompanied recitative. The ordinary means of dispatching narrative or dialogue, as opposed to arias, was *recitativo secco* (literally 'dry'), whereby the musical declamation, being merely accompanied by a chordal instrument with, say, a cello reinforcing the bass, permitted a brisk delivery without complications of ensemble. But the orchestrally accompanied recitative both enriched and slowed the music and greatly raised its emotional power. This was a resource young Wolfgang was quick to use, and it is the presence on his doorstep of Eberlin and what must have been good string players (to have encompassed such music) that set him on his way.

But it was to Leopold himself that Wolfgang owed not only an outstandingly devoted and meticulously organised international education, but also the home lessons on violin and keyboard (the latter doubtless shared with his sister) and in counterpoint and composition. One cannot help feeling that if Leopold's name had not been 'Mozart' more of his music would be available in print. Volume 9/ii of the *DTÖ* gives a selection of them. Two keyboard sonatas of 1762 show 'Mozartisms'; the last movement of that in F is a *Presto* interrupted by a minuet-like *Andante grazioso*, a precursor of such interruptions in Wolfgang's violin and other concertos; and the B flat sonata delays the cadences in its last movement, as countless of Wolfgang's arias were to do, by spectacularly jumping up from the expected last note to repeat the approach. The Divertimento for String Trio in G (1760) has a minuet and trio in G minor in the truly pathetic style which Wolfgang was to make his own in that key. The satirical high-jinks and buffoonery which obviously ran in the family in both musical and verbal forms come out in a truly funny Sinfonia Burlesca (1760 again) with no violins (to have the violas leading is presumably part of the burlesque), wrong-note cadences and a general disproportion and irrelevance which stands out in someone not given to either. In serious vein the Litany of the Blessed Sacrament (c.1768) contains in its 'Viaticum' a powerful short funeral march which would not be out of place alongside Wolfgang's C minor Mass, and its fugal 'Pignus' is a well-sustained and varied contrapuntal argument which must have achieved some fame as several old manuscript copies of it exist. At this level and in this genre Leopold had every right to appear on the same programme as his son (in Munich on New Year's Day, 1775), and one of his offertories, *Convertentur Sedentes,* was good enough to be mistakenly printed, as K.177, in the original complete edition of Mozart.

Archbishop Schrattenbach, all things considered, dealt justly and humanely with the unusual family. They lived on the third floor of 9 Getreidegasse (the upper of the two floors now devoted to the birthplace museum). This they rented from a grocery merchant, Johann Lorenz Hagenauer, who lived below, and who was sufficiently prosperous to own numbers 7 and 8 and a suburban house in Nonntal, then on the leafy outskirts of the city though only just on the far side of the fortress-dominated Hohensalzburg. Contemporary portraits of Hagenauer and his wife show them as solid citizens indeed. Hagenauer helped Leopold through the financial complexities of the international journeys, and it is clear from Leopold's letters to both husband and wife that the families were intimately friendly, sharing jokes, pastimes, gossip and solicitudes for the Mozarts' canary. Looking at the rooms today we can admire the concentration and orderliness and family equanimity which both Mozart parents must have contributed to the making of a happy home there which also had to serve for authorship, composition and teaching. Of southward view there was little, but northward towards the river Salzach which divided the town there was the open space then called Löchelplatz but now, appropriately, Hagenauerplatz.

How the first signs of Wolfgang's musical genius must have thrilled and transformed the life and ambitions of Leopold! Indeed it would hardly be an exaggeration to say that thereafter the father only lived for, and had ambitions for, the son—but we must not forget that Nannerl showed sufficient gifts on the keyboard to demand of Leopold their professional nurture. But Leopold's proud annotations of Nannerl's music book tell their own tale: for instance, 'This Minuet and Trio was learnt by Wolfgangerl inside half an hour on 26 January 1761, a day before his 5th birthday, at about 9.30 at night.'

The first of the journeys involving Wolfgang took place in January 1762 when Leopold took the two children to Munich to appear before the Elector of Bavaria. We have no details of this, and need not suppose that Wolfgang remembered anything significant about it. But we must face here the question why the journeys took place which, with or without Leopold, were to occupy so much of the next twenty years of Wolfgang's life. Some writers, followed by much sentimental opinion, have seen Leopold's share as an exploitation verging on tyranny. But one had to make money in order to make the journeys, and the frequent and detailed references to money in Leopold's letters back to Salzburg from the London expedition, for example, are both explained and necessitated by their being addressed to Hagenauer, whose arrangements for credit, to say nothing of friendly trust, depended on such knowledge. The earlier journeys, such as the first encounter with the Imperial court in Vienna later in 1762, were an attempt to impress upon the powers most directly to hand the gift (and therefore the responsibilities) bestowed on them. The much longer journey to Paris and London appealed to Europe's recognition as a further claim on the home powers, but also afforded the precious experiences of musical grist to Wolfgang's mill, that extraordinarily prehensile and quick-moving mind that justified such an undertaking at an age some ten years younger than would befit a young nobleman on the European Grand Tour. The Italian journeys add specific hopes, all dashed, of appointments in the country which most musicians regarded as the centre of the musical world. Wolfgang's final journey to Paris without Leopold represents a more hectic, less systematic attempt to escape Salzburg, which sometimes includes despairing cross-purposes between father and son. Leopold doubtless made mistakes. He seems sometimes to have had one skin too few. To his own tireless sense of responsibility Wolfgang's tendency to happy heedlessness appeared, in the end, as sheer fecklessness. The unprecedented gifts were ultimately too much for father and son.

So, then, the education proceeded with a visit to Vienna involving the whole family's absence from Salzburg from 18 September 1762 to 5 January 1763. With them went as factotum Joseph Estlinger, who was also a bassoonist and music copyist. The journey involved no leave from school; there is indeed, as already stated, nothing to show that Wolfgang had any formal schooling in his life. We know from Leopold's letters to Hagenauer that he had twinges of gout en route, that Wolfgang caught a cold at Linz, and that they had a wet steamer journey by the ordinary boat. A charming indication of family intimacy occurs in the letter of 16 October: 'We ask God to keep her [Frau Hagenauer] and all her loved ones well and strong for many future years and to invite us all in due course to play cards in Heaven.' Wolfgang eased their way through the customs by giving the officer a minuet on his little fiddle and the main object of the expedition was achieved: the Mozarts were received at court at Schönbrunn by Francis I and Maria Theresa, and Wolfgang must have been one of the few of Maria Theresa's subjects to give her a hearty kiss. What is more, the Empress sent both children gala court costumes. Leopold again: 'Wolfgang's is of the finest lilac-coloured cloth. The waistcoat is moiré of the same shade, and both coat and waistcoat are trimmed with wide double gold braid. It was made for Archduke Maximilian. Nannerl's dress was the court dress of an Archduchess and is of white broché taffeta with all kinds of trimming.' Wolfgang's dress is shown in a portrait, probably the work of Pietro Lorenzoni, made in Salzburg in 1763. After a second visit to Schönbrunn Wolfgang had to spend ten days in bed with a rash (*erythema nodosum*) caused by a streptococcal allergy. Concerts by the children helped pay the family's way; one of them evoked a printed poem by Puffendorff in honour of Wolfgang, and another, given before the French Ambassador, brought an invitation to Versailles, shortly to be followed up. Leopold, at least, heard Gluck's *Orfeo* at the opera and it is not unlikely that Wolfgang heard something of it, perhaps at rehearsal.

A Viennese correspondent, quoted in the *Augsburgischer Intelligenz-Zettel* of 10 May 1763, voices the astonished admiration that was to greet the children, but of course Wolfgang especially, wherever they went, London included. Gifted pianist that she was, Nannerl will have to excuse us for concentrating on her brother:

We fall into utter amazement on seeing a boy aged 6 at the clavier and hear him, not by any means toy with sonatas, trios and concertos, but play in a manly way, and improvise moreover for hours on end out of his own head, now *cantabile*, now in chords, producing the best of ideas according to the taste of today; and even accompany at sight symphonies, arias and recitatives at the great concerts . . . . Furthermore, I saw and heard how, when he was made to listen in another room, they would give him notes, now high, now low, not only on the pianoforte but on every other imaginable instrument as well, and he came out with the letter or the name of the note in an instant.

Soon after their return to Salzburg the birthday (28 February) of the Archbishop was celebrated in two ways: first by promotions, including, to Leopold's relieved gratification, his own to Vice-Kapellmeister, second by a gala-dress assembly of the Court (the Vienna dresses doubtless to hand) at which, says the Court chronicle, both the children played to everyone's astonishment, 'so that the birthday celebrations had a happy end'. Schrattenbach's generosity of spirit contributed to the happiness; he had after all rewarded more than three months' absence with promotion, and Leopold's cup must have been full enough for the time being.

3

The Great Family Journey

1763–66

The invitation of the French Ambassador in Vienna bore quick fruit in Leopold's mind. He must have determined upon, and made plans for, the family trip immediately. It was the act of a brave man and a trusting wife to embark upon the physical discomforts, even dangers, and the financial risks such an adventure entailed. Yet even in February Leopold was writing to his Augsburg publisher Lotter that he expected to see him soon en route to fulfilling their undertaking to the Ambassador. 'We are only awaiting the arrival of the swallows.'

They set out in their coach on 9 June with Sebastian Winter as servant and hairdresser. At Wasserburg, some forty miles north-west of Salzburg, they had an enforced stay with a broken wheel, and Wolfgang took the opportunity to play the organ. Leopold explained the use of the pedals, but Wolfgang's legs were not long enough to play them sitting down, whereupon he pushed the seat back and gave a standing performance (*stante pede*, as Latinist Leopold has it). They spent the first day after their arrival in Munich visiting one of the most notable emulations of Versailles, the Nymphenburg palace and park and bath-room of the Elector of Bavaria, and immediately that evening they were summoned to perform for him. It would be hard to imagine a more elegant background, or more in keeping with the lighter style of 'modern' mid-century musical taste. The stay at 'The Golden Stag' was lengthened by awaiting a second command performance presenting Nannerl, who was crowded out by Wolfgang at the first. Throughout the journey Leopold took notes, mainly of names and places, but we are also able to see some of the journey through Nannerl's eyes, through her intermittent diary. What struck her in the Nymphenburg included the Amalienburg with its kitchen 'where the princess herself has cooked', the marble bath of the Badenburg, and the 'chapel made of shells'.

So to the 'Three Moors' at Leopold's birthplace, Augsburg, where the children gave three concerts, Leopold going out of his way to remark to

The Mozarts' kitchen at 9 Getreidegasse

The Mozarts' Salzburg landlord and friend, the grocery merchant Johann Lorenz Hagenauer, and his wife Theresia

This oil-painting dated 1763, probably by Pietro Lorenzoni, shows the court-dress given to Wolfgang by the Empress Maria Theresa (see page 32). The sword was obligatory but presumably not dangerous

The sort of scene to which Wolfgang and Nannerl contributed at the Nymphenburg Palace, Munich (see page 34)

The Hall of Mirrors of the Amalienburg, a hunting-lodge of the Nymphenburg Palace. It was built by François Cuvilliés in 1734/9, and shows rococo architecture and decoration at its zenith

In this picture of a musical tea-party *chez* Prince Louis-François de Conti, painted by Michel Ollivier in 1766, there is doubtless some sentimental licence in making ten-year-old Wolfgang so diminutive a figure at the keyboard

The watercolour of Leopold, Wolfgang and Nannerl painted by Louis de Carmontelle (see page 41) at Baron Grimm's instigation. Nannerl's long dress sets off Wolfgang's short legs

Hagenauer that the audiences were almost entirely Lutheran. For keyboard practice on the tour he bought from the maker Stein a portable clavichord (he called it 'Clavierl').

At Ludwigsburg the family met the celebrated opera-composer Jommelli, whom Leopold suspected of obstructing their getting a quick hearing from the Duke of Württemberg. He went further and suspected Jommelli of helping Italian musicians to 'do down' the Germans in their own country. But they also heard and enjoyed the playing of the Italian violinist Nardini. By 14 July they were in Schwetzingen, the summer residence of the Elector of Mannheim, about nine miles away. Here they heard for the first time the admirable flautist Wendling, whose family were to be intertwined with the Mozarts much later on. But, perhaps more important, they heard the Mannheim orchestra, which Leopold roundly declares as 'the best in Germany. It wholly consists of people who are young and upright, not drunkards, gamblers and rakes.' This letter ends with a tribute he was not to pay in Paris, but which reflects the Elector Karl Theodor's enthusiasm for bringing Versailles to Mannheim: 'it is time to go to the French theatre, which could not be bettered, especially in its ballets and music'.

At Heidelberg they inevitably went to see the Great Tun, the recently installed huge wine-barrel. Nannerl's diary naturally mentions it. But it was then quite a recent tourist attraction, the Elector Karl Theodor having built it in 1751. At Mainz there were two foretastes of things English. Nannerl had a present of an English hat, whose floppy wide brim was in marked contrast to the Salzburg caps which dragged the hair back close to the skull. It was doubtless the sort of thing which so charmingly crowns Gainsborough's portraits. Leopold comments on Nannerl's hat: 'if we had been walking the streets of Salzburg there would have been as great a commotion of sight-seers as if a rhinoceros had arrived.' Englishmen staying at their hotel evoke his comment on the grotesque length of English clothing, and the following rings very true: 'one of them at least every other day went to swim in the Main before dinner and arrived at table like a baptised mouse.' The Mozarts left their heavy baggage at Mainz and paid a visit, by boat, to Frankfurt on Main. Here at the lodging in 3 Bendergasse we see Leopold as a posterity-conscious vandal, for he scratched the following on a window there: 'Mozart Maitre de la Musique de la Chapelle de Salzburg avec Sa Famile le 12 Aout 1763.' The Historisches Museum at Frankfurt now houses the *graffiti*.

At least five concerts were given in Frankfurt, and at one of them one wonder-boy was heard by another. Goethe told Eckermann in 1830: 'I still quite clearly remember the little fellow with his wig and his sword.'

Beset by bad weather they went down the Rhine to Cologne where Leopold commented adversely on the cathedral: 'dirty', 'God's temple looking like a stable' and the 'singing being mere howling'. Of more than a month's stay in Brussels little is recorded, but a keyboard sonata *allegro* in C was written into Nannerl's music book by Leopold and recorded as 'di Wolfgango Mozart, 14 October 1763 in Bruxelles'. This with two other movements from the same book was furnished with an accompanying violin part and became, with a new final *allegro*, the first published work, K.6. But these attributions must be taken with a pinch of salt. The *allegro* of K.8—'di Wolfgango Mozart à Paris le 21 Novembre 1763'—is claimed by modern criticism to have been actually composed by Leopold. Further, even if this were not the case, we should still be left to conjecture by what sifting these early pieces reached the manuscript page, let alone the printed one. The brilliant and exact studies of Wolfgang Plath have at any rate established to a large extent what early works are in the handwriting of father or son, or indeed of both or neither of them, the latter being of obvious importance in the matter of authenticity.

The family arrived in Paris on 18 November 1763, and their initial welcome was a German-speaking one. The Bavarian ambassador, Count van Eyck, took the family into upstairs lodging in his residence called the Hotel de Beauvais, and the Countess who was a native of Salzburg lent them her two-manual harpsichord. They were also befriended and energetically championed by the writer and literary critic Friedrich Melchior von Grimm, to whom we owe vivid descriptions of what Wolfgang could do. 'It means little for this child to perform the most difficult pieces with the greatest accuracy, with hands that can scarcely stretch a sixth; but what is really incredible is to see him improvising for an hour at a time giving rein to his inspiration and to a mass of enchanting ideas, which moreover he knows how to connect with taste and clarity.' 'I wrote him a minuet tune and asked him to put a bass to it; he took a pen and without approaching the harpsichord, fitted the bass.' 'He knows the keyboard so well that when it is hidden by a cloth he plays on this cloth with the same speed and precision.' This latter was a party-trick that both Nannerl and he were to captivate the London public with.

Earlier in the same year (1763) came the end of the Seven Years War, in which France had been a member of an alliance whereby Maria Theresa had sought to curb the ambitions of Frederick the Great of Prussia. Almost needless to say, England had joined the opposite side to the French, and by acquiring French Canada and, in effect, command of India, had acquired disproportionate spoils, when the others had to content themselves with little more than the *status quo ante*. It might be thought that the German-speaking Mozarts would meet more xenophobia than usual in Paris, the language representing either the enemy Prussia or the inefficient ally, Austria. But though it had been, to an unprecedented extent, a 'world war' the eighteenth century saw to it that it was kept in its place. Frederick had built himself a 'Versailles' at Potsdam with a French name—Sans Souci—and an obligatory use of French by his court. Paris in a sense reciprocated by housing and esteeming composers who were Teutonic by birth and French by manners—Schobert, Eckardt, Honauer and Raupach. Pieces by these four figure in the pasticcio piano concertos (K.37, 39, 40, 41) which Leopold and Wolfgang were to arrange between them on their return to Salzburg, and Schobert and Eckardt are amongst those who presented their published compositions to the children, thereby doubtless sparking off Leopold's publication at his own expense of four sonatas for keyboard 'which can be played with violin accompaniment'. The first two (K.6 and 7) were dedicated as op. I to Madame Victoire, the second of the four daughters of Louis XV whom Leopold called 'le [sic] 4 Mesdames de France' in his travel notes; the dedication speaks of 'the kindnesses with which you have loaded me'. The pair forming op. II (K.8 and 9) were dedicated to the Countess de Tessé, both dedications being the work of Grimm. The modern piano and violin having gone their separate assertive ways, the notion of the former being 'accompanied' by the latter may seem odd. But the harpsichord or indeed the emerging piano could both have their tone enriched by the violin, which in the years before the demands of the concert-hall led to higher bridges and metal strings was able to merge discreetly with the tone of either keyboard instrument particularly in the 'tune' register (the octave and a half above middle C) which stood in most need of warmth and carrying power. The charming water-colour made by Carmontelle immediately the Mozarts arrived gives some idea of the combination, though it also includes Nannerl singing. It is this picture which Leopold had engraved by Delafosse in 1764 and used for publicity and for sale as a souvenir in London.

The four sonatas each have a pair of minuets. One briefly explores the plaintive depths of B flat minor—the five flats momentarily furrowing the painted brows of the salons— and in the last, with no time for proof-reading, Wolfgang according to Leopold let slip some bad musical grammar, 'which at least shows that he wrote the sonatas', a statement which incidentally does not accord with Leopold's authorship of the first movement of K.8. Schobert, whose melodic grace and clarity of design sets him above the other émigré composers, has a connection with op. II, for he was the musician to Prince Conti, whose mistress was the dedicatee, the Countess de Tessé. A thin-skinned suspicion caused Leopold to call Schobert base ('niedertrechtige', underlined), but Wolfgang seems to have admired his music. Indeed it is Leopold who uses some chauvinism-in-reverse towards things French. On their piety: 'I can assure you it is not difficult to fathom out the miracles of the French women saints; those who work the greatest wonders are neither virgins, nor wives, nor widows, and all the wonders occur while the body is still alive.' On the singing in Versailles chapel: 'Everything sung by individuals and supposed to resemble an aria was empty, frozen and wretched—in a word, French. But the choruses are good.' It must be remembered that artistic Paris was still hotly engaged in the aesthetic battle between Italian and French musical style, a battle in which Grimm took a prominent anti-French part, and that for Leopold, stoutly patriotic though he was, only the Italians could and should win.

But royal receptions at Versailles could not suffice. The Mozarts also depended on recognition in the salons of Paris. The scene is conjured up by a picture painted by Ollivier in 1766 of a tea-party at the Prince of Conti's with Wolfgang looking very small at the harpsichord. A verbal picture can be found in Harold Nicolson's *The Age of Reason*. 'It was in the salons that the thinkers of the century, who were generally men of humble or at least provincial origin, acquired the polish and self-confidence of men of the world. But, said the Comte de Ségur, "it was not so much equality as familiarity".' One of the hostesses was a widow, Madame Geoffrin, of bourgeois origin and never received at Court, who wrote in 1768 to one of her ex-habitués Prince Kaunitz, Prime Minister of Austria, urging help and protection for the Mozarts. Wistfully she ends: 'they will be happy, far more than I, for whom nothing remains but a sad remembrance of my past happiness.' Nicholson tells us of this past happiness that the house (372 rue Saint-Honoré, still partly extant till 1939) was 'well-heated, the arm-chairs plentiful and soft, the pictures, tapestries and mirrors excellent in design and colouring. She had one of the best chefs in Paris .... Every Monday she had a dinner at which artists could meet patrons and purchasers and she financed and assisted Van Loo, Boucher, Chardin, Latour and Vernet ... Rameau was a frequent visitor.' That Madame Geoffrin, who was almost illiterate, should be able to join in so distinguished a fashion the ranks of the blue-stockings ('les précieuses' as they were mockingly and affectionately called) is tribute to the adaptability of this particular civilisation. Les précieuses were enthusiastic for precision in such matters as language and pronunciation, and this not for pedantry's sake but for communication with elegance and precision—not a bad epitomisation of the subsequent Mozartean style.

Thanks to efforts of Grimm, and the astute use of ladies to sell some of the tickets, two concerts in Paris had brought in enough money to encourage the continuation of the journey to England which Leopold says he had only half decided upon when he left Salzburg, and the family left Paris on 9 April 1764, though clearly intending to return, as they left some of their luggage there. Sebastian Winter had by then left them to go to his native Donaueschingen with a new master. In his place as hairdresser was taken on Jean Pierre Potivin, bilingual in French and German, coming from Alsace. But they also took with them to England an Italian named Porta who had done the journey to England eight times already and did all the bargaining for them. With Porta's help the intrepid Leopold hired a private boat to take them across a sea which none of them had seen before, in more comfort than the regular, crowded packet-boat. The child's first wonder at the sea is touchingly recorded in Nannerl's diary: 'at Calais I saw how the sea runs away and comes back again.' Leopold's first letter to the Hagenauers from London begins with vintage ironical humour. 'Thank God we are across the little brook of Maxglan [a suburb of Salzburg] though not without vomiting to which I contributed most. However, we saved money on emetics. Anyone with too much money need only do the journey from Paris to London.' He was not slow to notice the richness of the landscape—Kent after all was the garden of England—nor the fickleness of the climate. The meat he pronounced the best in the world, and the beer astonishingly strong and good. The Englishman's cheerful disdain rings very true when he writes: 'if the street lads see anyone in Frenchified dress they shout [and here he transliterates] *Buger French.*' Nor does he fail to note the tea kettle on the fire all day. Their first lodging was with Mr John Couzin, hair-cutter, in Cecil Court, off St Martin's Lane. The family arrived in London on 23 April 1764, as it was beginning to empty after the winter season, but Leopold did his best by arranging the first public concert of his own promotion for 5 June, reckoning that most of the nobility would have to come back for the king's birthday on the previous day. By then the children had already played at Court twice, the warmth of their reception doubtless partly deriving from the pleasure which George III's queen had in hearing her native language spoken by the 'wonders of nature'.

But a name almost immediately crops up which represents the greatest influence on Wolfgang's music so far, a name which he was to continue to venerate, that of Johann Christian Bach, the youngest son of the great but then virtually unknown Johann Sebastian. He had come to London, after an Italian training, in 1762, and had quickly launched himself on a career with works ranging from operas and symphonies to popular songs to delight the customers of the Vauxhall pleasure-gardens. His capacity for limpid songfulness and sensuous colour simply bowled

Wolfgang over, so much so that we illogically call Johann Christian's turns of phrase 'Mozartean'. Leopold says in another letter to Hagenauer: 'Wolfgang greets you from the clavier, where at the moment he is playing through Kapellmeister Bach's Trio.' Bach had published as his op. 2 in 1763 six sonatas for violin (or flute), cello and keyboard, and it is almost certain that one of these is the trio, and that Leopold and Wolfgang got from them the idea of publishing as op. III a similar set for the same combination dedicated to the Queen in January 1765.

But meanwhile there were the summer pleasures to be explored, notably the public gardens of 'fauxhall' and 'ranelagh' which both figure in Nannerl's diary. Leopold describes Ranelagh, immediately west of the Royal Hospital, Chelsea, with its huge Rotunda holding three thousand people comfortably. A programme of music from 7 till 10 p.m. was followed by 'Quartets played by Horn, Clarinets and Bassoon'. The sensuous sound must have intoxicated the boy from clarinet-starved Salzburg. There were alcoves and a great enclosed hearth in the middle around which people promenaded. For the entry-price of half-a-crown there was tea, coffee, butter and bread *ad lib*. 'The entrance-fee makes every man an equal—no standing with bare head before a Lord.' It was on the organ here that Wolfgang played in aid of the 'Lying-in hospital', that being 'the way of an English patriot and the way to the hearts of this quite unusual nation.'

Vauxhall on the other side of the Thames took Leopold's breath away. 'I thought I was in the Elysian fields with a thousand glass lamps turning night into day. In the middle there is a sort of high open summer-house with an organ and music with trumpets and drums.' Rowlandson's famous drawing shows Mrs Weichsall singing in the 'summer-house'. The admission to Vauxhall was only a shilling. 'But after a bottle of wine and a couple of chickens, what does it cost to get out?' The gardens were graced by Roubiliac's famous statue of Handel, now to be seen at Novello's, and Hogarth's paintings decorated the loggias. Amongst the singers were Cecilia Young, the wife of Dr Arne, the official Vauxhall composer, who figures on Leopold's 'London list' in his journey notes. Also listed are two renowned castrati: Manzuoli, the expensive star of the opera season during the Mozarts' stay, who comes into the tale on several subsequent occasions, and who gave Wolfgang singing lessons, and the redoubtable Tenducci, an intimate friend of J.C. Bach whose splendid portrait by Gainsborough (another intimate friend) now hangs in the Barber Institute of Birmingham University.

Alas, in July Leopold caught a chill at the Earl of Thanet's and was stricken with a severe inflammation of the neck. He suffered the usual drastic eighteenth-century remedies, and was brought 'an hour out of town' by sedan chair to recuperate in the country at 5 Fields Row (now 180 Ebury Street). In a letter from Chelsea he gives exhaustive and fascinating details of the eating and drinking habits of London (coffee, light beer, and, quoted in English, Roasted Beef and Plumb-pudding). He was evidently much taken with cider: 'it has spirit and is clear as gold.' Frau Mozart took to cooking for the family at Chelsea. She still knew no English but 'past ten a clock' from the night-watchman, 'Good morrow Sir', 'How do ye do, Sir?' and 'Very well, at your service.' We do not know what English Leopold knew, though we can be sure that he was not the man to be lazy about anything that might help the expedition. He did write into his journey-notes eight lines from the Merchant of Venice, act V, scene 1, from 'the man that hath no Musick in himself' to 'let no such man be trusted'.

Whilst concert life was at a halt in Chelsea Wolfgang took to composition. Nannerl in her memoirs published long afterwards in the Leipzig *Allgemeine Musikalische Zeitung* of 22 January 1800, states: 'When our father lay dangerously ill in London we were forbidden to touch a piano.' And so, to occupy himself, Mozart composed his first symphony for all the instruments of the orchestra—especially for trumpets and kettle-drums. 'I had to copy it out as I sat beside him. Whilst he composed and I copied he said to me "Remind me to give the horn something worthwhile to do".' Certainly the symphonies K.16 in E flat and K.19 in D were written at this time, but Nannerl is wrong about the trumpets and drums, unless there were other lost compositions. What is true is that the first two symphonies were 'London' symphonies. We can't tell how 'helped' these symphonies were. But the first (K.16) shows a typical opening, a unison fanfare followed by quiet descending chordal sonorities, the masculine and feminine which we get for example in the piano concerto in the same key, K.482. If we were told that this symphony was by J.C. Bach it would have to be disproved on other than musical grounds. In the slow movement the first horn has 'something worthwhile to do', singing the four-note phrase—*d, r, f, m*—which rings out in the last movement of the 'Jupiter', so that a bit of the last symphony is embedded in the first. The symphony K.17 is spurious. K.18 is by Karl Friedrich Abel, the distinguished player of the viola da gamba, who was chamber musician to the Queen, and who was to join Bach in the famous subscription concerts which began in 1765. But it should not be omitted from our account, for it not only affords the sound of the clarinets, but in its first movement's secondary paragraphs takes a delight in silencing the strings so that we hear the 'wind band' of two clarinets above the single bassoon, supported by the horns. This slow movement, in C minor, could well have taught Wolfgang a lesson in decorative langor. The symphony K.19 in D begins with a rapid alternation of *forte* and *piano* over a drumming bass, again typical of Bach, and taken over by Wolfgang into many opening movements. But so far are we from the conscious drama that builds up to a dénouement in the recapitulation of the opening subject, that this is omitted altogether, and we end with a deliberately pat 'signing-off' gesture.

J.C. Bach's six symphonies op. III were published in London in 1765 whilst the Mozarts were there. In the *andantino* of the fourth occurs one of the most indelible of all Mozart's fingerprints—the yearning, love-melting phrase with which Tamino greets Pamina's picture in the sixth bar of his first air in the *Magic Flute*, a phrase moreover which Mozart used in the slow movement of his 40th symphony. What is more, the key (E flat) is the same in all three cases! Other works of Bach certainly known to Mozart, and published in London in 1763, were a set of keyboard concertos. The beginning of the jig-type *presto* of no. 4 turns up shortly afterwards in the last movement of the symphony in B flat, K.22 written in The Hague, then reappears in Bach's key of G as the introduction to Figaro's announcement that the wedding band are ready to hand.

This is not mere resemblance-fancying. The styles were sometimes deliberately interwoven. Grimm reports in his *Corréspondance Littéraire* (1766): 'In London Bach took him between his knees and they played alternately on the same keyboard for two hours extempore before the King and Queen.' This was presumably some 'question and answer' game, phrase by phrase, with doubtless deceptive modulations thrown in. The differences of musical style between J.C. Bach and his father have caused some historians to regard him as a surprising if not illegit-imate musical son. But in all but his most hurried and superficial work there is a continuation of German workmanship below the Italianate sensuousness and glitter. The riches of the orchestration of the operas, for example, led Dr Burney to say of *Orion* that 'the arias in the opera, being indifferently rendered, were more admired as instrumental pieces than compositions for the voice.' Incidentally, Burney also notes this as being 'the first time that clarinets had admission in our opera orchestra'. The opera was produced at the King's Theatre on 19 February 1763 before the Mozarts' arrival, but we know that Leopold possessed a copy of Walsh's 1763 publication 'The Favourite Songs in the Opera call'd Orione'.

A notable event in January 1765 was the publication as op. III of six sonatas (K.10-15) by Wolfgang dedicated to the Queen, 'for the harp-sichord', the title-page states, and 'which can be played with the accom-paniment of the violin, or Transverse Flute'.

Although the title-page does not say so, there is actually a cello part as well. Wolfgang received 50 guineas for the effusive and elaborate dedication, of anonymous concoction. The violin is clearly the intended 'accompaniment' as the part contains such impossibilities for flute as double and treble stops and notes below the compass, but this violin part differs from the Paris sonatas in offering from time to time complementary material of a more systematic and characteristic kind, amounting occasionally to a real dialogue with the keyboard right hand, without which the music though complete is the poorer. See for instance the close imitations in the Menuetto (in G minor) of K.11 and the *andante* (in F minor!) of K.13. The cello is a different matter. It hardly ever plays a note which is not in the left-hand part, and is a typical and effective aid to a thin keyboard bass, the more necessary as the violin becomes a real contributor. The cello's most effective moment is perhaps its total silence in the 'Menuetto II en carillon' of K.14 when in musical-box style the keyboard part shifts to the top of the compass and is accompanied by the violin's pizzicato.

A benefit concert for Nannerl and Wolfgang was announced for 21 February at the Little Theatre, Haymarket, at which, said the Public Advertiser, 'all the Overtures will be from the Composition of these astonishing Composers, only eight Years old'. The advertisement was wrong about Nannerl, and for that matter Wolfgang was already nine, but it is very probable that both the K.16 and K.19 symphonies figured here. The use of Overture and Symphony as synonymous had a straightforward reason. An overture in an opera-house probably received scanty attention before curtain-up. Its future life, if any, would be entrusted to the public concert where it might be called a symphony or simply still an overture. After running a further gauntlet in esteem it might achieve print in a collection of 'Favourite Overtures'.

Interest was high enough in op. III for Leopold to reprint in London opp. I and II with a new joint title-page, but by then the Public Advertiser was already mentioning a farewell concert. This took place in Hickford's Guest Room in Brewer Street on 13 May, billed to include 'Concerto on the Harpsichord by the little Composer and his sister, each single and both together, etc.'. A piece specially written for this sort of occasion must have been the Sonata for keyboard duet, K.19d. The piece contains the eye-catching technique of crossing hands, as shown in the later family-portrait picture by della Croce (1780/1). With few if any examples to his hand Wolfgang shows a wonderful sense of the effective deployment of the colours and textures available. The last movement is a bring-the-house-down rondo, running along like clockwork until a sudden stop in mid-phrase, whereupon the only slow music intervenes, a solemn tune with weighty harmonies, which accidentally or not is a striking reflection of the *andante* of Bach's overture to a *pasticcio* comic opera *La calamità de' Cuori*, put on in London in 1763.

Before the Mozarts left, the price of hearing the children play had dropped from the original half-guinea to five shillings, and then to a final half-crown at the Swan and Harp tavern in Cornhill in the last few weeks of their stay. Just before they left, Leopold presented to the recently-founded British Museum the engraved volumes of all the Mozart works published so far in Paris and London, and also the only Mozart setting of English words, a so-called madrigal 'God is our refuge' (K.20). If the Museum thought they were getting an autograph composition they were mistaken, since, as we know from Wolfgang Plath, the clefs, key signatures, some of the words and some of the music are all in Leopold's hand. In the circumstances Wolfgang's share in the authorship remains too problematical for further attention to be paid to the piece. So they left England, stopping at Canterbury for a day at the races. What might have happened had Mozart returned in maturity? England had in quick succession taken to her on the whole generous bosom two German musicians—Handel and J.C. Bach—who spoke musical Italian for her benefit. Perhaps had Mozart followed them, as he once suggested in a letter, he would have found in England the rewarding outlet for his restless spirit.

They had an easy crossing—three-and-a-half hours—to Calais, picked up their own coach again and headed not for Italy, which was their original intention, but for Holland on a last-minute request from the Dutch envoy. With various stops for illness and organ-playing they reached The Hague on 10 September 1765. But there plans were thrown into confusion. Nannerl fell ill with intestinal typhoid and after some five weeks was actually given extreme unction. She was hardly on her feet before Wolfgang caught the same disease. But somehow he was well enough to write a symphony (K.22 in B flat) by the year's end. In its first movement, as in K.19, we seem to be doing without a recapitulation of its main subject, but we find it used instead as a 'signing-off' device to mark the ends of the two main paragraphs. This use of the beginning tune for the end recurs in some mature works, and even in these early days reads far more like a sophistication than an irregularity. The slow movement is in G minor, not perhaps in itself worth mentioning were it not for the large proportion of mildly chromatic harmony and the patches of successive string entries making a pleading accumulation which foreshadows the slow movement of the great G minor symphony no. 40. This was doubtless played, with other 'Overtures of the Composition of this little Composer', at one of the two concerts at Amsterdam.

Gainsborough's painting (c.1770) 'The Harvest Wagon' shows the English summer countryside as the Mozarts would have seen it

Engraving after Canaletto showing the interior of the Rotunda at Ranelagh Gardens (see page 44), with the music podium on the left

Rowlandson's watercolour of Mrs Weichsall gracing the 'summer-house' at Vauxhall Gardens with her singing

Six
SONATES
pour le
CLAVECIN
qui peuvent se jouer avec
l'accompagnement de Violon ou Flaute
Traversiere
Tres humblement dediées
A SA MAJESTÉ
CHARLOTTE
REINE de la GRANDE BRETAGNE
Compoſées par
I.G. WOLFGANG MOZART
Agé de huit Ans
Oeuvre III.
LONDON *Printed for the Author and sold at his Lodging*
at Mr. Williamson in Thrift Street Soho

Left: Gainsborough's portrait of Tenducci conning a part gives a striking—perhaps even slightly sardonic—impression of the artist who would expect his arias to be tailor-made
Right: Title-page of Wolfgang's six sonatas (K.10–15) dedicated as Op.III to Queen Charlotte

The Verona portrait by Saverio dalla Rosa (see page 64): the inscription describes Wolfgang as 'dear to the kings of France and England'

The interior of La Scala, Milan in the mid-eighteenth century

The Villa Poggio Imperiale at Florence, summer residence of Grand-Duke Leopold of Tuscany, where Wolfgang gave a concert in April 1770 before going on to Rome

The delays through illness at any rate meant that the Mozarts were still on hand at The Hague for the great festivities to mark the coming of age and installation as Stadtholder of William V of Orange. The occasion was marked for Wolfgang by publication of two sets of keyboard variations: K.24 on a patriotic song written by the Court Kapellmeister Ernst Graf, and K.25 on the Dutch national song 'William of Nassau'. The former set is at times elaborate, and shows the traditional procedure of starting with slow note-values and speeding them up as the variations proceed. There is a slower variation towards the end, as became Mozart's regular practice in solo variation cycles. But we can hardly quarrel when Leopold says: 'they are trifles.'

Slightly more weighty was another publication, op. IV, a set of six sonatas (K.26-31) dedicated to the Princess of Nassau, the sister of William V. Mozart's mark was sufficiently made in Paris for their reprinting there in 1767. The violin is still announced as accompanimental, but there is a fitful advance: whilst nowhere does the keyboard accompany the violin, there are frequent passages of dialogue. But as Einstein points out, in the six variations which close the set the violin never emerges from the subsidiary role.

But there was limelight for Leopold too. He was presented at Haarlem with a finely-printed Dutch translation of his *Violinschule*. The other product of the stay in Holland was a squib of a piece, jointly written out and probably jointly composed by father and son, called 'Gallimathias Musicum' (K.32). The opening three movements are like a tiny symphony but then the gallimaufry begins with bag-pipe imitations, horn-calls, a banal harpsichord solo, and various other abrupt fits and starts ending with a quite substantial fugue on 'William of Nassau'. It was the sort of humorous hotch-potch at which Leopold was adept.

The journey back to Paris was quick, with occasional concerts but no long stays, and they arrived there on 10 May 1766 at lodgings found for them by the faithful Grimm. They went again to Versailles but little is known of this second Paris stay. One work dates from this time, however, a Kyrie (K.33) for voices and strings. Again it is a 'mixed' manuscript, Wolfgang's hand being confined to one page of music and the superscription, which reads: 'Mese à Paris le 12 juni di Wolfgang Mozart 1776' (the first word probably means 'Mass', but if so it was never proceeded with). It can hardly have been meant for Paris in any event. Three days before, Leopold had written to Hagenauer of their intention to leave, and furthermore since Louis XIV's time the custom there was *Messes basses solennelles*, in which only a motet or cantata was 'à grand choeur', the rest of the music being on the organ or sometimes other instruments, so that there was no occasion for settings of such items as the Gloria or Sanctus. Nevertheless there is something French to be seen in this Kyrie. Its rhythm savours of the sarabande, and it has graceful, short, conjunct phrases with a few chromaticisms in the middle, giving the words a modest and precise declamation with no trace of Italian flowering of ornamental expression.

Their way home brought them concerts at Dijon and Lyons. At Dijon the last of Leopold's travel notes on the journey ends with an English word: 'Hautbois—Deux freres—Rotten'. Writing from Lyons Leopold turns his eyes wistfully towards Italy: 'don't you think it very heroic and magnaminous of us to abandon going to Turin . . . and then, after seeing the Ascension Festival in Venice to return home through the Tyrol? . . . But I have promised to go home and shall keep my word.' This resolution might have sprung from a consciousness of long absence from duty, but might it not have been reinforced by a sudden travel-weariness from the heroic Frau Mozart? At all events they passed through Switzerland, missed seeing Voltaire at his Château de Ferney near Geneva because of his illness, met their ex-servant Winter at Donaueschingen and played twice at the Bavarian court in Munich. There is a strong tradition that whilst they were in Bavaria Wolfgang composed an offertory *Scande coeli limina*, K.34, for the monastery of Seeon at Chiemgau; furthermore that he did so 'on the sill of the window on the right as you leave the refectory'. There must be some caution as to its outright authenticity, as it does not occur in Leopold's catalogue of his son's works up to 1768. But it is musically remarkable and historically interesting. In the celebration of a mass the activities at the altar at the Offertory allow time for musical expansion instead of the usual plainsong versicle. The music here often became a joyous relaxation, a letting of the hair down. In Italy at this period it sometimes took the form of a virtuosic solo cantata, of which *Exsultate* (K.165) is a famous example. In France it was often a loud piece on the organ, as in Couperin's two 'organ masses', where the offertoires 'sur les grands jeux' are *grands jeux d'esprit*. In Germany the use of choirs expanded the Italian resources and so we get the mixture of chorus and solo which is Mozart's standard use away from Italy. The offertory K.34 is in honour of St Benedict. The saint's soul winging to heaven comforts the earth-bound ones lamenting their untransfigured state, curiously enough with the plural prayer given to the solo and the saint's reply given to the chorus. But it is, as Kurthen says, a musical and verbal counterpart to the embellished ecstasies of the late baroque altars of this part of Europe.

The family arrived back in Salzburg on 29 November 1766, after an absence of more than eighteen months. Not knowing exactly what the aims of the expedition were, we cannot know how satisfied Leopold was.

We might allow the faithful Grimm a final comment: 'If these children live, they will not remain at Salzburg. Before long monarchs will vie to possess them.' An irony, indeed.

4

The Salzburg/Vienna/Italy Rondo

1766–73

Apart from the Hagenauer letters some news of the achievements of the journey must have percolated back. The Salzburg Court Diaries record a 'small *Cammer-Musique*, composed by the young son of Mozart' which was performed on 3 January 1765. This must have meant something from the Paris publications. A glowing report from London, perhaps from Leopold, appeared in the *Europaeische Zeitung* of 6 August 1765 in Salzburg. But naturally Archbishop Schrattenbach and the court were agog to see and hear for themselves. Wolfgang wrote two occasional pieces (K.36 and K.70) each consisting of a recitative and aria to mark the Archbishop's consecration anniversary and birthday. More substantial was a 'sacred musical play' (*geistliches Singspiel*) performed on 12 March 1767 in the Rittersaal of the Residenz. The enticing title is 'The Obligation of the first Commandment' (*Die Schuldigkeit des ersten Gebots*). It was home-made with a libretto by Herr Weiser who had a textile factory, and performed as to the principal parts by leading members of the musical establishment. Wolfgang set the first part; the other two parts, of which the music is lost, fell to Michael Haydn and Adlgasser. Leopold's hand appears in the score, providing not only the words of the recitatives but also note-corrections and other musical details. The 'characters' in Wolfgang's share are Justice, Mercy, Worldliness, Christianity. We are obviously far from what the composer of *Figaro* would have called characterisation, and the dramatic stage interest is nil, with the characters often addressing the audience at length rather than each other. But the music shows an aptitude for picking up the baroque language of simile, with illustrations aplenty of roaring lions, laughter, trembling, howlings in hell, and the like. One of the most interesting traits of the orchestration is the association of a florid trombone solo with judgement day, an idea deriving from Eberlin which Wolfgang reverted to in the Requiem.

The story that Schrattenbach as a true test had Wolfgang shut up for eight days of unaided composition to a given text most probably refers to the Passion cantata composed for Holy Week, K.42. Its title, *Grab-musik*, makes it likely that it was performed at the 'holy grave' in the cathedral. The Soul in anger at the sight of the Saviour's body calls down rock-splitting thunders (a very usual reaction, as for instance in Bach's St Matthew Passion). The Angel calls upon the Soul rather to reflect on its own guilt—a pathetic air with a slight premonition of the 40th symphony. There follows a lyrical duet offering and accepting forgiveness. There is much less extravagance and more beauty of line than in *Die Schuldigkeit*; in short, a less frontal assault on the public ear. When Lent was over, Wolfgang supplied the music for *Apollo and Hyacinth* (K.38). This was again a home-made affair, a musical intermezzo diversifying a Latin comedy put on by students of the Gymnasium, a school under the tutelage of the University. (The morning classes, incidentally, had been shortened to allow time for routine blood-letting.) The music is again shapely, but far from involvement with real characters, and the Latin adds to the distancing.

Of far greater importance, historically, are four keyboard concertos (K.37, 39, 40, 41), each of three movements. One of the movements remains unidentified, but the others are all made out of solo keyboard pieces by Raupach, Honauer, Schobert, Eckardt and C.P.E. Bach (the first four, in spite of their Teutonic names, Parisians by residence and clientele). They were presumably put together as repertoire for Wolfgang. The score is again jointly written, Leopold's substantial share including corrections, for the better, of some of the keyboard writing. Whether the eleven-year-old boy received substantial help or not is not of crucial importance compared with the fact that in making first movements with orchestra out of solo movements he came to immediate grips with the formal problems of what to many are the climax of his instrumental works, the piano concertos. The main problem was the balancing, without mere equal-handed duplication, of the music for orchestra and soloist so that each had something characteristic to say, and the rounding-off convincingly of an inevitably larger design. In the K.39 concerto, for instance, the orchestra begins with the principal subject, from Raupach's sonata op. 1 no. 1, but it takes care not immediately to follow the original in a swing away from the home key; this will be reserved for when the soloist emerges. But neither is this tutti a duplication of the sonata without that modulation; it subtracts and it adds, notably a piquant new falling motif, really Mozartean in its syncopated chromaticism, with which the music is sewn up after the cadenza. On a smaller scale there are bar-by-bar felicities of orchestral accompaniment-motifs throughout the concertos. Whether by intuition or teaching, the basics for the mature concertos are miraculously there. The slow movement of this concerto derives from Schobert, and with its repeated triplet chords and slowly-rising arpeggio bass might have been the germ of the accompaniment of the slow movement in the same key of the piano concerto K.467, though it lacks almost any hint of the latter's marvellous melody.

The family's next visit was to Vienna, leaving Salzburg on 11 September 1767 and arriving on the 15th. It was a fiasco. They presumably went to cash in on the audiences and demand for music occasioned by the festivities for the betrothal of Ferdinand IV, King of Naples and Sicily, to the sixteen-year-old Archduchess Maria Josepha. But as Leopold put it in a letter to Hagenauer, 'the Princess-Bride has become a bride of the heavenly Bridegroom.' She died of smallpox on 15 October. The family, like many others, fled Vienna and got as far as Olmütz (now Olomouc) where Wolfgang fell ill. One thinks back to Leopold's letter from Paris (22 February 1764): 'Do you know what people here are always wanting? To persuade me to let my boy be inoculated with smallpox. But I have now sufficiently shown my dislike of this impertinence.' Of course Jenner's invention of the vaccine from cowpox was only to come after Wolfgang's death, and the French were talking of actual smallpox taken from a sufferer from it. We have to thank in the main two people for Wolfgang's survival: a Dr Joseph Wolff, the physician, and the Dean of Olmütz, Count Leopold Anton von Podstatzky, who rescued them from the 'Black Eagle' inn. Leopold again: 'I should like to know how many people would receive into their house a whole family with a child in such a condition, from no other motive than human compassion.' Leopold never wrote the biography of Wolfgang in which he vowed he would record this compassion for posterity. There is a further outbreak of 'Te Deum' in a letter from Olmütz of 29 November, Nannerl having got over the smallpox safely, 'a sign that the few spots she had in her childhood were not the real thing'. We might feel with our post-Jenner knowledge that they probably *were*.

At about this period came the first of the Vienna symphonies (K.43 in F) and the first to have a minuet making the third of four movements. There is a very pretty orchestration (muted violins for the tune, mainly pizzicato accompaniment) of the serenade-like slow movement which is largely derived from a duet from *Apollo and Hyacinth*, an excellent example of the aria-for-orchestra which throughout Mozart's lifetime continued as an alternative to the more argumentative, motivic and 'instrumental' type of slow movement. Leopold had a hand in this score as well.

At last, on the afternoon of 19 January 1768, the Mozarts were received at court by Maria Theresa and her son Joseph II, the new

Emperor, but there seems to have been little upshot, with Maria Theresa basically apathetic and Joseph miserly. There are two church works from this period the occasions for which are unknown, though the whole ethos of the times makes it unlikely that they were merely speculative investments: a 'Veni Sancte Spiritus' (K.47) shows strong affinities with Leopold's own church music, with energetic parts for orchestra including trumpets and drums, and small but well-judged bouts of counterpoint within paragraphs of time-saving chordal treatment. The other work is a Missa Brevis in G (K.49) for which K.47 may have served as a Whitsun Offertory. The *missa brevis* was a definite genre; it called for concision, which meant that there had to be a preponderance of chordal writing and a minimum of repetitions of words, particularly in the Gloria and Credo with their longer texts. This caused problems of cohesion to a composer of integrity, who would seek to achieve it by consistent use of accompaniment-figures, and by transference of motifs from one 'movement' to another. Again in this example the son learns from the father. But he also learnt the church-music trade by copying the works of others in his own hand, a process which has naturally aggravated the problems of authenticity. For instance, to this end he made himself study-scores of two psalms by Carl Georg Reutter and at least four works by Eberlin, all of which can be found in current editions of Köchel's catalogue.

Leopold was in a dilemma; the longer he stayed in Vienna, the less inclined he was to go home with nothing to show for his increasing expenditure. The pressure increased when Schrattenbach very reasonably stopped his salary, but not his appointment, from 1 April. But suddenly we hear that the Emperor had, rather loosely, suggested that Wolfgang should write an opera. This he did, and at speed, completing *La finta semplice* (K.51) between April and June. But here was another fiasco; in spite of a petition from Leopold the Emperor had not the will, nor did he elect to use the financial muscle, to insist on the performance, which d'Affligio, the lessee of the Burg and Kärtnertor theatres, managed to thwart. The financial risks, it seems, would have been his in any case. There are good reasons why the singers should doubt, with d'Affligio, whether the work would be worth doing looked at from the ordinary stage view-point. It was not succinctly characterised, and it was musically elaborate, even granted that its technical demands, being a comic opera, were less than for *opera seria*. The plot, adapted from Goldoni, used the same comic ploys repeatedly. But to us there are some hints of later magic, particularly of *Così fan tutte* in the heroine's night song in E major invoking the hovering Cupids whilst sensuous thirds on the bassoons alternate with divided violas. The finales keep the pot boiling, but not by the continuity of the action as in Mozart's superb mature examples. The old buffoon's music is what comes most naturally to the boy's hand; he does not seem to have committed himself otherwise to more emotional insight (why should he, even supposing he could?). Leopold hastily and probably unjustly ascribed the non-performance to Gluck but he was surely nearer the mark—how it rings true even today!—when he wrote: 'If a man has no talent that is unhappiness enough, but if he has talents envy pursues him in proportion to his ability.'

Some slight operatic recompense was the performance of *Bastien and Bastienne* (K.50) in the garden of Dr Anton Mesmer, the magnetist affectionately guyed in *Così*. The libretto can be traced back to the deliberate naïveties of Jean-Jacques Rousseau, and recounts how the estranged and ingenuous country lovers are reconciled by an old shepherd, Colas, who is a bit of a conjuror. The dialogue is spoken, and the songs, except for Colas's mock-bloodcurdling invocation, are in the charming countrified style which Rousseau would recognise as befitting his 'Back to Nature' call. But he would have had to acknowledge a compensating tendency towards sophistication in orchestral resource which is one of the reasons why the piece is still sometimes to be heard.

Otherwise the only opportunity to make a public display came when in the presence of the Empress the church at the Vienna orphanage in the Rennweg was consecrated on 7 December. The Jesuit priest in charge, Ignaz Parhamer, had two passions: military exercises for the boys and music for all. He was a friend of the Mozarts; Leopold and Wolfgang had attended the laying of the foundation stone in the Emperor's presence. Now, with parades and festal cannonades as prelude and postlude, Wolfgang was to produce and conduct a mass and an offertory. According to most critical opinion, the Mass was the C Minor, K.139, and the offertory was 'Benedictus sit Deus', K.117. This was emphatically not the occasion for a *missa brevis*. We still have to reckon that Leopold may have helped Wolfgang with the 'set-piece' fugues which would be a touchstone to the connoisseurs in the audience. We can easily imagine the tension and excitement of the opening bars. For the Mozarts this was the last opportunity to capture the public; for the public there was the presence of the Empress, two Archdukes and two Archduchesses, the famous orphans' choir and the prodigy-conductor. Yet what the audience first heard was the trombones adding a Gluckian, even tragic tone, and the plaintive unusual sound of divided violas in the minor key. For those who had recently heard Gluck's *Orpheus* and *Alceste* it must have conveyed a surprising unsuitability. But the 'unsuitability' is there deliberately to enhance the onset of the *allegro* in the major key. In the 'Christe' section of the Kyrie the shapely and euphonious roulades of the soprano/alto and tenor/bass duets are made to please. Thus even in the Kyrie we have three styles, all having to be bulls'-eyes, so to speak: the pathetic, the festive, with four trumpets, and the Italian-sensuous. A fourth style, of the obligatory fugues, is much stiffer. Their archaic subjects remain a feature till the end of Wolfgang's career, with the Requiem a notable example, but by then, partly through instinct and partly through the revelation of Bach and Handel, their treatment is far less symmetrical and elongated. For the 'Crucifixus' there is a return to the Gluckian style of trombone solemnities, but also muted trumpets, a colour borrowed from Leopold's own Missa Solenne in C.

The offertory 'Benedictus sit Deus' starts with a festal chorus containing a balanced mixture of counterpoint and harmony, the latter enlivened with rushing violins. The central section is a true concerto movement for soprano solo, including orchestral paragraphs and a cadenza; its recapitulations are not exact but subtly altered beyond the needful minimum caused by key-changes. This kind of 'voluntary alteration', one of the most precious Mozartean features, is thus making an early appearance. The final chorus renews the brilliant violin accompaniment but also includes four entries of a traditional plainsong psalmtone, again following Leopold's example (in his 'Convertentur sedentes').

When the family returned to Salzburg on 5 January 1769 they had little enough to show for more than a year's absence, but amongst the several symphonies of this period there is one true landmark, K.48 in D which is dated December 1768, in which Wolfgang is finding his feet with the dramatic as opposed to the entertaining-decorative; though the latter aspects are still there, for if a symphony of that date were to be deemed neither entertaining nor decorative it would be thought pointless to write it. But in the first movement great play is made of abrupt alternations of loud and soft, and of major and minor harmonies. The *andante*, for strings alone, is ostensibly much more innocently tuneful, but fascinatingly refuses to speak in regular phrase-lengths. In these two movements, short as they are, we are on the threshold of 'music as drama', the essence of the classical symphonic style.

We do not know when in 1769 the intention to take Wolfgang to Italy crystallised, nor does it appear that there was any commission or even invitation, but we can be sure that Leopold, intent on recovering salary after his truancy, would in any case have been silent about it on their return to Salzburg. Two greatly differing masses signalised Wolfgang's reappearance. The first is a Missa Brevis (K.65 in D minor). Its unusual severity of key and style is explained by its being written for the opening of the forty hours of prayer in the University Church. The inclusion of a Gloria on a 'Lenten' occasion has caused some doubts. But the Salzburg church calendar makes it clear that the forty hours were spread over the Sunday, Monday and Tuesday before Ash Wednesday, making a preparation for, not an observance in, Lent, and a Gloria for Quinquagesima Sunday in the minor seems nicely to hit the liturgical nail on the head. The first choral D minor sound with the traditional trombone backing cannot but prefigure for us the last such sound in the Requiem. It is not the case of a temporary minor as in the festal orphanage mass. The opening *adagio* (incidentally without violins) gives way to a continuation in the minor with the tiny alleviation of the 'Christe' in two duet-phrases in thirds. But each movement is basically in the minor, from which neither the life of the world to come, nor the Sanctus, nor the usually jolly 'dona nobis pacem' can remove us. The melodies are sometimes gaunt and frequently vivid; but perhaps the most remarkable passage is the chromatic duet of the Benedictus, arrived at after the rejection of no fewer than three other versions. The pregnancy of this Missa Brevis and the brevity of the relieving solo passages brings to a head for the first time the 'demonic' mood which is far removed from the mere assumption of the pathetic vein.

In the greatest contrast is the so-called 'Dominicus' mass in C, K.66. One of Wolfgang's childhood friends was the son, Cajetan, of the Hagenauers. When the Mozarts heard in London that Cajetan had become a novice in the Benedictines 'Wolfgang burst into tears, thinking he would see him no more'. On 15 October 1769 Pater Dominicus, as Cajetan now was, celebrated at St Peter's, Salzburg his first solemn mass, to Wolfgang's music. The structure of the work is very similar to that of the orphanage mass, but now instead of the slightly self-conscious and opportunistic 'effectiveness' of the state occasion there is a more overt allure to the music, expressing a happy, sometimes ingenuous indulgence of youthful friendship. The waltz-like accompaniment of the secondary theme in the Kyrie is something to smile with, not laugh at. The 'Et incarnatus', compared with that of the orphanage mass, seems even to double its charm by turning the duet into a quartet, but still with the euphony of pairs of voices in thirds. Amusingly, the downward scale which was an orchestral unifying device in the earlier K.139's Credo is now an ascending one, particularly convenient for the Resurrection, and the life of the world to come is obviously envisaged as a fast minuet. It is worth remarking that there are clear signs, in a sketch of the Gloria's final fugue, of corrections in Leopold's hand, corrections moreover which are substantially accepted in the final version.

Schrattenbach had *La finta semplice* performed in Salzburg with Mrs Michael Haydn, *née* Lipp, as Rosina who feigns simplicity, and the chambermaid Ninetta played by Maria Anna Fesemayr who shortly

became the third wife of the organist Adlgasser at a ceremony with
Leopold as witness and Wolfgang as groomsman.

To the summer of 1769 almost certainly belong three instrumental
works called by the unusual title of 'Kassation'. The derivation of this
word is uncertain, some authorities referring it to the German word for
'street' (*Gasse*) and others to the French (*casser*) in the sense of a broken-
up or at least breakable suite. It seems certain at any rate that 'cassations'
are open-air music. These examples are provided with a march for entry
and exit, whilst in-between the stationary musicians play a suite like a
light, elongated symphony containing at least two minuets. Incidentally
this means the absence of the cello—which can only be played sitting
down, and the giving of the line called *basso* to the double bass and
probably the bassoon. The first two cassations (K.63 and K.99) are of
the species called *Final-Musik*, a term serving for two kinds of finality:
after supper, and after the end-of-term examinations, since they were
played by university students as festive and unintellectual homage to
their teachers and patrons. But perhaps no piece of Mozart can be wholly
'unintellectual', and the open-air treatment by no means precludes variety
and occasional subtlety in the scoring. Moreover the first minuet of K.63
uses canon between top and bottom in the manner of Joseph Haydn.
Nannerl's diary of 1775 records a *Final-Musik* in two instalments on the
one night, first in the Mirabell garden and then in the 'colegio'. The
third cassation is more elaborate, running to a (thus-entitled) Serenata
of eight movements after the March. It is formed from two elements
previously separated in Köchel's catalogue—the March K.62 and the
Serenata K.100. Its march was used again in *Mitridate*.

The first of the symphonies in C, K.73, may date from this Salzburg
period but it might already have been written in Vienna on the one hand,
or be one of the first 'Italian' symphonies on the other. It has even been
ascribed to 1772. If we hesitate to think of it as being written in or for
Italy, it is because its first movement at any rate has something of the
non-melodic drive of K.48, albeit few of its surprises. Where the Italians
might expect the secondary material to sing we have counterpoint for the
violins instead. Indeed the busy bass of the symphony's opening bars
occurs in Leopold's hand in a contrapuntal-exercise book of Wolfgang's.
It may be a far cry from this first C major symphony to the final
'Jupiter', especially comparing the pat and simplistic first rondo with
the latter's sublimities. But the combination of pomp and brilliance
associated with the trumpets and drums in this key is already in evidence,
to be met again, for instance, in the C major piano concertos, K.467 and
503.

A confidential letter from Leopold to Hagenauer from Vienna (11 May 1768) comments that going without salary makes it easier to undertake the journey to Italy which, he felt, could not be postponed. One of the reasons, clumsily put, seems to show him in a grasping light: that otherwise Wolfgang will have outgrown the capacity to attract notice as a prodigy. But the tenor of Leopold's words and actions all point to a dominating altruistic ambition, Wolfgang's education and career, and the Italian experience was now vital—and so, of course, was Wolfgang's earning capacity if a Salzburg salary could not be honourably asked for when it was not being earned. In fact Schrattenbach not only gave leave for the journey but also gave financial help from the Salzburg treasury. There would be a precedent for this, for in 1763 he had sent Adlgasser on a two-year study-leave to Italy. Wolfgang was named before departure as third Konzertmeister, with the shrewd provision that the salary should date from his return. There were also introductory letters from the doyen of Vienna composers, Johann Adolf Hasse, to his friend in Venice, Giovanni Ortes, who was an influential music-lover.

For the Italian journeys wife and daughter were left at home, not without pangs perhaps tinged with jealousy. Father and son departed on 13 December, with a concert at Innsbruck en route. By now Wolfgang is assisting in the recording of the journey by letters, by postscripts and by occasional entries in Leopold's journey-notes. A postscript to his mother from Worgl on the second evening away from home is typically boyish in mentioning the warmth and exhilarating speed of the carriage, but saying nothing of the scenery. So it was in the main to continue; Wolfgang's subject-matter was people, on or off the stage. Leopold comments on the plentiful snow on the way to St Johann, but the weather in crossing the Brenner Pass towards the end of December is not mentioned. He continued in this respect to be lucky and intrepid. They arrived at their first major Italian city, Verona, on 27 December. Here they were principally befriended by Pietro Lugiati, the provincial receiver-general, who commissioned one of his relatives, Saverio dalla Rosa, to make a portrait of Wolfgang. The music on the desk is the *allegro* K.72a, and we may assume that its very legible 'quotation' on canvas establishes the piece's authenticity.

Wolfgang's first concert in Italy was given on 5 January 1770 in the Accademia Filarmonica, and evoked two poems and an ecstatic review which Leopold sent home. From it we learn that the entertainment began with one of his 'overtures', and included playing at sight a harpsichord concerto and other pieces, extemporising and singing an aria to given verses (his Italian must have been good enough), improvisation on a given subject, and participation in a trio by Boccherini. The notice appeared in the *Mantua Gazette*, and consequently served as advertisement for a similar elaborate display-concert given in Mantua on 16 January, at which Wolfgang played a symphony with all the parts on the harpsichord, from a single violin part. This evoked another paean from the *Gazette*, and another poem, this time by a Signora Sartoretti who not only gave Wolfgang treatment for chapped hands, but also accompanied her poem with money. At Mantua they heard Hasse's opera *Demetrio*. Wolfgang shows how little the music as such means to him by confining himself, in a letter to Nannerl, to describing the performers in his racy way, for instance the prima donna who 'cannot open her mouth', whereas the 'seconda donna looks like a grenadier, with a powerful voice to match'. At Cremona he had his first encounter with the libretto of *La clemenza di Tito* as set by Michele Valentini. Again there is nothing about the music, and the most memorable comment is on the grottesco-dancer 'who whenever he jumped let off a fart', exactly the kind of remark Wolfgang would think suitable for a young female relative. But the Italian journeys spark off humorous letters, ranging from mish-mashes of German and Italian to outright bawdiness, and incorporating this kind of simplicity: 'Herr Gellert the poet has died at Leipzig and since his death has written no more poetry.'

At Milan we reach one of the centres of Leopold's hopes. The Mozart cause was energetically espoused by a native of Salzburg now Governor-General of Lombardy, Count Karl Joseph Firmian, at whose residence Wolfgang several times played. This is where the threads of the Italian education are rapidly drawn together. Wolfgang meets two leading Italian composers, Piccinni and Sammartini. He hears Jommelli's *Didone abbandonata* at La Scala. He is presented with Metastasio's complete works by Firmian, and doubtless as a proof of capacity for Italian serious opera, he introduces arias for soprano (K.73a, 77, 78) to words by Metastasio which are heard at Count Firmian's at a reception to which he invites a hundred and fifty of the nobility. The precious upshot of all this was a contract (*scrittura*) for Wolfgang to write the opera with which the next Milan season was to begin immediately after Christmas. The recitatives had to be in Milan in October and 'we must be there by 1 November so that Wolfgang may write the arias'. This to us unfamiliar procedure was both regular and realistic. The recitatives carried forward the action; they had to be learnt and got out of the way, but unless they were of the 'accompanied' kind they were nondescript and virtually anonymous. But the arias were made to measure; they had to be tried out by the singers and altered patiently and quickly in just the same way as their clothes at a costume-fitting. In both cases fluency in the language of the medium and dexterity in finding the *mot juste* for both character and situation were at a premium. A score in those days was not a tablet of stone handed down from Sinai; it was a last-minute record of a compilation, defined just in time for the orchestral parts to be copied.

So the Mozarts were entitled to rejoice on their way south, having determined to be in Rome during Holy Week. They were furnished with introductory letters by Firmian to influential patrons in Parma, Bologna and Florence. All these stays were brief. At Parma they were guests of the soprano Lucrezia Agujari, nicknamed La Bastardella, whose astonishing range Wolfgang notated in a letter to Nannerl. At Bologna another hundred and fifty of the nobility heard Wolfgang as did also the famous counterpoint teacher Padre Martini, who never ordinarily went to concerts, but who generously followed this one up with further tests and lessons for Wolfgang which were to bear fruit on the return journey. At Florence they were received at the Pitti palace by one of Maria Theresa's sons, the Grand-Duke Leopold of Tuscany, and met again the male soprano Manzuoli, last seen in London. Wolfgang also made a friend of a young English violinist, Thomas Linley, who touchingly got an Italian poet, whose splendid pen-name was Corilla Olimpica, to write him a farewell sonnet to deliver to Wolfgang.

A musical milestone was passed on the journey from Milan. Possibly under the influence of the lively instrumental music of Sammartini, Wolfgang wrote at an inn at Lodi his first string quartet (K.80). A final rondo was added some years later to its original three-movement plan, which began unusually with an *adagio* which was not an introduction but a complete design. Though we are obviously some distance from the poise and equality of interest of the mature quartets, and there are no clouds to diversify the extrovert cheerfulness, each movement has its patches of counterpoint, to a markedly greater extent than obtains, say, in the earliest quartets of Haydn.

They arrived at Rome on the Wednesday of Holy Week, 11 April, and went that same afternoon to the Sistine Chapel where Wolfgang heard the celebrated 'Miserere' of Allegri. That he was able subsequently to write down the jealously-guarded and unpublished music from memory was a feat which, thanks to Leopold, is the one the world most remembers of the 'prodigy' stage of Wolfgang's life, and one which probably accounts for the rushed journey to make sure they arrived in time for its achievement. Achievement it was, of a sort, but some qualifications attach to it. The music was not totally inaccessible other than by ear; the English musical historian Charles Burney had a copy; so, more importantly for the Mozarts, did Padre Martini with whom they were already on friendly terms. The setting involves chanting in chords, using similar successions each time; so that there was no contrapuntal weaving, though perhaps some melodic decoration of the cadences. Provided that the whole psalm was performed, even if only alternate verses were sung by the choir, Wolfgang would have heard the same formula ten times in succession, and we can certainly gather from Leopold's letter (14 April) that two performances were heard. The recognition of the chord-sequence would not be unduly difficult for a prehensile ear; the precise allocation of their constituent notes among the voices would be the major achievement. Wolfgang's postscript to the relevant letter invites his mother to imagine how little sleep he gets having to share a bed with his father, and describes how he kissed the foot of St Peter, having ignominiously to be lifted up to do so.

We also learn from Wolfgang of compositions in Rome. He used his Metastasio for a setting of an aria from Demofoonte (K.82), but the occasion is not known. There is also reference to symphonies, with his father as copyist, to save plagiarism. The chronology and places of composition of the Italian symphonies are problematical, but one whose parts are in Leopold's hand is K.81 in D. It has been published as Leopold's own composition, but recent critics assign it with confidence to Wolfgang. Comparing it to K.48 we see an altogether more easygoing content. Chameleon-like, the boy has immediately adopted the colouring of his surroundings. Charm and brightness is all. Short motifs are abundantly repeated; the ends of paragraphs are marked by emphatic hammerings-home of a key which was never in doubt in any case. The slow movement is all undemanding gracefulness, there is no minuet, and the jig-like finale is as regular and brash as any Italian opera overture. Much the same could be said of a pair of symphonies with very similar first movements, K.95 and 97, both also in D. They both have minuets. The slow movement of the symphony in C, K.96, takes on some local colour in employing the *Siciliano* rhythm. In a sense, then, these symphonies are a step back from purposeful drama. But all is grist to the mill, and it will not be long before charm and power cease to be alternatives.

On 8 May, the travellers left Rome for Naples in a small convoy of carriages to discourage the bandits, and arrived on the 14th. They visited the Prime Minister, Tanucci, who from Leopold's account was of far more consequence than the ineffectual King and Queen of Naples, and they also visited the English ambassador, William Hamilton. His knighthood and marriage to the famous Emma who became Nelson's mistress were events for the future. Meanwhile, it was the first wife, *née* Catherine Barlow, a good keyboard player though nervous of being heard by Wolfgang, who saw to it that there was a benefit concert and an audience at the palace of the Imperial Ambassador, Kaunitz. Although doubtless the Mozarts would in any case have gone the tourist round of Vesuvius and the two ruined cities of Pompeii and Herculaneum, William Hamilton's passion for volcanoes and antiquity must have confirmed and educated their choices, which included Pozzuoli and a boat-trip thence to Baiae, adding a second sea to the collection of the otherwise land-locked Mozarts. A possible commission for a Naples opera was precluded by commitments to Milan, so that the contacts and the sights were, in a sense, all that remained to the Mozarts as they set out for Rome where they arrived after a 27-hour journey on 26 June. They had only slept for two of the 27 hours, and Leopold undressed the snoring Wolfgang and put him to bed without the least sign of his waking up.

On that same day the official wheels had been set in motion by the Pope's secretary of state to decorate Wolfgang with the Cross of the Golden Spur. Two musicians had recently been so decorated—Gluck and Dittersdorf—but Wolfgang was at the higher grade of Knight of the Golden Order, in which his only musician predecessor was Lassus some two hundred years before. After the audience with Pope Clement XIV the travellers were hurrying back to Martini in Bologna. But on their way they went across to the Marches district on the Adriatic coast to visit, as piety dictated, Loretto, the place of pilgrimage for lovers of the Virgin Mary, whose Nazareth home was supposed miraculously to have been transported there in the thirteenth century. It is this place and this cult which give the names to the *Litaniae Lauretanae* of which both father and son wrote examples, Wolfgang's first, K.109, being written in Salzburg in May of the next year, 1771. They arrived in Bologna on 20 July, but a postscript from Wolfgang to his sister written the next day shows that he still did not know what opera he had to compose for Milan. The libretto eventually arrived on 27 July; it was *Mitridate* by Vittorio Cigna-Santi out of Racine.

Meanwhile, Leopold was ill at ease, still suffering from the effect of a gashed foot on the headlong journey from Naples to Rome. 'You can imagine what our household is like, now I can't get about. You know what Wolfgang is.' That last phrase from husband to wife helps us indeed to sense what Wolfgang by now is. Charles Burney encountered Wolfgang in Bologna on 30 August. His travel notes record: 'Who should I meet but the celebrated little German, Mozart, who in 1766 astonished all hearers in London by his premature musical talent . . . . The little man is grown considerably, but is still a little man . . . . There is no musical excellence I do not expect from the extraordinary quickness and talents, under the guidance of so able a musician and intelligent a man as his father, who, I was informed, had been ill five or six weeks at Bologna'. Meanwhile, we learn from Leopold's letter of 25 August that

Wolfgang is growing out of his cravats and shirts, and that he has lost his boy's voice: 'he has neither a low nor a high voice, not even five decent notes.'

The notable event of this second stay at Bologna was Wolfgang's admission to membership of the Accademia Filarmonica on 10 October. The qualifying test was the writing of an exercise in the strict contrapuntal style of sixteenth-century Italian church music of which Palestrina was the exemplar and Padre Martini the guardian (as far as eighteenth-century knowledge permitted). Wolfgang would be no stranger to these studies, for Leopold certainly taught him from Fux's *Gradus ad Parnassum*, the text-book which enshrines the technique. On the day of the test (9 October) Wolfgang found himself alone with a sheet of manuscript paper on which were already written the clefs for three upper voices, the time-signature, and the given bass part which was a plainsong made into long equal notes, to the words 'Quaerite primum regnum Dei'. The test was to add the upper three voices. What Wolfgang wrote is K.86, and the original is in the Conservatory library at Bologna. The proceedings-book of the Accademia is not whole-hearted: 'At the end of less than an hour Signor Mozart produced his attempt [?—'esperimento' is the original word] and having regard to the circumstances it was judged sufficient.' Mozart's effort would not normally have passed the requirements of the 'strict style'; the carillon-like sequence in the top part is engaging and enterprising but not Palestrinian, and there are other stylistic solecisms such as downward leaps of a sixth, close approaches to forbidden parallel intervals between voices where a miss cannot be said to be as good as a mile, and a good deal of domination by the treble to spoil the equilibrium—the tenor in particular having less than its share of interest. The test-piece thus comes rather short of Leopold's boast of Wolfgang's easy mastery, but the Accademia had the good sense to secure the immortality of its name by the election of its most famous member. (Incidentally, there exists a receipt made out to Padre Martini for 40 lire for Mozart's admission fee.) But a mystery then begins. There is extant in Martini's hand a reworking of Wolfgang's test which uses his opening gambit (but even here with the order of the entries improved) and which thereafter far from being a correction, as some have asserted, is quite different, and is stylistically almost impeccable even by modern musicological standards. One's first assumption is that this was a piece of teaching to show Wolfgang what could be done with the exercise. It is elegant, and pleasurable to sing. But on *this* version Martini has written: 'Del Sig. Cav. Gio. Amadeo Wolfgango Mozart fatto per l'ingresso nella Accademia di Filarmonici.' (?!) There exist two copies in Wolfgang's hand of this reworking; on the one which is now in the Mozarteum at Salzburg

Leopold actually wrote 'Scritto nella Sala dell' accademia filarmonica in Bologna le 10. d'Ottobre 1770' (N.B. the date is one day later than the test). Thus we have Martini actually saying his own work is Mozart's, and Leopold *almost* saying so. One can perhaps suppose that Martini's concern for the standards of the Academy led him to a kind—and for all we know, transparent—subterfuge; that the faults, as well as the virtues, of Wolfgang's own effort were evident to him at a moment's glance, and that he forthwith composed his own and got Wolfgang to set the record straight by copying it out then and there, before the final meeting authorising the diploma. But that rickety hypothesis is as far as charity need go.

Thus it was as Chevalier and Academician that Wolfgang returned to Milan to fulfil his commission to compose *Mitridate*. The letters home give a vivid account of the turmoil of preparations, of writings and rewritings. The first performance was due on 26 December, and the leading man, Pietro Benedetti, had not arrived even by 24 November, so that Wolfgang was 'anxiously awaiting his presence to measure his musical clothing to his body'. On the other hand the famous Antonia Bernasconi, who was taking the leading woman's part, 'says that she was quite beside herself with joy at the arias Wolfgang has made for her just as she had wanted them'. Ultimately, no doubt, this was the case, but there exist two completely composed and orchestrated, and quite different, versions of her very first aria. The first touches on a high B twice, but contains early on some arpeggios more suited to a pianist than a singer. The second, approved, version abounds in high Bs and has a couple of forthright high Cs, the first fairly early in the singer's first paragraph, calculated to bring the house down almost before it was erected, so to speak. In this version the florid runs are more scalewise, with more comfortable breathing places. Leopold may describe the demands of the singers with a father's jaundiced eye, and we may follow him from an unconsciously romantic viewpoint, but the surviving first drafts show that the changes *were* for the better. Nor does this detract from Wolfgang's achievement, not least in rewriting so well and so quickly instead of throwing down his pen. Wolfgang's favourite tribute must have been that of the leading man, who declared his satisfaction with the duet (which had already been completely written twice) with the words: 'if it doesn't go down well, I'll let myself be castrated again'. Of course a fourteen-year-old could not find from experience the nuances of sexual passion in what was, by *opera seria* standards, a good libretto, but though this places the piece at several removes from, say, *Idomeneo*, it shows a striking and immediate knowledge of how to express such passions in the current Italian style—which, after all, is what constitutes almost the whole (and perfectly valid) *opera seria* experience. Take, for instance, Aspasia's second air 'Nel sen mi palpita', not only for its pathetic and realistic vocal line, but also for the wonderful wailing of the bassoons in their tenor register, an effect of which Handel would be proud. What an orchestral opportunity it was, in any case! Leopold lists the forces as 14 first violins, 14 seconds, six violas, two [sic] cellos, six contrabassi, two keyboard instruments, two oboes, two flutes, to play with the oboes when there were no separate flute parts, four horns and two clarini [trumpets]. Interspersed with three ballets not of Wolfgang's composition the whole entertainment ran initially for six hours and had twenty-two consecutive performances. The first three were directed from the keyboard by Wolfgang, and we can accept Leopold's invitation to his wife and daughter to 'picture for yourselves little Wolfgang in a scarlet suit, trimmed with gold braid and lined with sky-blue satin'.

Relaxations afterwards included a dinner at Madame d'Asti's which featured liver-dumplings and sauerkraut, 'which Wolfgang had asked for'. Then there were expeditions to Turin and Venice. At Venice there were no great Mozartean musical activities but plenty of social ones: they went to a ridotto twice, and went in gondolas so often that at night the bed seemed to rock during their sleep. The happy time there must largely have stemmed from the real family warmth extended by a business colleague of Hagenauer's, Giovanni Wider, who had six daughters whom Wolfgang called 'pearls'.

The journey home was begun by hiring a private boat to go as far as Padua on the water-way called the Brenta. The Widers, hospitable to the end, had thoroughly victualled the expedition. Indeed the Widers and two 'pearls' went with them to Padua, and then Giovanni wrote to Frau Mozart to say what a pleasure it was to have befriended them.

The results of the tour, as far as commissions were concerned, were an opera for Milan due at the end of 1772, one for Venice which was not proceeded with, and an oratorio for Padua. The latter had no deadline and seems not to have been given there, but it was *La Betulia liberata*, K.118, to words by Metastasio. Its composition was in progress in the summer of 1771. Some of the score is in Leopold's hand. It treats the story of Judith, and the most notable feature is the noble severity of its overture leading to the first scene of an afflicted city, a potent reminiscence of Gluck's *Alceste*.

But when the Mozarts returned to Salzburg on 28 March 1771 (Maundy Thursday) there was a letter from Count Firmian, the Austrian minister in Milan, to say that the Empress had commissioned Wolfgang to write a stage serenata due to be performed in Milan on 17 October as part of the festivities for the wedding of her son the Archduke

Ferdinand to the Archduchess Maria Beatrice d'Este, Princess of Modena. This was to be a festal spectacle with dancing and chorus-work, allegorical rather than narrative, entitled *Ascanio in Alba*. The opera proper for the occasion was to be the work of the two Vienna doyens, Hasse the composer setting *Ruggiero* to a libretto by the Imperial poet Metastasio.

The Imperial word would secure leave of absence, and perhaps more, but the Mozarts were tactful enough to busy themselves with Salzburg duties in the twenty weeks they were there. Wolfgang's church compositions of this summer show that the Martini style was in every sense a thing of the past. The *Regina Coeli*, K.108, opens like an Italian symphony, with chorus added. The second movement is like a concerto slow movement for soprano solo, full of a sensuous delight in sound, the delightful roulades being set impartially to Mary's carrying of the Child and to His Resurrection, with the chorus, as it were, sealing and applauding the solo paragraphs with delightfully varied alleluias. Add to this the lovely scoring with two flutes, often doubled an octave below by two viola lines, and we can see here the true results of the first Italian journey, the 'beaker full of the warm south'. In the last 'alleluia' chorus there are traces of a musical reference back to the opening chorus, and a delightful 'ting-ting' figure on the violins which cannot but remind us of the second duet in *Figaro*. Another lively and joyous piece is an offertory in honour of St John the Baptist, *Inter natos mulierum*, K.72, but darkening characteristically for John's declaration 'Behold the Lamb of God'. The experience of Loretto, and the emulation of a similar work by Leopold, were the probable stimulus of *Litaniae Lauretanae*, K.109. The stereotype of a litany is solo invocation and choral response, but Wolfgang uses a much more flexible distribution. It is, for instance, the chorus who invoke Mary as 'virgo potens', but the soloist who sings 'rosa mystica'. The Agnus Dei of a litany does not end with 'dona nobis pacem', often the signal for final jollity in a mass, but with 'miserere nobis'. Here there is a strikingly sombre ending, low in the voices and mainly in the minor key.

Wolfgang also occupied himself with symphonies that summer, and here we begin to see the new power of counterpoint applied to living, not antiquarian, material. For instance, in K.75 in F, the middle of the first movement is enlivened by strenuous discussion, the point additionally made by launching into it without the customary full-stop and repeat at the end of the exposition.

Leopold and Wolfgang set out on their second Italian journey on 13 August 1771, with mother and daughter left wistfully at home. Either the speed of their journey or their glossy condition induced Leopold to say 'we are like two deer, but not ruttish'. They arrived in Milan on 21 August, and on the 24th Leopold says that they had not yet received the libretto of *Ascanio* from Vienna where it would have to be passed as suitable. 'Until it comes the costumes cannot be made, nor the staging and other details settled.' There is never a hint that the music cannot be done in time! Amongst the preparations for the festivities that Leopold noted were twenty thousand pounds of wax candles. Our fire regulations hardly permit us to envisage the golden light that such a serenata as *Ascanio* would thus be seen in. Wolfgang's postscript to his sister concentrates on matters to hand: 'We have a violinist upstairs, another downstairs, in the next room a singing teacher giving lessons, in the opposite room an oboist. Good fun when composing! Plenty of ideas!'

The decorative combination of dancing and chorus-work is evident at the beginning of *Ascanio*. Leopold describes the overture as an *allegro*, then an *andante*—to be danced, but by a few people—then instead of the last *allegro* a sort of *contredanse* with chorus which is danced as well as sung. Thus is set the festal Versailles-like tone, as opposed to the realistic launching of an opera plot in recitative. True to the requirements of the situation the music is rarely more than decorative, often with true allure, although towards the end the emotions are momentarily deepened. The title-part, obviously representing the Archduke in allegory, was sung by an old London friend, Manzuoli, also engaged for Hasse's opera, but Wolfgang tells us that he subsequently behaved 'like a true castrato': he had a dispute over his fee and stormed away without taking any of it. Wolfgang also, it appears, composed the music for the ballet between the acts, but all that remains of it is a bass part not in his hand. The return to Salzburg was not immediate, as Leopold was awaiting the return of the Archduke from visits outside Milan. Meanwhile, Wolfgang had written, probably for a benefit concert, the first version (it was later more fully scored) of the Divertimento in E flat, K.113. Leopold wrote on the score 'Concerto ò sia Divertimento à 8', thereby pointing to the individual nature of the wind parts. Here we have Wolfgang not merely writing for the first time for clarinets—unavailable in Salzburg—but revelling in them. The piece adheres to the four-movement shape associated with the symphony, not suggesting the tendency of the Austrian 'open-air' music to spread into a suite of more than four movements.

The reason for the delayed departure for Salzburg seems all too clear: Leopold was waiting for the upshot of Ferdinand's suggestion to his mother that he might take the Mozarts (presumably both of them) into his service. Her reply, in French, effectively put an end to the second

Italian journey: 'I don't know why you want to, not believing you have need of a composer or of useless people . . . if they are in your service it degrades that service when these people go about the world like beggars.'

The Mozarts were back in Salzburg on 15 December, and the next day their world suffered another shock: the kindly and patient Schrattenbach died. His successor was Hieronymus, Count Colloredo, one of a wealthy family which had given long service to church and state in the Austrian Empire. He made his state entry to Salzburg on 29 April 1772. One of the pieces performed in the Residenz in his honour was a 'serenata drammatica' by Wolfgang: *Il sogno di Scipionie* ('Scipio's Dream'), K.126. The libretto was by Metastasio, again, after Cicero. Scipio has a dream in which he has to choose between the goddesses of Fortune and Constancy, with incidental help from his ancestors and from the music of the spheres. As all good Archbishops should, he chooses Constancy, to the fury of Fortune. Thus ran this one-night show, and hence a string of arias the most interesting feature of which is that Salzburg was able to deploy musicians with the technique to sing and play them (for the orchestrations are sometimes elaborate). The overture originally consisted of an Italian-style *allegro* which led into a charming slower movement to introduce the dream. Wolfgang thought highly enough of it to add a finale a year or so later, so that it could be used as a symphony. Wolfgang was correct in assuming the Italian tastes of the new Archbishop, shown for instance in his appointment to his establishment later in the year of yet another Italian as a second Kapellmeister, one Domenico Fischietti, to the chagrin of Leopold. The Kapellmeister was the music director, and there was a second because Lolli, though not dismissed, was deemed no longer capable. But by now Wolfgang was growing up apace as a composer. Leopold's tireless efforts in Italy, though they had not brought about any appointment, had educated Wolfgang to a mastery in writing for what could fairly be claimed to be some of the best professional forces of the day, and we are now beginning to record a seemingly unquenchable flow of disciplined composition in an ever-increasing number of genres. For instance, the Salzburg symphonies of this summer contain in K.129 in G a really witty work, with sharp rhythmical gestures and contrived collisions of unexpected entries; the sharp twists and chuckles of comic opera are already there, with no-one on the stage. In K.130 in F four horns lend a festive richness, and the finale has grown up into an extended and witty piece enlivened with sudden rests, echoes and *fortes*. It is the idiom of an athlete sure of his training. There are four horns again in K.132 in E flat. Here the slow movement has a 'coming-of-age' moment where in its recapitulation the main theme is surprisingly extended; we

An anonymous oil-painting of 1777 showing Wolfgang as a Knight of the Golden Spur. As befits a papal decoration and an Academician twice over, plainsong notation figures on the music-stand

Guardi's painting of a regatta on the Grand Canal, Venice is dated about 1780 and represents what Leopold and Wolfgang could well have seen, looking towards the Ponte di Rialto

Ceremonial portrait (1772) of
Hieronymus Count Colloredo
wearing the pallium as Prince-
Archbishop of Salzburg

The disciplined but convoluted
Mirabell Gardens of the
Archbishop's summer residence.
The palace itself dates from 1601,
but was remodelled in 1721 by
Johann Lukas von Hildebrandt

The house on Hannibal-Platz in Salzburg (now Makart-Platz) where the Mozarts lived from autumn 1773, occupying eight rooms on the top floor. Leopold died there in 1787

The Benedictine monastery of St Peter at Salzburg, where the C minor Mass was first performed

Tiefer Graben, the street in the Inner City where Leopold and Wolfgang lodged on their 1773 Vienna visit

Loretogasse, Salzburg (now Paris-Lodron-Strasse). The Haffner family's summer residence (see page 96) is the second three-storey house on the left, opposite the monastery which gave the street its original name. The picture dates from c.1755

are in a new time-dimension, where there might have been merely a pretty symmetry. Again in the trio of the minuet, the place where one expects the most popular kinds of tuneful, rhythmical regularity, there is an outbreak of six-bar phrases and no 'tune' in any Salzburgian or Italian sense. The last of this set, K.134 in A, completes the impression of the finale having grown up; the symphony contains many rhythmical surprises, and we encounter what, in the piano concertos especially, will turn out to be a Mozartean fingerprint: themes which are omitted from the expected places and which turn up elsewhere.

In the lighter field of the Divertimento this too was a noteworthy summer. We don't know the occasion of it, but in June Wolfgang wrote a Divertimento in D, K.131 in which what might have been a symphony was extended into a suite by the inclusion of two minuets, one with no fewer than three trios, the other with two. There are four horns again, but these by no means merely enrich the total sound; they are featured, sometimes alone and usually spectacularly. Indeed this work quite surpasses any predecessors in its delight in varied instrumental colour. Three other works called Divertimenti (K.136/8) are of a quite different kind; so far from being extended suites they are three-movement pieces without a single minuet between them, and they are written for strings alone, though whether they are for string orchestra or string quartet is not obvious. Alfred Einstein may be right in suggesting that Wolfgang took them with him to Italy ready to turn into symphonies by the mere addition of such wind instruments as were available and suitable. Be that as it may they are the first pieces of Wolfgang's concerted instrumental music still regularly programmed; especially frequent is the first, in D, though if we take the notation at face-value, the virtuosity of the up-bow-staccato scales called for in its opening *allegro* makes us doubt whether it is an orchestral piece.

In church music, before Colloredo had ever appeared on the scene, Wolfgang had written, again with a work of Leopold's to emulate, the first of his two *Litaniae de venerabili Altaris Sacramento*, K.125. The March dating means that it could have been the 'Litany with numerous and well-founded music' which we know was the culmination of the forty-hour prayer of Holy Week. Wolfgang's score contains additions in Leopold's hand of tempo-marks and other details, and indeed a few musical corrections. The usual set-piece fugue for the words 'Pignus futurae gloriae' is long and conventional, the choruses are mainly fillings-in of a basically orchestral conception, and the solos are Italianate and ornamental, but have no obvious connection with feeling.

There is another setting of *Regina Coeli*, K.127, to the same words as K.108 of the previous year. There is plenty of orchestral glitter and the opening chorus is in effect a rich symphonic movement. The soprano solo at 'Ora pro nobis' develops into an out-and-out concerto-*adagio* for the voice, complete with space for a cadenza. The prayer is not over-laden with a consciousness of sin, but rather of virtue or at least virtuosity. The date on the score, May, makes it likely that Colloredo heard it. The unclouded relations between him and Wolfgang were presumably rendered yet more happy when in August Wolfgang's appointment as Konzertmeister was at last made a paid one, at a salary—150 florins a year—which was neither extravagant nor negligible.

Father and son set out over the Brenner pass yet again, leaving Salzburg on 24 October 1772 and arriving in Milan on 4 November, where they lodged near the d'Astis, of liver-dumpling fame. Madame d'Asti lent them comfortable pillows instead of the Italian ones, which they found too hard. After all, Madame came from Salzburg herself. Their object was to fulfil the commission for the opening opera of the Carnival season, beginning on 26 December. On the way, at Bolzano, Wolfgang, according to Leopold, was 'whiling away the time writing a quartet'. Bolzano was obviously the butt of family jokes: 'dreary', and 'pigsty' are some of the epithets, and Wolfgang in a postscript even contributed a doggerel (or perhaps one should say piggerel) poem about the unfortunate town. But it has its undying distinction in being the launching-pad for a series of six string quartets, K.155 to K.160, in which, as with the symphonies of 1772, Wolfgang came of age. The first of them may begin like a Mannheim symphony with drumming under-parts on repeated notes, but then there emerge snatches of tune for second violin and indeed virtuoso passages for viola which certainly would not be written for any orchestra Wolfgang would envisage at this date. Though the works may not yet match the extended range of thought and depth of feeling of later sets, they already show an intuitive sense, with few models to hand, of the balance of four solo strands, and although some of the movements are short-winded by later standards, each is a 'character'. This sudden hitting of the essential nail on the head constitutes the sort of 'Wunderkind' leap which would remain, even were every work of Mozart's contemporaries analysed down to the last semi-quaver in a search for precedents.

On 21 November Leopold writes with tenderness partly disguised with pseudo-pedantry about their silver wedding anniversary: 'It was, I believe, twenty-five years ago that we had the good idea of getting married—in fact, we'd had the idea many years before that, but all good things take their time!' Typically, this passage is not at the head of the letter beneath the all-important date, nor even in a separate paragraph, but comes between comments on the lodgings—the bed is wider than the last one—and on the arrival of the leading male soprano, Venanzio Rauzzini. The principal singers gradually assembled, which at any rate allowed Wolfgang to concentrate on their arias individually, but the tenor Cordoni, who was to have sung the title-role, fell ill and his place was taken by an inhabitant of Lodi, Bassano Morgnoni. This meant some swift composition—we read of two arias in one day—and his arias are by far the least demanding. Morgnoni's inexperience led to a contretemps on the first night, when his over-acting of rage set the house laughing and quite put the prima donna, the famous Anna d'Amicis, off her stroke, so that she had to be mollified by a personal reception at Court the next day. Nor was this the only mishap on the first night. It began two hours late because Archduke Ferdinand was 'detained by official matters'. One can well imagine the emotions back-stage and in the pit. With three long ballets between acts the performance ended at 2 a.m. The music of *Lucio Silla*, K.135, *qua* music, contains the richest and most distinguished passages of any of Wolfgang's stage works so far, but much of it, by its very elaboration, is at odds with any sense of characterisation and interaction. For instance, the first two arias are long and brilliant concerto movements for two different sopranos, each stopping for *two* cadenzas. They are succeeded by two more arias for two more sopranos. At the end of the first act there is a duet for two sopranos (one female and one male) who, when they sing in thirds, seem to be pre-echoing the sensuous intoxication of *Così fan tutte*, though without its deft characterisation. As the libretto makes its seemingly inevitable way towards the beloved prison-scene over which death looms, the young Mozart, in his 'now-or-never' position, invests the emotions with all the music he can throw in. Heroism, love, terror, self-sacrifice—all the larger-than-life attitudes have their larger-than-life music. The opera was given twenty-six times, and indeed the first night of the second opera, Paisiello's *Sismano nel Mogol* was put back a week till 30 January. Leopold had attended some of a rehearsal and liked its music, and adds: 'In this opera there are to be twenty-four horses and a great crowd of people on the stage, so that it will be miraculous if some accident doesn't happen.' He leaves his family to speculate on what sort of accident he means.

Meanwhile, Rauzzini had sung in the Theatine Church a work which Wolfgang had written for him, and which, while *Lucio Silla* has remained virtually unperformed, has become one of the best-known of all the solo cantatas, *Exsultate jubilate*, K.165. Mention was made in Chapter 3 of some of the forms taken in Italy, France and Germany in Mozart's time by concerted music during the Offertory, at a moment for a letting down of the hair, between that part of the Mass which culminates in Gospel and Creed and the central drama of which the preliminary is the bringing in of the bread and wine. If we think of a jubilant intermezzo, we shall not be far from the effect of the *Exsultate*, and of the several other such works by Wolfgang called 'Offertorium'.

Leopold himself did not attend the Paisiello first night on 30 January. He was in bed with feigned rheumatism. He had by now to have a reason for their not coming back to duty at Salzburg. It seemed all too certain more than a month after the first night of *Lucio Silla* that there would be no Milan appointment although neither he nor Wolfgang could have done more, and he was desperately clutching at a possibility, with Count Firmian as go-between, of an appointment at the court of Archduke Leopold at Florence. His letter of 27 February abandons all hopes of Florence, and therewith, as it turns out, all hopes of Italy. 'You can't imagine my distress at our departure; it comes hard, having to leave Italy.' It is not often that Leopold, with his 'stiff upper lip' training, writes like this. The rheumatic delay also held up negotiations for the Mozarts to move into the first floor of a house in Hannibal-platz (now Makart-platz) on the other side of the Salzach. It was to give the family eight rooms, and the move eventually took place in the late autumn. For the last time they saw Verona, and for the last time climbed from Trent to Bressanone to the Brenner. They arrived in Salzburg on 13 March 1773, the day before the celebration of the first anniversary of the new Archbishop's enthronement. But although Wolfgang had left Italy, Italy in the musical sense was never to leave Wolfgang.

Wolfgang threw himself for a while into a study of Salzburg church music, copying out works by Michael Haydn and Eberlin. There seemed little enough else to throw himself into. But the largest authentic church work of his of this date seems not to have been written for the cathedral. For one thing it contains no solos. It is the Mass in C, K.167, written 'in honorem SS: mae Trinitatis' and probably for the Trinity church. Its editor for the New Mozart Edition, Walter Senn, calls attention to the fact that it has a *missa brevis* shape but with *missa solemnis* orchestration. The choir writing is almost all chordal except for the traditional fugues at the end of Gloria and Credo, and, in this case, Agnus Dei. The orchestra, though there is no viola part, is made festive by the addition of drums and four trumpets. Two of them are ordinary ones at the usual pitch but the other two are written in the *bass* clef. There were such things as bass trumpets at the time, and the Salzburg Museum possesses one made in 1763. The musical excitement they lend is modest as between them they employ only four notes. The total effect of the mass, though bustling and brilliant where necessary, is rather empty, as though the heart is not in it.

But the genre of major importance in the output of 1773 was the

Symphony. Before the year is out there will be a peak unclimbed before. These symphonies show the marriage of the Italian style to Wolfgang's own growing personality. The chameleon is becoming Mozart. Four symphonies ascribed to this year, K.162, 184, 199 and 181, are all restricted to the three-movement norm of Italy, sometimes with one movement leading into another, as often in opera overtures, and they end with happy-go-lucky last movements, in a jigging style. The first of them, K.162 in C, though giving no hint of intellectuality in its breezy style, has its first movement held together by cross-references of its rhythms from one part of the design to another, and it is rounded off by reverting to the opening bars of its main theme which somehow had failed to be recapitulated at the 'right' place. In K.184 in E flat, the first movement again uses apparently superficial materials and joking loud punctuations of its second theme, but surprising clouds of minor harmonies come and go, and the movement suddenly leads straight into an *andante* where the minor tonality has come to stay. Its melancholy is made almost hypnotic by an insistent rhythmic figure which is rarely absent, no matter where we are in the design. The gem of K.199 in G is its truly charming *Andantino grazioso*: in the strings the violins are muted, the others *pizzicato*. There are deceptive cadences which somehow manage to repeat their surprises, but again all is held together by rhythmic figures which, however, always avoid insistence. We don't know what the immediate stimulus for these works was, whether an Italian commission or the prospect of Salzburg performance. But we cannot help sensing, in the light of the future, that this application of a more powerful organising personality to entertainment music simply had to take place at this juncture.

After only four months back in Salzburg father and son were on their travels again.

5

Excursions to Vienna and Munich

1773–77

The exact reason for the visit to Vienna is not known. The Mozarts were received in audience by the Empress, but Leopold seems not to have cultivated the nobility particularly. What is clear is that Leopold was not showing off an infant prodigy, but seeking to introduce to a metropolitan centre a young man who by proven experience and reception elsewhere could claim to be treated as a metropolitan musician.

They left Salzburg on 14 July 1773 and arrived in Vienna on the 16th. They lodged with Gottlieb Fischer, one of a family whom the Mozarts had known since the 1768 visit; the address was 322 Tiefer Graben, an open place in the inner city. Apart from the Fischers, the family most often mentioned in the letters home are what Leopold collectively called 'die Messmerischen', centred on a man who has given his name to the language, Dr Franz Anton Mesmer, who founded the study of what he called 'animal magnetism'. He had lived in Vienna since 1759, practised healing by laying on of hands, and had built himself a 'little magnetic hospital'. He had a good tenor voice, and played the cello and harpsichord as well as an instrument of tuned wine-glasses called a 'glass-harmonica'. Wolfgang of course tried his hand at this, and indeed was ultimately to compose for the instrument.

The first letter home from Vienna mentions sending off to Salzburg the first instalment of the Final-Musik (graduation celebration) for Judas Thaddäus von Andrettern. The music comprises a March (for entrance and exit), K.189, and the Serenade proper, K.185. The outer movements are like the Salzburg symphonies we have discussed, blithe and attractive but firmly and wittily constructed with nothing reach-me-down about them, and the mélange of many-coloured movements in between contain two featuring a violin solo. It is clear that in spite of the music being due in Salzburg at the beginning of August, there was nothing put down in usable form before the Mozarts left there.

On 5 August the Empress gave them an audience. Leopold says she was very gracious but does not mention the upshot of any request they may have made. Remembering her letter to Archduke Ferdinand this is hardly remarkable. There may be a hint in a letter of 4 September which mentions Florian Gassmann, who the previous year had been made Kapellmeister to the Imperial court. Leopold says Gassmann had been ill, but was better. (In fact he died in 1774.) 'I do not know what sort of connection this should have with our stay in Vienna. Fools everywhere are the same!' These enigmatic remarks are perhaps the nearest we get to the purpose of the visit. In any case the postscript says they will not be staying much longer.

Compositions that can certainly be dated in this period are six more string quartets, K.168–73. They have enough resemblances, sometimes even amounting to turns of phrase, to Haydn's set of quartets, opp. 17 and 20 to make it certain that Wolfgang was acquainted with them. It is noteworthy that they should have been written so quickly, with the first four dated in August and the other two almost certainly in September. What is more, some movements look rather hastily put together, especially when compared with the more purposeful part-writing and formal coherence of Haydn of this date. It is possible that Leopold, having failed with personal demonstrations of Wolfgang's talents, was determined to renew publication of 'post-prodigy' music. He had already made an abortive approach to Breitkopf at the end of the second Italian journey, but in fact this famous firm never published a note of Wolfgang's music during his life-time. But if chamber music was to be published sets of six were the norm. It is however possible that at this stage they were simply materials for musical evenings at the Teybers, who figure prominently in the letters home. Matthäus Teyber was a violinist in the court orchestra, and one of the daughters, Therese, was to be Blonde in the first performance of *Die Entführung*. The most individual movements of Wolfgang's set are the minuets, where he is emboldened by Haydn's example, if example he needed, to write pithily and surprisingly, sometimes turning the dance into a string of instrumental epigrams. The most consistently interesting quartet is perhaps the last. Here for the first time he writes a quartet in the minor key—and in a thoroughgoing way with three of the four movements in D minor. In the first movement the frequent unisons and unaccompanied phrases (as of some singer left palpitating and unsupported on the stage) add to a sense of pathos and unease, and the last movement, though a fugue on a conventional subject, has enough resource and drama to hold our interest, which is clinched by the quiet, resigned ending. There was no immediate publication.

The letters home, though they do not give much detail about music, give precious glimpses of local colour in the family life. For instance, the family journey to England is doubtless responsible for the name of the Mozarts' dog. Wolfgang asks in a postscript dated 21 August: 'How is Miss [sic] Bimbes?' [N.B. not Fräulein Bimbes] and incidentally besides writing date and place backwards signs himself 'gnagflow Trazom'. (This to his sister of course, not his long-suffering mother.) In the next letter Frau Mozart is upbraided by Leopold for missing an opportunity of sending by a friend his 'English red-brown coat with the golden spangles'. In the same letter he promises to do what he can about getting bonnets and the like for Nannerl, but his purse is getting emptier as his figure is getting stouter. There is a tantalising sentence on 28 August: 'Tomorrow we dine with Monsieur Novere.' This must have been Jean Georges Noverre, the famous dancer and ballet-master. If they had talked of artistic matters at all might they not have spoken of the narrative, dramatic uses of dance of which Noverre was a pioneer, and perhaps even of Don Giovanni, whose tale had been vividly told by Noverre's choreographer colleague Angiolini and Gluck in a ballet put on in Vienna in 1761?

Amongst the sparse news of concerts we learn that Leopold conducted the Dominicus Mass, K.66 in the Jesuit church in the square called 'Auf dem Hof' on 8 August; this was only a month before the expulsion of the Jesuits from their monastery there. The suppression of their order in the Austrian Empire with effect from 10 September—arising from Pope Clement XIV's Brief 'Dominus ac Redemptor' dated 21 July—was an event greeted with a mixture of piety and *Schadenfreude* by Leopold. They left Vienna on 24 September, travelling by the direct route, although at one time Leopold had thought of a detour along the Wolfgangsee, 'to show our Wolfgang the pilgrimage church of his patron saint at St Wolfgang, and St Gilgen, the famous birthplace of his mother'. They arrived back in Salzburg, to greet Miss Bimbes amongst others, on 26 September.

The impetus to symphony-writing seems to have renewed itself immediately, for the score of the next, K.182 in B flat, is dated 3 October 1773, just seven days after the return—though we must not forget Wolfgang's capacity for composing in his head in all sorts of circumstances. It has an exceedingly pretty *Andantino grazioso*, but does not differ greatly from its three-movement predecessors. But it is quite otherwise with the G minor symphony, K.183, dated *two days* later, in which we are suddenly plunged into a turbulent emotional world rendered all the more powerful by the formal rigour with which it is controlled. Because of *the* G minor symphony (K.550) it is sometimes referred to as the 'little G minor'. There is nothing little about it, not even in its dimensions if the repeats are properly observed. This is Wolfgang's first

symphony in a minor key, and like the D minor quartet it makes a
thorough job of it, with the finale unrelieved by any relaxation into G
major. It bears the full symphonic weight of four movements, and its
minuet only relaxes momentarily in its all-wind trio. Just as the Eliza-
bethans and their Italian contemporaries enjoyed laments, so perhaps did
educated Europe enjoy turbulent passion in the 1770s, when *Sturm und
Drang*—storm and stress—became a catch-phrase. After all, in the
following year young Goethe was to lay waste the adolescent hearts of
half Europe with 'The Sorrows of Young Werther'. Even so, there could
hardly be a greater stride away from communal entertainment than this
symphony with its palpitating syncopations, tenderly sighing slow movement and the use of four horns to ensure the punching home of the severe
main themes in the minuet and the final *allegro*. We do not know for
whom the symphony was written (if indeed for anyone).

In contrast, the Symphony in C, K.200 inhabits an entirely happy
world. The courtly minuet has pre-echoes of the 'Jupiter' symphony,
and the last movement is a truly fleet *presto* which brings the house
down with a crescendo like an opera finale. The trilogy closes with the
A major symphony, K.201 whose grace and vivacity assures it of a regular
place in the concert repertoire. In the first movement there is some close
imitation between the melodic voices, but it is an elegant adjunct, not a
demonstration. In the last movement the new-found tight control of shape
and argument makes all the more telling the momentary stoppages when
the violins turn the small upward run of the main subject into virtuoso
rocket-like scales. To these masterpieces the Symphony in D, K.202
forms a rather inconsequential appendix, and then perhaps not surprisingly there are no more symphonies until the 'Paris' of 1778.

But before the end of 1773 Wolfgang had written his first works in
two new genres. Perhaps spurred by a recent work for the same
combination by Michael Haydn, he wrote a string quintet in B flat,
K.174. The main consequence of adding a second viola to the string
quartet was to ensure a fuller harmony when the first viola (as often in
this piece) alternates melodically with the first violin, to charming effect.
The style sometimes verges on the orchestral; there are a few places in
the part marked *basso* where a double-bass would not come amiss, and
Wolfgang wrote a complete version each of the trio and final *allegro*
before arriving at the ultimate text.

The mature flowering of the string quintet was a long way in the
future. Of more immediate consequence was the first of the piano
concertos, K.175 in D. (We can view as preparation for this composition
the making of three more father-and-son concertos, K.107, this time
arrangements of the beloved J.C. Bach, three of whose op. 5 keyboard

sonatas supplied the raw materials. They were probably intended for use on the Italian visit of 1772. In the scores Wolfgang wrote the three string parts which constituted the concerto frame—for instance, the opening *tutti*, additional themes, accompanying figures and a bed of harmony for the solo to lie on. In Leopold's hand is the solo part, sometimes having to be crowded into Wolfgang's previously written bars.) Wolfgang seems to have written K.175 for himself to play, or else his sister. He must have had a soft spot for it, as he played it several times later in his career, supplying it with cadenzas and writing a new last movement for a performance in Vienna (the Rondo K.382). This must have been a concession to Viennese taste, as the original finale is an exhilarating example of a sonata form always willing to dash off into counterpoint.

Amongst the church music of this summer Wolfgang writes a Dixit Dominus and a Magnificat, K.193, a solid piece of counterpoint with 'the humble' offering the only real surprise. But a second *Litaniae Lauretanae*, K.195, is a different matter. It is extended and elaborate, full of ornamental devotion. In the final Agnus Dei the chorus themselves break into flower, so to speak, with rapturous and quiet roulades. This expansion is in marked contrast to the feats of compression required in two works called 'Missa Brevis', in F, K.192 and in D, K.194, both written for Salzburg Cathedral. This is perhaps the place to quote before its chronological time from a letter sent in the name of Wolfgang but written in Leopold's best hand to Padre Martini in September 1776: 'Our church music is very different from that of Italy, for a mass with all its music—Kyrie, Gloria, Credo, the Epistle Sonata [a one-movement instrumental interlude of which there survive seventeen by Wolfgang], the Offertory or Motet, Sanctus and Agnus Dei—even the most solemn one must not last more than three quarters of an hour when our Prince is celebrating it.' It does indeed need 'un Studio particolare' as the Mozarts put it. These two works are technical feats but also compelling music. Leopold conducted them both in the Hofkapelle in Munich in February 1775. The F major is of particular interest because its Credo enshrines the 'Jupiter's *d r f m* signature-phrase which carries interjections of the word 'Credo' throughout the movement. It is also the theme of other clauses and of a fine 'amen' fugue (since space is somehow made for counterpoint) and the choir sings it to 'credo, credo' as a sly, soft postscript. This technique of interjecting the word at intervals survives in Beethoven's Missa Solemnis.

But the autumn of 1774 must have been largely occupied by the composition of another commission, this time for the Elector of Bavaria in Munich, Maximilian III Joseph. It was for once not a stately *opera seria*, but an *opera buffa*, *La finta giardiniera* ('The mock gardening-girl'). Presumably again with the Archbishop's blessing, father and son set out for Munich on 6 December. Their lodgings were to be with a canon of the Frauenkirche, Johann von Pernat. From the very first letter home (14 December) it is clear that Nannerl was hoping to join them somehow for the opera. But Leopold points out that Munich is like Salzburg, that is, emphatically not like Milan, in the infrequency of repeat-performances of operas, due to a lack of paying customers. Indeed the first performance was postponed from the original date and there were only three altogether, of which the second suffered cuts with a singer being ill. By 16 December a lodging had been found for Nannerl at the 'Spatzenreiter house in the square' where lived in great respect-ability the widow von Durst, a 'brunette with dark eyes, sensible, well-read, aged 26 to 28, who doesn't care for philanderers'. Frau von Durst was making a harpsichord available. But these admirable arrangements were only the preliminaries to a flood of advice and instructions. 'Nannerl really must learn to do her own toilette including making-up her face; she should also practise the clavier' (these last two injunctions actually come in the same sentence in that order). She should wear fur boots, not felt shoes, for the journey, and she should have hay in the bottom of the coach to bury her feet in. Finally, there were minute and fool-proof instructions on how to find the lodgings in Munich. In the event von Pernat's servant was also sent to meet the coach to make doubly sure.

But there was also music to be sent. Both Leopold's and Wolfgang's (K.125) settings of the *Litaniae de venerabili* were to be performed, presumably in the Frauenkirche, so 'see that all the parts are with them'. In this connection there is one interesting combination of musical and domestic detail. The shortened form of Wolfgang's 'Pignus' fugue from K.125 is required: 'it will be found in the middle drawer above the desk, the one that doesn't shut properly . . . . If you can't find it in that drawer where the toy coach and horse are, I don't know where it is.' Nannerl has to bring with her Wolfgang's written-out piano sonatas and some variations, but 'not many concertos are required, and we have Wolfgang's with us' (clearly K.175). There are again enquiries after Miss Bimbes, who appears now to be spelt 'Pimpsess', and a laconic postscript from Wolfgang: 'I have toothache.'

Nannerl's escort was an old Salzburg friend, Frau Robinig, with her daughter Louise. Nannerl was of course 'so well looked after all the way, I couldn't possibly have frozen.' She renewed acquaintance with the Nymphenburg, and Leopold mentions that she went to a masked ball as an Amazon; 'it suited her well'—a claim which from her pictures we find hard to believe.

But meanwhile, *La finta giardiniera* had added to the list of successes without upshots. (Though it was later, in 1779, taken up by a touring company in German with spoken dialogue, a form of entertainment known as a *Singspiel*.) The original, however, was an *opera buffa*—all sung, in Italian, with stock characters based on Harlequinade: for instance, an old man making himself ridiculous in love, a scheming and pert maidservant, all contributing to an *imbroglio* of unexpected events leading to finales in which the stage gradually fills with the cast. This particular libretto divides the roles into serious and comic ones, perhaps to the detriment of the Mozart setting, inasmuch as Wolfgang so enriches some of the sentiments of the 'comic' characters as to make their reversions to comedy incongruous and unconvincing. The finales lack his later genius for quick cumulation and changes of groupings while the action continues; the characters tend instead to take it in turns to sing rounded and balanced sentences. But the music is delightful. The arias include a conducted tour of the orchestra, and of European styles of love-music with a blunt English example, and one precursor of the catalogue music in *Don Giovanni* when Il Contino Belfiore enumerates his ancestors. On the 'genuine' side the rival women have arias of real passion. The orchestration is far more thoroughgoing than that of contemporary *opere buffe*; there can be few viola parts like Mozart's of this date. When Leopold announces the postponement by a week of the first performance (in fact it was again put off till 13 January) it is 'that the singers may learn their parts more thoroughly'. With this music added to the complications to be enacted we can well understand, but we can also realise that such postponements might well be counted to the discredit of Wolfgang, who saw so much deeper and further, and who could not forbear to explore and express such insights, whether the libretto or the occasion was suitable or not. In comparison with Italy the whole operation must have seemed sadly marginal. The opera was not even given in the Residenztheater, but in the Assembly Rooms in the Prannerstrasse. The Archbishop of Salzburg was indeed in Munich for part of their stay, but not on a date when he could have heard the opera. He would have to be content (if that is the word) with second-hand accounts of his employee's work.

It was probably early in 1775, during this Munich stay, that Wolfgang committed to paper the first six of the regularly-recognised piano sonatas, K.279–84. His extempore powers would normally suffice him for concert work, so that their systematic arrangement by keys (C, F, B flat, etc.) and their number (six) may point to intended publication. The use of these sonatas as teaching materials tends to prevent their proper assessment. Their *allegro* movements, for instance, are far less vehement and ebullient than those of the early Beethoven sonatas to which piano students aspire to graduate. Thus one tends to overlook the subtlety and indeed profusion with which their undemanding, entertaining ideas are set out. If we look at the exposition of the first sonata (K.279 in C) and count the number of different melodic ideas we shall find seven at least, with a plausible case for nine. After the double-bar it is instructive to count them again, and see in what order they reappear, and note the surprising ways in which they are altered. If gravity is required (perhaps a mistaken search, as though sad-sounding music is somehow 'deeper' than blithe-sounding music) then there is the F minor slow movement of K.280, whilst the *andante* of K.281 has serenade-like reminiscences of clarinets singing in thirds. Incidentally the expression marks, especially the surprising alternations of *forte* and *piano* in the course of a phrase, make them quite unsuitable for a harpsichord, which is not of course to say that they were never played on a harpsichord.

The Elector having expressed a wish to hear what Wolfgang could do in the contrapuntal line, he speedily wrote *Misericordias Domini*, K.222, which was given on 5 March 1775. It is a remarkable piece of sustained workmanship, rearranging and expanding minimal materials (five Latin words in all, two to chords and three to counterpoint) so as to achieve 159 bars of coherent music. It is resourceful rather than endearing, but it evoked a handsome testimony from Padre Martini, to whom it was sent with the letter about the brevity of His Grace's masses. If Wolfgang had thought of the piece as in some way an essay in the old style he must have been surprised at Martini's choice of words at the beginning of his encomium: 'I was exceptionally pleased with it, finding in it all the requisites of Modern Music.'

But by the time the letter was sent to Martini (4 September 1776) another long summer had been spent at Salzburg, another operatic occasional piece had had no more effect than had the state banquet with which it was doubtless equated, and the letter accordingly contains complaints about meagre operatic resources, and a pretty explicit plea for some new métier particularly in beloved Italy. Immediately on the return of the three Mozarts on 7 March, Wolfgang was set to work by the Archbishop to compose Metastasio's *Il re pastore* as a festal entertainment for the visit of the Archduke Maximilian, Maria Theresa's youngest son, that same Maximilian whose court dress had been inherited by Wolfgang in Vienna in 1762. He was on his way back from Paris to Vienna, doubtless as part of the periodical effort to keep the two centres of the Habsburg-Bourbon families from being at loggerheads. To sing in the opera and in other musical entertainment for the Archduke the castrato Tommaso Consoli who had sung a principal part in *La finta giardiniera* was brought across from Munich, together with a flautist, Johann Becke. It looks as though Leopold arranged this, for the Archiepiscopal accounts show him being reimbursed for food, drink, etc. served by the Sternbräu (Star Brewery) to the 'two virtuosi engaged from Munich'. Considering that the opera was a short occasional piece—two acts, one night—it is of a superior workmanship, though not really engaging Wolfgang's dramatic instincts. It is a succession of solo airs with a duet as climax to the first act. At the end the five characters sing a finale which is more extended and varied than the usual lining up for an easily-memorised jubilation. Two of the characters begin as shepherds but have higher matters thrust upon them. Wolfgang does not do much to convey the pastoral scene, but the routine contrasts of love and duty are dispatched efficiently, and an aria with muted strings and violin solo, 'L'amero', has remained a concert favourite. Another aria to be rescued from oblivion was 'Aer tranquillo' sung at Mannheim in 1778 by Aloysia Weber. Its opening bars had a speedier resurrection than this, however. They reappeared, slightly altered, as the opening subject of the G major violin concerto, K.216, one of the five which Wolfgang wrote in 1775. He was a Konzertmeister, it will be remembered, a term which would normally be applied to what we would call the leader of the orchestra. It is unlikely that Wolfgang, though capable of it, had such a function at Salzburg by way of duty, since the Court Calendar of 1775 shows Michael Haydn the organist and composer, but with no reputation as a violinist, in the same honorific but not necessarily honorary position. But Wolfgang certainly at this stage did regard himself as a potential concert artist on the violin. He may well have written the concertos for himself, but they were obviously also used by another artist, Antonio Brunetti, who from 1777 was also a Salzburg Konzertmeister. Wolfgang wrote him a new middle movement (K.261) for the A major concerto, K.219, because according to Leopold he found the original one 'too studied'. Both the original and the substitute have their surprises which are obviously timed and thought about, but that an experienced professional should call 'too studied' what most listeners would nowadays regard as 'heaven-sent' is a measure of the gradient of the uphill path Wolfgang had to climb.

At nineteen years old, with a genius enriched by more experience of professional music-making and world-travel than anyone of his age could have expected, Wolfgang in this music is already showing us touches of irony, though humorous and affectionate rather than bitter, using the formal clichés of everyday music to surprise us. In the slow movement of the G major concerto the soloist re-emerges to sing once again a parting phrase of the heavenly tune as though he cannot bring himself to say good-bye to it. Yet this occurs after the cadenza at the very moment when he ought to be mopping his brow. The end of the same concerto is a throwaway gesture on the wind instead of an applause-catching *tutti*. The D major concerto, K.218, begins with the most ordinary of fanfare-motifs, the sort of thing that any princeling might expect to make an entrance to. But there are no trumpets in the score, only their imitation by a generous use of open strings; when the soloist emerges he restarts the fanfare two octaves higher, out of trumpet range, but with a neighbouring grace-note attached to the first note which sounds like a well-observed imitation of the 'split note' which would be the likely result of a trumpet trying to start at that altitude. Three of the rondo-finales in these concertos contain a feature which may have been suggested by one of Leopold's own keyboard sonatas—the one in F (1762). Their course is suddenly interrupted by 'popular' music in a quite different and strongly-marked tempo. For instance, the A major, K.219, bursts into 'Turkish' music including a theme which Wolfgang had copied down from the ballet *Le gelosie del Seraglio* which diversified *Lucio Silla* in Milan.

So the Salzburg round resumed. Some of it is catalogued in what survives of Nannerl's very laconic diary. For instance, the only recorded event for 3 May 1776 is 'an elephant arrived here' (it left on 15 May). The 16th was busier: 'a litany by Fischietti was sung in the Mirabell palace' and 'Today my brother fell in the dung.' On 25 May there was a one-day visit from their old friend Dr Mesmer.

But thwarted of opera the springs of creation merely flowed in other directions in 1775–77. Perhaps symptomatic of the home milieu is one of the shortest of all masses: K.220 in C. It takes further Wolfgang's interest in rounding out the music by adopting Michael Haydn's device of ending the Mass with the music of the opening. This mass has been nicknamed 'The Sparrow' because the violins have a cheeping motif in the Sanctus and Benedictus—a repeated high note with a grace-note beneath it. There may be a family joke here: three such cheeps begin the 'Teutscher Tanz' in Leopold's famous 'Musical Sleigh-ride', and they were later to introduce (in the same rhythm) the second of the three simultaneous dances in Don Giovanni's ballroom.

In marked contrast to the 'Sparrow Mass' is another mass in C, K.262. It bears the title 'Missa Longa' in Leopold's hand, perhaps in jocular distinction from the plethora of examples of *missa brevis* which surrounds it, for there appears to be no such recognised category as a *missa longa*. This example, two big fugues apart, is in many respects merely a blown-up version of a *missa brevis* with the soloists used in the main only as incidental colour. The petitions in the middle of the Gloria have touches of unusual harmony. It was probably written for the consecration in the cathedral, as Bishop of Chrysopel, of Ignaz Joseph Count von Spaur, who had been for many years a family friend. If so, the date, 17 November, would make it one of no fewer than four masses occupying the last two months of 1776. The others are all *missae breves*, K.257–9, and they are all in C, but nothing need be read into the key beyond the fact that they were all enlivened with trumpet parts, and C was clearly the natural key of the Salzburg instruments. They are emphatically not dispirited hack-work; apart from their many felicities their very variety shows a welling-up of creativity in spite of identical texts and basically identical formats. In comparison with former masses they are more sheerly tuneful, perhaps as a result of the succession of serenade-like music in this crowded year. The orchestra, though important and enlivening, is also more distinctly accompanimental. In K.257 'credo' interjections are very much in evidence, and the $d\,r\,f\,m$ motif (yet again) begins the Sanctus. There is an extended Agnus Dei as though Wolfgang has suddenly realised he has time to spare. In K.259 the organ in the Benedictus is released from its supporting function and it purls along in accompanying the four soloists. In Salzburg Cathedral the soloists would be standing by their own 'solo' organ, thus enhancing their differences from the *tutti* with a spatial effect. There is a magical moment at the end of this Benedictus when they end their quartet with what amounts to a written-out cadenza for the four of them above a low pedal note. This is at the furthest remove from routine. It is impossible to suppose that *no-one* had ears in the cathedral for this beauty, nor that the Archbishop himself, who liked music, could not have taken pleasure in it. The *music* does not in the least suggest the caged bird trying to escape; the creative well begins to flow immediately the occasion (dutiful or congenial) sets it off, and it miraculously channels itself in the right directions.

Very different in kind is *Litaniae de venerabile Altaris Sacramento*, K.243, first heard on Palm Sunday, 1776. Not being tied to the formal ceremonial of a mass, but serving as a musical climax of, and release from, a day-long roster of prayers, such music can expand, and can make up the traditional text into a mélange of different movements. In this setting the tenor solo 'Panis vivus' is one of the jolliest of all pleas for mercy. As with some other works of this period it is marked *Allegro aperto*, and it does indeed have an 'open' extrovert exuberance. The later descriptions of the Sacrament as 'tremendum' and as a 'viaticum' on death's journey rouse Wolfgang suddenly to vivid utterance, and the soprano solo 'sweetest banquet' has a lyrical minuet on muted strings for background music—a celestial *Tafelmusik* as it were. The final 'miserere' uses the same quiet phrases as the opening. A personal devotion suffuses these Mozart litanies. Wolfgang was not to know it, but he had already written the last of them.

But the 1776–77 period at Salzburg was also rich in secular music, particularly Divertimenti and Serenades. At this time and place the Serenades have strings as their basis, with wind added (though this does not hold good later on) whereas the Divertimenti would either employ these forces or a wind sextet of two oboes, two horns and two bassoons. Obviously the wind ensemble would be suitable for open-air work, but we would be wrong to suppose that in summer the Salzburg ambience could not be quiet and balmy enough for strings *al fresco*. The works themselves could either be miniature symphonies in four movements or less, or grow into suites with at least two minuets in them. It might depend on the amount of the commission, or on the depth of the friendship. But what all the music has in common is a purpose which is almost impossible to mention nowadays without seeming pejorative— entertainment. Leopold gives such a vivid picture of one such Salzburg entertainment, albeit one that went wrong, that it is worth quoting here, though it refers to the summer of 1778, when mother and son were in Paris. Count Czernin is the arranger of a serenade for Countess Lodron.

Czernin looked up at the window, then called out 'Straight through!' Then came Menuet and Trio—just once through, then an Adagio which he played with great diligence and terribly badly—talking all the while to Brunetti standing behind him; then he cried out 'straight through' and then 'allons! marche!' and he and the musicians disappeared in a trice. No one could have devised and carried out a better way of turning a serenade into a public insult, for half the town was there. And why?—because he imagined that the Countess was not at the window, in which misconception Brunetti supported him. But the Countess and Dean Breiner were at the window and everyone else had seen them there. A couple of days later . . . the Countess gave Brunetti a terrible dressing-down, and since then the Archbishop has had nothing more to do with him.

It was this same redoubtable Countess for whom Wolfgang wrote two Divertimenti, both for two horns and strings: in 1776 K.247 in F, one of the jolliest of such confections, and in 1777 K.287 in B flat, whose last movement is led into, and later interrupted by, a mock-dramatic recitative which takes the first violin to melodramatic heights, increasing the bathetic humour of the country-dance subject which Einstein says is a South German popular tune 'D'Bäuerin hat d'Katz verlorn' ('the land-girl's lost the cat'). The Divertimento in D, K.251 is generally supposed to have been written to celebrate Nannerl's being twenty-five in July

1777, though perhaps it was also used as a Final-Musik the following summer. It adds a prominent oboe part to horns and strings. The *andantino* between the two minuets is one of his most delicious tunes, and the march is a reminder perhaps of days in Paris; entitled 'Marcia alla Francese', it is obviously an affectionate parody (for a family 'in the know'), and is inevitably full of spiky dotted rhythms, with the comic incongruity of a momentary turn into a gavotte. But the divertimenti for wind are not inferior in charm, for instance that in F, K.213 (1775)—true garden-music, with a final 'Contredanse en Rondeau', which epitomises the high jinks that are always likely when six happy wind-men get together—and K.270 in B flat (1777), a delicate miniature symphony.

But this side of Wolfgang's art is seen at its most ample to date in the famous eight-movement Serenade in D, K.250—with its March K.249. It was written for the wedding of Elizabeth Haffner in July 1776 to Franz Xavier Späth. Elizabeth was the daughter of a deceased Burgo-master of Salzburg, and her bridegroom was a forwarding-agent. Her brother Siegmund had commissioned it, and it was played in the garden of his summer-residence. Siegmund deserves well of us, as he also commissioned the symphony in D, K.385, to mark his own ennoblement in 1782. Not only does the 'Haffner' Serenade include movements of a style and range which would be proper to a symphony of the 'festal entertainment' type, but like several of its predecessors it has 'violin-concerto' movements. One of them, the well-known and brilliant Rondo, demands a degree of technical skill beyond anything in the concertos proper. If indeed in this Salzburg period the symphony, properly speak-ing, was lying fallow, the later riches that were to spring from this soil make it impossible to regret the seeming contraction of horizons. One cannot experience the charm and examine the workmanship of all this lovely entertainment-music and be persuaded that Wolfgang found the writing of it uncongenial. If this 1776-77 is a routine period, who needs inspiration?

But 1776 has begun with *three* piano concertos in successive months. In January came the B flat concerto, K.238. Wolfgang must have written it for his own concert use; he played it at both Munich and Augsburg in 1777, and Rose Cannabich, the daughter of the Mannheim Kapell-meister, played it on Wolfgang's visit there in 1778. Its first movement shows Wolfgang's delight in pouring out plenty of material and then rearranging it. We could call it a jig-saw were that not a contradiction. The slow movement is another example of the growing penchant for delightful sound. The February concerto is for three pianos (in E flat, K.242). It was written for Countess Lodron and her two daughters, Aloisia aged thirteen and Josepha aged eleven. Josepha had an easier part, for instance omitting successions of quick staccato ornamental notes in the slow movement, so her part was easily dropped when Wolfgang made the piece into a two-piano concerto (probably in 1779 to make a pair with K.365). Here again the slow movement is the most charming; all the music is comparatively easy-going, and why not? It would have been a poorly-executed commission which turned out to be over the heads of two-thirds of the soloists. The March concerto is K.246 in C, written for Countess Antonia Lützow, the wife of the commandant of the Salzburg fortress, and probably a pupil of Leopold's. This is technically the easiest of all the piano concertos to play. Wolfgang used it for teaching others, but he also wrote two quite large cadenzas for it. He eased the Countess's path in another respect. Instead of writing a figured-bass—a short-hand for the accompanimental chords the piano was to play in the orchestral *tuttis* which any professional would be expected to handle—he wrote in the suggested chords for her right hand.

But these concertos pale before the one that Wolfgang was to write at the year's end, K.271. It was commissioned by a French pianist who came then to Salzburg on a concert-tour; her name was Jeunehomme, but by the Mozarts she was usually called 'Jenomy'. Wolfgang clearly reckoned it a crown of his efforts in the genre so far. Here we reach the start of the regularly-played canon of the piano concertos, and with justice. Too much has been made, perhaps, of the surprise of the piano solo interrupting the opening fanfares without waiting for a seemly time to emerge, but the richness and profusion of the themes, to which is now added much quicker changes of their colourings in allotting them to piano or orchestra—all this is on a new plane. So is the combination of emotion with filigree in the darker-coloured *andantino*, which twice ends its paragraphs with imitations of recitative—perhaps another whimsical reference to the Paradise Lost of opera? Certainly it must have made Mlle Jenomy seem like an operatic heroine holding the centre of the stage, with the muted violins using sighing rests and sobbing accents as the supporting cast. The final rondo is interrupted by a minuet; but unlike the violin concerto interruptions this is no longer 'popular' in style. Its phrase-lengths have been made irregular and its decoration is both elaborate and, to a perceptive player, capable of expressing emotion—in fact it would certainly qualify for Brunetti's description: 'too studied'. One other composition-provoking visit in 1777 must be mentioned, that of the Czech pianist and composer Franz Xaver Duschek, and more particularly his wife Josepha the singer. For her Wolfgang wrote K.272, a fine 'concert' recitative and aria: 'Ah, lo previdi'. This was one of a genre Wolfgang made his own, a vocal concerto movement without stage action, but expressing the intensity of operatic passion, *faute de mieux*,

by music alone. *Faute de mieux* must remain the watch-word in opera
for some years yet.

We cannot be sure when during this period Leopold determined that
another 'make-or-break' tour for Wolfgang was a necessity. We know
of a petition (though it is not extant) to the Archbishop as early as 14
March 1777, but it mentioned the failing family circumstances and asked
for increased salaries for both of them, without, as far as we can tell,
raising the question of leave. Perhaps the Archbishop's refusal precipitated the thoughts of touring. On 1 August there was another petition
bearing every mark of Leopold's composition, written in Leopold's hand
but signed by Wolfgang. It refers to Leopold's intention in June to ask
for a few months' leave to earn some more money, but the Archbishop
had then ordered additional orchestral preparations for a possible visit
of the Emperor, Joseph II. (He was indeed in Salzburg on 31 July on
his way back from Paris—where he followed his youngest son on a
conciliatory visit.) In the final paragraph Wolfgang announces his resignation, to ensure that he at least can leave. The Archbishop cannot
have failed to recognise Leopold as the author, and must have found
certain allusions ill-judged, to say the least. For instance, the Archbishop,
a professional celibate, is treated to a homily on parenthood and on the
parable of the talents: 'The parents go to great pains to enable the
children to earn their own bread: they are responsible for that both to
themselves and to the State. The more talents the children have from
God the more their duty is to use them to improve the lot of themselves
and their parents, to comfort the parents and to provide for their own
development and for the future. Thus the Gospel teaches us.' This last
lesson in theology is too much for the Archbishop who minutes on the
petition: 'In accordance with the Gospel they are both free to seek their
future elsewhere'—that is, both discharged.

This dismissal was a thunderbolt which laid Leopold low. A neighbour
from their Getreidegasse days, Joachim von Schiedenhofen, records in
his diary of 6 September how he found Leopold ill for that reason.
However, Leopold was reprieved. If in his vexation the Archbishop had
ever intended the dismissal, he never put any machinery in motion to
carry it out. Leopold had to decide that Wolfgang and his mother must
go. Significantly, to send the young man by himself, now in his twenty-
first year, was never for a moment considered. Leopold must have stirred
himself over a multiplicity of arrangements, though Schiedenhofen still
reports him with heavy catarrh on 19 September. A loan had to be
negotiated with a family friend, Joseph Bullinger, and letters of credit
arranged as before through Hagenauer.

Meanwhile it is perhaps not too fanciful to see three more church works as private farewell offerings. The Missa Brevis in B flat, K.275 was apparently performed only after Wolfgang's departure. The music is in a simple lyrical vein, with something of a childlike piety expressed in it. The Benedictus has a shapely soprano solo which Leopold tells mother and son that the new resident castrato, Ceccarelli, sang excellently. But it is the final 'dona' which gives the mass its 'farewell' quality; all four soloists and the chorus keep taking up its happy haunting tune as though they cannot bring themselves to put it down. It must have been hard to realise that its composer was indeed gone from them. A short piece in similarly simple and limpid melodic style is the offertory that probably went with the mass: 'Alma Dei Creatoris', K.277. Finally, dated 9 October, there is 'Sancta Maria, mater Dei', K.273. Its words are personal, not liturgical. 'I owe everything to thee, but from this hour I devote everything to thy service . . . . Protect me, in life and death.' There are no soloists; only the choir with string orchestra support sing the tune from the heart, in a work which can best be likened to a young man's equivalent of the last such motet: 'Ave verum corpus'.

6

To Paris: One Single, One Return

1777–79

The fateful day was 23 September 1777. As we know from a subsequent reproachful letter to his son, Leopold was still doing Wolfgang's packing at 2 a.m., ill as he was, and at six he was up again, to see that everything was in order as they left, in the family's own carriage. In his anxiety and wretchedness he realised that he had let Wolfgang go without a father's blessing, and hurried to the window where there was a view of their outward road the other side of the river. But it was too late. He said his morning prayers, went back to bed, read and fell asleep over the book. The dog came in to tell him she wanted to go out, and thus he knew it was nearly noon. As for Nannerl, her diary tells us that for most of the day she was in bed with pains in stomach and head. Leopold spent the afternoon praying and reading, but the kindly Bullinger visited them. In the evening Nannerl felt better, and they played Picquet and supped. 'Then', writes Leopold, 'we went to sleep in God's name and thus passed the sad day I never thought I should have to undergo.' But after this, in the same letter, the administrative man of affairs takes over, discussing hotel costs, whom to meet, organs to play, and offering such reminders as 'make sure Wolfgang has the boot-trees put in his boots'. The news of son and mother on that day is of a determined cheerfulness, in Wolfgang's letter from the 'Star' at Wasserburg where they made their first night stop. 'I am the second Papa, and keep my eye on everything.' As for Mama, 'she has just visited the little house, and is now fully undressed.' The next afternoon they alighted in Munich at the 'Black Eagle', whose landlord, Franz Albert, was an enthusiast for music and gave weekly concerts at the inn.

There is a straw in the wind in Wolfgang's first letter from Munich. On the first morning there they got up at 7 a.m., but Wolfgang's hair was so untidy that he couldn't make his call on Count Seeau, the supervisor of the Court entertainments, before 10.30 a.m., by which time he was out hunting. This would surely not have happened had Leopold been in charge. One can imagine him grinding his teeth in Salzburg, with time being money—borrowed money. Yet 'Patience!' is all that Wolfgang adds to this unsatisfactory passage, which hardly explains the lapse of three and a half hours—untidy hair or no. Wolfgang saw the Count the next day and took the opportunity to remark, at a first conversation, that a first-rate composer was badly needed in Munich. It needs little worldly wisdom to see the likely consequences of impugning the judgement of those who had installed the second-raters—and what would those Mozart-styled second-raters do but close ranks? The fact that compared with Mozart most of the rest of mankind *is* second-rate is neither here nor there. However, Wolfgang says, 'my heart is as light as a feather now I have got away from all that [Salzburg] chicanery'. 'Too light', we may perhaps hear Leopold say.

Seeau did in fact speak to the Elector at the Nymphenburg. 'Too soon! Let him go to Italy and get a name!' 'Such Italy-paroxysm!' was the comment of the young man who had gone to Italy and who had got a name. Wolfgang personally spoke to the Elector. 'No vacancy.' It was as though *La finta giardiniera* had never been. Wolfgang had an idea of offering his services to Seeau, for a retainer, as an opera composer, especially to capitalise on the new-found interest in *Singspiele*. Another idea sprang from Herr Albert, to persuade ten music-lovers to make an annual money contribution whereby Wolfgang could stay at Munich. Not unnaturally Leopold was against everything except a real position. His letter of 4 October bids them continue north and west, away from Italian penetration of the musical establishments.

Although he played in a few houses, Wolfgang gave no public concerts in Munich, and consequently took no money. But one of the private concerts at Albert's must have been a great occasion for those who had ears to hear, containing as it did the three latest piano concertos, K.238, 246 and 271—the last being the 'Jenomy'.

The 'Black Eagle' was also the scene of one of those thumbnail-sketches which leap out from the pages in Wolfgang's letters, bespeaking the future master of comic opera. He is Councillor Öfele. 'Just picture him, very tall, well made, pretty fat, with a perfectly absurd face. When he crosses the room to go to another table, he puts both hands to his belly, bends over them and heaves it up, and nods his head and very quickly draws back his right leg. He performs this for every person in turn.' Leopold replies by return post: 'I should think I do remember Öfele'; he goes on, perhaps to Wolfgang's surprise, to say that he sang a cantata as a treble at Öfele's nuptial mass when he married the beautiful Lepin, a merchant's daughter who sang and played the clavier well.

'What is more she had more than 30,000 florins ... sic transit gloria mundi!' Leopold can usually be relied upon for well-worn Latin tags.

There was a brief flurry of a possibility of an opera contract for Naples through the good offices of Joseph Mysliwecek, a Czech composer who had lost his nose through horrific treatment of bone-cancer. But the mere possibility of the engagement moves Wolfgang to something which comes from the heart: 'I have only to hear an opera talked of, I have only to sit down in a theatre and hear the orchestra tune up, to be immediately beside myself.'

Meanwhile at home Nannerl tells of Miss Bimbes still living in hopes and sitting at the door half an hour at a time 'hoping you will arrive at any moment.' With Mamma away Nannerl has become the martinet. 'Our maid Tresel finds it very funny that Nannerl should constantly be poking her nose into the kitchen and daily scolding her about dirt.' Mamma has meanwhile told Leopold with her usual solicitude: 'Please tell Nannerl not to get cross with you and to take care that you don't worry.'

But to stop Leopold worrying was not in anyone's power, especially as the expedition's purposes were flagging already. On 13 October he writes: 'I expected to hear from Augsburg, but you are still in Munich. If you stayed almost three weeks in Munich where you could not hope to make a farthing, you will indeed get on in the world!'

But by this time they had moved to Leopold's choice of the 'White Lamb' in Augsburg, Leopold's birthplace, where his bookbinder brother, Franz Aloys lived, whose nineteen-year-old daughter Maria Anna Thekla emphatically moved into Wolfgang's ken as the Bäsle (little cousin). Wolfgang describes her to Leopold: 'like me she is rather a scamp', and the mention of her sends Wolfgang off into the sort of verbal jokes, often scatological, which the whole Mozart family, Mamma included, obviously take in their stride. Apart from her the figure who contributed most to the Augsburg stay was the piano-maker, Stein. Wolfgang's praise of Stein's latest instruments centres on the recently-invented escapement action which prevented the hammer remaining against the string to thwart repetition. In Wolfgang's words, 'when you touch the keys the hammers fall back the moment after striking the string, whether you hold down or release the keys'. But the crux of the matter was the tone: 'However I touch the keys the tone is always even, never crude, never too strong or too weak, and never failing to sound.' This unforced naturalness is part and parcel of Wolfgang's philosophy as well as his music. On being made to hear a concerto for two flutes by Friedrich Graf, the Augsburg Kapellmeister, Mozart delivers to Leopold the ultimate in condemnation: 'It doesn't please the ear at all; it isn't a bit natural', and—almost worse—'The poor chap must have taken a great deal of pains over it.' At Wolfgang's main public concert the opportunity was seized to combine business with pleasure by demonstrating three Stein instruments with the triple concerto, K.242, played by Demmler (the cathedral organist), Wolfgang and Stein himself; but this was only one item in a Mozartean feast which elicited a paean of a review in the *Augsburgische Staats- und Gelehrten Zeitung*. The concert evidently lived up to Wolfgang's promise in the advertisement to 'entertain his compatriots right royally for a few hours'. Unknown to Wolfgang, his Paris friend Baron Grimm was at this concert on a one-night visit to Augsburg.

In another concert at the Holy Cross monastery, Wolfgang played his G major violin concerto, and left there, to be copied for the monks' use, scores of two masses, K.192 and 220, and the offertory 'Misericordias Domini' K.222. The Bäsle was deputed to see that the scores came safely back.

So at last there was some replenishment of the family purse, though not enough to break even, because of the unnecessarily long stay in Munich, as Leopold did not fail to point out. They left on 26 October, Wolfgang having written the previous day in his cousin's album:

> Si vous aimes, ce que j'aime
> Vous vous aimes donc vous meme
> votre
>   Tres affectioné Neveu,
>   Wolfgang Amadee Mozart.

To call himself her nephew would be a typical parting shot, but shots in the shape of nonsense-letters were to rain on the Bäsle from time to time, with jokes which always included the lavatory; a non-ornithologist might well call them dung-chat.

The pair journeyed to Mannheim by way of the beautiful walled town of Nördlingen, whence they made an abortive expedition to Hohenaltheim to renew contacts with the Prince of Wallerstein, who had heard Wolfgang in both Rome and Naples. But the Prince was in distracted mourning for his wife and would hear no music, and what is more, Mamma caught a horrible cold. They eventually arrived at Mannheim on 30 October and stayed initially at the 'Pfälzer Hof', not the much dearer 'Prince-Friedrich' where the whole family had stayed before. On the very next afternoon, Wolfgang went with the famous Mannheim Kapellmeister, Christian Cannabich, intending to hear in rehearsal Part I of Handel's *Messiah*, conducted by the Abbé Vogler, the Vice-Kapellmeister. But

Vogler was also rehearsing a work of his own, which took precedence over Handel's for nearly an hour, by which time Wolfgang had had enough, his impatience doubtless spurred by the desire to get a letter to Bäsle in the post, which went at six.

The musical glory of Mannheim was its orchestra, which had never looked back since the Elector Karl Theodor had appointed Johann Stamitz to direct it some thirty years before. Charles Burney had called it in 1772 'an army of generals', and that was Europe's opinion. Wolfgang called it 'very strong' and give its composition as: ten or eleven violins on either side (that is, firsts and seconds), four violas, two oboes, two flutes, two clarinets, two horns, four cellos, four bassoons, four double-basses, and also trumpets and drums. At first sight this seems, clarinets excepted, somewhat smaller than the orchestra Milan assembled for *Mitridate*. But of course not only was Mannheim's orchestra a regular, salaried, cohesively disciplined body, but its regular métier was what we would recognise as a 'symphony concert'. The regular home of an Italian orchestra was a pit. There is a puzzling aspect to Wolfgang's experience of the Mannheim orchestra; he did not write a single symphony there, nor is there a record of any of his earlier symphonies, several of which he had brought with him, being played on this visit. There is something to be said for calling Wolfgang's next symphony, the 'Paris', a transplanted Mannheim piece.

Choral music was evidently not Mannheim's *forte*. 'You can't conceive anything worse than the voices here', and in any case there were only six of each on the establishment. German opera might have offered some prospect to Wolfgang, but he did not think kindly of it in comparison with Italian. Soon after their arrival they attended a German opera by Ignaz Holzbauer, now in his sixties and for eminence and long service reckoned as an Oberkapellmeister without infringing Cannabich's executive direction. The opera was *Gunther von Schwarzburg* and in his dedication to the Elector Holzbauer records his protection under which 'the Palatine Stage for the first time sang a German hero'. The work is, not surprisingly, fully scored, with the orchestra enthusiastically underlining the many moments of drama. Holzbauer as a composer elicited Wolfgang's genuine admiration. So did Cannabich, particularly as an orchestral trainer. Early in the visit, Wolfgang tells Leopold that he is daily with Cannabich who was apparently milder—'quite different from what he used to be'. Wolfgang having played all six of the Salzburg piano sonatas at Cannabich's, the daughter Rosa became his pupil, and for her he wrote down the new C major sonata, K.309. One says 'wrote down' because the basis of the outer movements was an improvisation at the last Augsburg concert, with the rondo 'full of din'. Wolfgang sent a copy of this sonata by instalments back to Salzburg, with an underlined admonition to Nannerl that the *andante must not be taken too fast.* Incidentally, he said that Rosa was just like the *andante.* Nannerl confessed that this movement 'requires great concentration and accuracy', and even before receiving the rondo, said: 'One can see from the style that you composed it at Mannheim.' When the whole is before him Leopold says: 'Your sonata is out of the ordinary [the German is 'sonderbar']. It has something of the *mannered* style of Mannheim, but so little that your own good art is not spoilt.' Perhaps the main Mannheim element consists in the unmistakable passages in 'full orchestra' style—sudden outbreaks of martial sound, quick crescendos and drumming basses. But perhaps they also meant the increasingly convoluted variations of the basically simple song of the *andante.* Traces of the same orchestral style of unbuttoned brilliance can also be found in another piano sonata of presumed Mannheim origin, K.311 in D, particularly in the imitation of tremolando violins in the rondo.

As early as mid-November, Leopold is anxious about the whole enterprise and makes the first mention of Wolfgang's going on to Paris, which does not seem to have been envisaged when he and his mother left Salzburg. On the same day (13 November) that Leopold is writing in a care-worn strain, Wolfgang is giving an account of his own antics on the organ at mass: 'I came in during the Kyrie, and played the end of it; and after the priest had sung the intonation of the Gloria I made up a lead-in which was so different from what they are used to here that they all looked round, especially Holzbauer . . . the people were ready to laugh. From time to time the music was marked pizzicato, whereupon I gave the keys little slaps. I was in my best mood.' But as this took place in the Court chapel one wonders what sort of recommendation it could have evoked from Elector or clergy for the one role, that of organist, in which Mannheim seemed to be deficient by the best standards.

The Elector was being evasive about employment, but his cousin-wife, whom Wolfgang called 'the stern Electress', was evidently more amenable since she was insisting on teaching Wolfgang how to knit. Curiously enough, it was she rather than her husband who partly evoked some composition at any rate, for Wolfgang decided to dedicate to her a set of six violin sonatas, K.301–6. In fact, according to him, four were written in Mannheim and two in Paris. We loosely call such things 'violin sonatas' but Wolfgang called them 'Clavier duetti mit violin' (14 February 1778) and even 'Clavier sonaten' (28 February). They were eventually published by Sieber in Paris in November 1778 as 'Avec Accompagnement D'un Violon'. This being so, it is those places where the instruments equally share the material that catch the eye as breaking new ground, rather than those where the violin has more than its share of subordination. But in any case the violin envisaged for this music was more fitted for accompaniment, with its lower bridge and gut strings, than the far more assertive instrument enforced by modern concert conditions.

The first movement of the first sonata (K.301) reverses a normal Mannheim orchestral procedure by starting with a flowing symmetrical tune, as though charm were to be all; this is *followed* by abrupt 'orchestral' unisons, and then the tune is resumed as though the interruption hadn't happened. Here is another example of the wit involved in the observation of externals and the ironic-humorous rearrangement of them into a personal idiom. The later progress of the piece shows why the orchestral 'irrelevance' is there. It fulfils all sorts of functions except that which it first had. There is another witticism in the form of the third sonata of the set, K.303. It starts *adagio* with an unhurried tune. Is it an introduction, or a slow movement taken out of the expected order? It turns out, almost too late for the device to be convincing, to be the true first subject of an *allegro* which is otherwise twice as fast. But the little gem of the set is the E minor, K.304, its opening subject a soft, sad version of a rising unison fanfare which turns the conventional 'Mannheim rocket' into a poignant witticism. Here too the violinist, far from accompanying, takes part in quite trenchant contrapuntal discussion, and the plaintive mood is carried over into the final *Tempo di Menuetto*, despite one melting section in the major. Wolfgang follows tradition in restricting five of the sonatas to two movements, but the sixth goes further into the realm of concert music, in not only having a third movement but equipping it with a cadenza which is larger than many which he sketched out for piano concertos.

Political uncertainties were added to the rest on this ill-starred journey when on 30 December 1777 the Elector of Bavaria (Maximilian III) died. Carl Theodor succeeded him, thereby joining the courts and dominions of Mannheim and Munich, with the likelihood, which indeed became fact, that most of the Mannheim musicians would be transferred to Munich. The family letters anxiously exchanged comments on rumours of war. Joseph II in Vienna might accept the succession, or most of it, but Frederick the Great of Prussia was another matter. Indeed in July 1778 Frederick did go to war, invading Bohemia, but things were patched up, Carl Theodor and Munich were undisturbed, and Salzburg continued its usual enjoyment of provincial seclusion.

But Wolfgang's letter of 17 January 1778 for the first time mentions a name of far more fateful and immediate effect—that of Weber. Friedolin Weber was a lowly musician of the Mannheim establishment, who had he lived would have been the uncle of the great composer. One of his daughters, Aloysia, was then aged seventeen—though for some reason Wolfgang says 'fifteen'—and her agile voice and her looks were enough to throw Wolfgang deeply in love. He had taken with him the concert-air 'Ah, lo previdi', written originally for Josepha Duschek, which Leopold had suggested would suit Consoli, the Munich castrato who had sung in *La finta giardiniera* and *Il re pastore*; but it was to Aloysia that Wolfgang gave it to learn, later adding explicit instructions from Paris: 'Put yourself into the person and situation of Andromeda' and 'Reflect on the sense and force of the words'. In February Wolfgang composed another such piece, 'Non so d'onde viene', K.294; it was written as a deliberate exercise in new invention under the shadow of a setting by J.C. Bach which he knew and admired. It was intended for the singer Anton Raaff whom Leopold had insistently recommended as a Mannheim contact. But as the composition proceeded, Aloysia and the vision of what she could do with it took over—and what she could do with it clearly included a fast scale up to the E flat above the treble stave which was nevertheless part and parcel of a basically lyrical love-song. The opening words, 'I do not know whence comes this tender feeling' and the change in destination from Raaff to Aloysia tell their own tale, as indeed Wolfgang artlessly told it to Leopold. Incidentally, Cherubino expresses the same sentiments in the same key in his first song in *Figaro*, though in a more fluttering, boyish style. But Raaff was properly recompensed; within three days he had a concert-air of his own—'Se al labbro mio non credi', K.295. Wolfgang offered to alter it in any way required, but Raaff only asked for a shortening 'because nowadays I haven't so much capacity for sostenuto'. He was by now sixty-four. Incidentally, Metastasio called him 'the most excellent of singers, the coldest of actors'. This flurry of arias also included one (K.486a) to words from Metastasio's *Didone abbandonata* chosen by the singer Dorothea Wendling, wife of a Mannheim flautist. She was later to be the first Ilia in *Idomeneo*. Dorothea had a daughter, Elisabeth Augusta, whose voice Wolfgang admired, and whom, Frau Mozart says in a postscript, 'that Bach in England wanted to marry'.

All four of these concert-arias would drastically tax the techniques of modern singers, but Wolfgang is never content with virtuosity as an end in itself. As usual he is merciless about the wretched Vogler on the subject. Vogler sight-reading the piano concerto in B flat, K.246, played the first movement '*Prestissimo*, the Andante *Allegro*, the rondo even more *prestissimo*. Well, what good is it? To me that sort of sight-reading is on a par with shitting. The listeners who are worthy of the name can't say more than that they have *seen* the music and the playing; hearing, thinking and feeling they experience no more of than he does.'

The one opportunity to make some money in Mannheim, even then only partly taken, was a commission arranged by Dorothea's husband for Wolfgang to write for a Dutch flautist and music-lover named De Jean 'three short easy concertos and a pair of flute quartets'. Eventually De Jean got according to Wolfgang two concertos and three quartets, but only one in each category survives complete, of undoubted authenticity and originally written for the advertised medium. De Jean eventually paid less than half the fee, to the impotent fury of Leopold. Wolfgang claims in a letter that he cannot stand the flute. But the listlessness which overtakes him—'fecklessness' to Leopold—though it may have been compounded by an uncertain future added in his mind to a present failure to launch himself, must have mainly sprung from love, perhaps even then not truly requited. Hitherto, a commission—almost any commission—would release instantly the happiness of creativity. Now for the first time the balance is gone; he is 'bowled over'.

The flute quartet K.285 is dated Christmas Day 1777, and contains an *adagio* in which the flute is accompanied as it were in a serenade of great beauty which all too soon, by what sounds like an impatient *coup de théâtre*, breaks off into a silence out of which springs the last rondo. Neither here nor in the concerto K.313 does the well-turned characteristic writing show any lack of sympathy. Perhaps to call the concerto's first movement *Allegro maestoso* is a sly dig at the unmajestic flute. We might rather have expected its carefree nonchalance to be called *aperto*, but if we suppose that this breezy style is all that Wolfgang thought the instrument capable of, we are confronted in the slow movement with an intensely personal utterance of a deeper kind, too deep apparently for De Jean, as the Andante in C, K.315, is obviously an easier substitute—'easier' we may say, but were the other movement not written we should find nothing untoward in the very shapely substitute. The other flute concerto, K.314 in D, seems beyond doubt to be a reworking of an otherwise unknown oboe concerto written for the Salzburg player, Giuseppe Ferlendis. This very agreeable piece has a tune in its last movement which Wolfgang rescued for Blonde's air in *Die Entführung*—'O what bliss, what joy'—which it fits so well that one can't believe it is second-hand.

If Wolfgang really felt an antipathy to the flute it is perhaps because its comparatively narrow emotional and dynamic range prohibited its solo use on an extended scale, and this may have defeated even a Mozartean fecundity when mass-production was needed. But rather than thus blaspheme against his capacities one prefers to think that he was oppressed, like the Flying Dutchman, with the feeling that here he had no abiding place, and that the situation could perhaps be remedied only at the cost of leaving Aloysia.

As late as 9 February 1778 Leopold is writing to Wolfgang yet another list of useful contacts in Paris, whilst constantly advising him against undue familiarity. 'You can always behave quite naturally to people of high rank; but with all the others *make yourself an Englishman.*' But he is writing thus in ignorance of the thunderbolt about to land on the doorstep in Hannibalplatz. Wolfgang proposes not to go to Paris with two stars of the Mannheim orchestra, Wendling the flautist and Ramm the oboist, in whose characters he has suddenly found flaws, but proposes instead to go on musical travels with the Weber family. Leopold is asked to get Aloysia engagements in Italy, and having despatched Frau Mozart in advance to Salzburg, they will call in en route to let Leopold hear and see the marvel which with Wolfgang's help is to save and renew the fortunes of both families. Leopold on 11 February: 'My dear son! I have read your letter of the 4th with stupefaction and horror. I am beginning to answer it today, having not slept all night, and I'm so tired that I'm writing word by word, and it will take me till tomorrow to finish.' A scornful enumeration of Wolfgang's temporary lady-loves follows, and the crux is 'Off with you to Paris! Aut Caesar aut nihil.' Again the Latin tag when all else fails. At the very end, in the last sentence on the cover of the letter: 'Mamma is to go to Paris with Wolfgang.' Mamma had tentatively suggested it a week before, for the first and only time as far as we know. It must have been a measure of her love and anxiety that the good woman brought herself even to that measure of independence in proposing what was literally to become a self-sacrifice.

The last days in Mannheim brought one further composition, a sonata for piano and violin in C, K.296, dated 11 March and inscribed 'Pour Mademoiselle Therese'. She was fifteen, the step-daughter of Councillor Serrarius, who for most of their stay had given the Mozarts lodgings in return for her lessons. The sonata was the parting gift—with, typically, commissioned work for De Jean left uncomposed—and they left on 14 March, still in the family carriage, though it was now sold to the coachman as part of his hire for the long drive to Paris. With a trembling heart Nannerl had actually lent some of her own money to further the enterprise.

The journey to Paris took nine and a half days. Wolfgang mentions only the boredom of it; his mother mentions the fair weather of the first eight days, with very cold mornings and warm afternoons, but thereafter the wind and the rain soaking them. The lodging had been arranged by

Leopold through an Augsburg merchant, Joseph Arbauer, and was at the house of his Paris agent, a man named Mayer. Here the hall and stairs were so narrow that it was impossible to get a keyboard instrument up to their room, so that apart from the absence caused by Wolfgang's having to make himself known, Mamma did not even have her son composing at home. With a burst of candour she writes: 'I sit alone in the room the whole day as if I were in gaol, and as the room is very dark and looks out on to a little yard I don't see the sun all day, and don't even know what the weather is like; with a great effort I manage to knit by the light that does struggle in.' The privations extended to food as well, but they were shortly to go to other lodgings, Frau Mozart's last, found for them by Madame d'Epinay, Grimm's mistress and a friend from the 1766 visit. Meanwhile Wolfgang went for an instrument to the house of Monsieur Le Gros, who had begun his career as a tenor, but who was now the Director of the Concert Spirituel. This series was founded in 1725 by the composer Philidor and constituted the first regular public concerts in Paris. As the name implies, the original object was sacred works for choir and orchestra, but by now the scope had extended to what we should call symphony concerts. From Le Gros Wolfgang experienced the usual alternation of enthusiasm and chicanery. Almost immediately it was arranged that Wolfgang should write a good deal of additional material for a performance of a Miserere by Holzbauer; in the event only half of it was performed. A Sinfonia Concertante for wind instruments and orchestra (whose original version is now lost) was accepted with alacrity; its orchestral parts were seemingly not even copied out, let alone performed.

Even in the early letters from Paris there are various strands which run contrary to Wolfgang's desire to reassure Leopold. There is real xenophobia about French musicians—and it must have been noticed in the transparent Wolfgang, and reciprocated by the alert victims. For instance, on 5 April he writes that he is in a place where money can certainly be made

but only at a cost of frightful trouble and labour; but I'm prepared to do it all to content you. But what annoys me about the business is that our French gentlemen have only improved their goût to the extent of managing to listen to good stuff as well. But that they should realise that their own music is bad, or at least to notice any difference—Heaven preserve us!—and their singing!—oimè!—if only no Frenchwoman sang Italian airs I would even forgive her French squalling, but to ruin good music!—that is unbearable.

Another worry, despite heroic reticence, is coming into the open. Frau

Mozart's postscript of 1 May says that she has for three weeks endured tooth-ache, sore throat and ear-ache. Leopold's immediate reaction is, with underlining, 'do not forget *to be bled*'. Even so, this operation did not take place till 11 June.

As for opera, at one stage Wolfgang is expecting a two-act libretto, but nothing came of it. As far as we know, the only notes of Mozart heard at the Paris Opera were his contributions to Noverre's ballet *Les Petits Riens*. The *Journal de Paris* of 12 June does not mention the music in its report, but goes into interesting detail about the plot: 'Two shepherd-esses fall in love with the supposed shepherd, who, to undeceive them, eventually bares her breast .... We must add that at the moment where Mlle Asselin enlightens the two shepherdesses several voices cried *bis*.' It is impossible to guess from the music where this dénouement takes place, still less whether it is in Mozart's part. But he can hardly have set much store by the music, which occurred as after-piece to an opera, *Le finte gemelle*, conducted by its composer, Nicola Piccini. Parisian opera had always been the home, not so much of music, as of controversies about it, and unfortunately for Wolfgang its clientele was currently indulging itself in a battle of taste between Gluck and Piccini, which was dubbed the 'Guerre des Bouffons'. It is not to be supposed that Wolfgang did not take the opportunities to go to the Opera, though he doesn't give any details; what is more, two of Gluck's weightiest shots in the campaign had very recently been published: *Alceste* (in its French version) in 1776, and *Armide* in 1777. If Mozart the spectator could distance himself from Mozart the crowded-out composer he would have been bound to renew his respect for Gluck's serious and undoubtedly powerful emotional realism.

As far as daily bread went, lessons—with the expenditure of time and effort getting to them and enduring them—seem to have been the sole means for most of the time. The Duke de Guines, whom Wolfgang called an incomparable flautist, had a daughter who played the harp 'magnifique'. Thus came about the famous concerto for flute and harp, K.299, which incidentally was still not paid for four months later. The ear for French taste is clearest in its final rondo, based on the beloved gavotte rhythm. But the Duke also wanted composition lessons for his daughter. One can almost hear Wolfgang grinding his teeth as he tells Leopold about them: 'If she gets no inspirations (and at present there are no signs of any) then it is all in vain, for God knows I can't give her any.' Leopold's sensible suggestions as to how to continue the lessons using the expectations of an ordinary mortal make it the more certain that he was the better teacher of the two!

Recent researches—see the next chapter—have displaced from Paris four well-known piano sonatas, rendering this depressing period emptier still. The apparent survivor is a piece without precedent in the genre, the A minor, K.310. The whole sonata is given over to a fateful intensity, including at the height of the first movement's storm two passages with the comparatively rare mark of *ff*. In this movement the 'Mannheim' thrumming of a repeated bass has become the throbbing of persistent chords and the 'military-march' dotted rhythms have become something relentless. The consolation of the slow movement is interrupted by more throbbings, and the momentary gleam of the major key in the final *presto* is quickly lost again in a movement by turns shadowy and turbulent.

Only once, it seems, did a firm offer of a position present itself in France. According to a letter of 14 May, Wolfgang was definitely offered the organistship of Versailles. It would have meant only six months of residence for half a year's salary, and of course it would have assured him of the Royal ear. If there had been composing duties they might well have been light, since choral and orchestral masses were not, as in Teutonic countries, a feature of French religious life. One can't help feeling that if such an arrangement could have been made with Salzburg as a base the Mozarts would have leapt at it, with its complete freedom for half a year making an ideal compromise between patronage and freelancing. The only risk, not to be foreseen, was that of the office, if not its holder, being guillotined in or after 1789. In all probability the all-sufficient deterrent was six months out of the likely milieu of Aloysia. She and her future career were always foremost in Wolfgang's mind, and whilst in Paris he began to write for her the concert-aria 'Popoli di Tessaglia', K.316, to words from Calzabigi's libretto to Gluck's *Alceste*. From the expressive power of the recitative, containing modulations of extraordinary freedom, and the agility and range of the *allegro*, twice going higher even than the Queen of the Night in the *Magic Flute*, we can get some notion of the technical powers that bewitched Wolfgang.

But the work of Wolfgang's to which the name 'Paris' has become attached is the Symphony in D, K.297, written for the Concert Spirituel and first performed on 18 June 1778. Wolfgang's autograph shows the pains he took over this 'now-or-never' work, particularly in the tautening of the design of the first movement by sternly cutting attractive material already sketched. Curiously enough, although clarinets are available the individuality of their voices remains almost unexploited. Independent passages for them are very rare, and they are not even used in the slow movement. It is the richness and force of the wind-band as a whole that has excited Wolfgang. What we have here is the first Mozartean symphony deliberately designed in its outer movements for performance by a large orchestra, of nearly 60 players. The eight woodwinds (a pair each of flutes, oboes, clarinets and bassoons), together with the brass (two horns and two trumpets) constitute the forces of Beethoven's first two symphonies. Their use *en bloc*, sometimes contrasting rhythmically with the strings, sometimes clamorously reinforcing them, was designed for, and achieved, Parisian applause. Wolfgang is quite sardonic to Leopold about indulging French taste. On 12 June he writes: 'I have not failed to include the Premier Coup d'archet [the unison attack at the opening by all the strings]—and that's enough. The fuss the oxen here make of it! What the devil! I can't see any difference—they all begin together—as they do in other places.' Coming from Mannheim of all places, he would expect such unanimity as a matter of course. In the last movement, playing with such expectation, he starts instead with a quiet dialogue of unaccompanied violins, to reap the more applause from the oxen as the *tutti* sets in. But of course there is more to the music than mere parody. In the first movement the *premier coup* turns out to be the *dernier* as well, and serves both punctuation and argument in the middle. The final *allegro* balances the first in weight and in strenuous contrapuntal argument in its central section. Wolfgang having observed the decided French preference for symphonies of three (not the German four) movements, there is no minuet, and there are alternative *andante* movements. The one heard at the first performance was deemed unsuccessful by Le Gros, and Wolfgang meekly wrote another, somewhat simpler and more in minuet style, for the second performance on 15 August; it was this second *andante* which figured in the printed version put out by Sieber, who was also printing the sonatas which were to be presented to the 'stern Electress'. Wolfgang appears as a very human figure both before and after the first performance. Before, he suffers the agonies of bad rehearsal; afterwards, he celebrates by going to the Palais Royale and having an ice-cream, then says his rosary 'according to his vow', then goes home.

But the very letter (3 July) which describes this begins with an untruth: 'my dear mother is very ill'. She was dead as he wrote the words, but he could not bring himself to tell his father then and there. Instead he wrote the news at 2 a.m. on 4 July to Abbé Bullinger, begging him to use his judgement in breaking things to father and sister. Meanwhile, the ironies of time and space meant that on 13 July Leopold was beginning a letter to Paris wishing his dear wife 'happinesses by the million' and congratulations on being able to celebrate her name-day once more. But directly after the first paragraph the fateful letter of 3 July arrived. Leopold had the presentiment of death already, and before the letter was finished Bullinger came with the confirmation. Pressed for details by Leopold, Wolfgang harrows himself and us with an account of internal inflammation, diarrhoea, momentary deafness, shivering and fever—then breaks off in mid-paragraph to a rambling discussion of his own affairs. Their very inconsequence betrays how his spirit's stamina has been undermined, and his recognition of a rudderless course seems encapsulated in a postscript of a pathetic, wry cheerfulness: 'yet another mishmash!'

A friend at the death-bed, and a witness at the burial in one of the cemeteries attached to St-Eustache, was a Czech hornist and trumpeter, Franz-Joseph Haina, who kept a music and instrument shop and whose wife, Gertrude, was a music publisher. At this time Paris could claim to be the music-publishing headquarters of the world. Engraving of music was a process which, compared with movable type, greatly increased legibility, and had the precious advantage of being a loophole in the Royal monopolies. The Haina ménage is thus symbolic both of the musical opportunities which attracted foreigners from all over Europe (but which could not support a Mozart!), and of the commercial market for publication, used also by composers like J.C. Bach, who had no intention of settling in Paris. In both these respects—publishing and performing—the connection with Mannheim was close, the Parisians regarding the latter as a musical suburb. Figures from *L'Almanach Musical* of 1783 show that in Paris (a city then of some half-million people) there were 194 composers, 63 singing teachers (plus 5 who advertised themselves as teaching in the 'goût italien') . . . 93 masters of the violin, 42 of the cello . . . 12 organ builders and no fewer than 32 professional music engravers, the latter figure not of course including people (like Leopold) who knew how to do it for themselves. At the time of Wolfgang's visit, there was indeed another orchestra, about 80 strong, started in 1769 by, amongst others, the redoubtable composer and conductor, Gossec, yet another import. This was the Concert des Amateurs. Wolfgang comments on the handsome fees they paid for new symphonies, but records no approach in either direction. It seemed to be all there for the taking, but all taken.

It was also the hey-day of the private concert. One such noble patron was an old acquaintance of Wolfgang's, the Maréchal de Noailles, to whose daughter, the Countess Tessé, the two boyhood sonatas K.8 and K.9 had been dedicated. Towards the end of August, Wolfgang visited the Maréchal at St Germain, together with old London friends: Bach himself, in France to hear the singers for his forthcoming opera *Amadis des Gaules*, and Tenducci. We hear (27 August) that for Tenducci Wolfgang is writing a Scena with piano, oboe, horn and bassoon. What a loss that not a note of it survives! The constellation of so many good executants had led to the rise of the *sinfonia concertante* for two or more soloists with orchestra, in which an Italian, Giuseppe Cambini, had both a vested interest and the ear of Le Gros. It seems for once that Wolfgang was right in suspecting machinations when his own Sinfonia Concertante was dropped by Le Gros in favour of one by Cambini for, mysteriously, exactly the same combination of instruments and performers.

After his mother's death, Wolfgang was taken into the joint ménage of Madame d'Epinay and Baron Grimm. What kind of pressures and rivalries caused Wolfgang's relations with Grimm to become thread-bare can only be guesswork, but the eventual incompatibility doubtless had right on both sides, and can perhaps be summed up in a sentence from each. Grimm wrote on 27 July to Leopold, who quoted it back to Wolfgang: 'He is too true-hearted [Grimm uses the German "zu treuherzig" in a letter otherwise in French], too inactive, too easy to trap, too little occupied with the means towards making his fortune.' An impatient Wolfgang writes on 11 September: 'Mr Grimm may be able to help *children*, but not adults.' This is in a letter in which he has accepted that he must return to Salzburg. That Leopold had secured from the Archbishop, at some loss to his pride, a paid appointment for Wolfgang as court organist, with some composing duties, and that he should have persuaded Wolfgang to accept this, represents a comparatively rare triumph for his diplomacy. As far as 'netting' his son goes, the overriding argument was that if he settled in Paris he could say good-bye to Italy, or even Munich, of whose chief musicians moved thither from Mannheim Leopold cannily gives a list which includes 'Weber-basso' (Aloysia's father). It is agreed that the homeward route should be through Munich, but Wolfgang asks if he could make the detour through Mannheim if it transpires that the Webers are still there. Leopold rules this out as quite impracticable. Wolfgang goes to Mannheim, 'on advice' as he says.

Wolfgang left Paris on 26 September; that he only arrived in Salzburg nearly four months later (15 January) shows the uncertain equilibrium between the call of a motherless home and a repugnance towards Salzburg's artistic life. The latter is perhaps best expressed—though incoherently—in a letter to his father from Strasbourg (15 October) where he gave poorly attended concerts to help with his journey expenses: 'At Salzburg I never know what I am—I am everything—and also sometimes nothing at all—but I don't ask for myself *so much*, nor yet *so little*—but just something—if only I am something . . . .'

At Mannheim he found that the Webers were not there, having gone to join the musical establishment at Munich—Aloysia with a good salary. Cannabich also had gone to Munich, and Wolfgang stayed with Frau Cannabich, who was still in the old house at Mannheim. Perhaps the need to be mothered kept him there, though he did toy with a suggestion that he should compose a 'melodrama', a piece in orchestrated recitative, but with the latter spoken, not sung. At least he was wise enough not to commit himself far in this without the guarantee of payment. The whole incident seemed to Leopold vexatious and inexcusable. On the Munich visit Wolfgang presented to the Electress the sonatas for pianoforte and violin (K.301-6) which Sieber had engraved in Paris, and he completed Aloysia's 'Popoli di Tessaglia', but in his three weeks there he does not record anything musical which truly required his presence. We may well ask with Leopold the reason for this new and fruitless delay when an impatient Archbishop might already be revoking an appointment which was being so cavalierly treated. The three weeks at Munich probably represent either the time of hoping against hope or of recovery of so much of Wolfgang's spirit as remained after it had become obvious that Aloysia Weber, if indeed she had ever fully reciprocated his love, had certainly cooled and was content to let him go. She was on her way up as an opera star, and he was on his way to be an organist in Salzburg. This was the journey's final loss, the nadir of an apparently disastrous experience. To spend three weeks over such an accumulation, even with the comfortings of the Bäsle from Augsburg whom Wolfgang had sent for, seems an excusable delay before the onset of what he had now talked himself into regarding as a servitude of unknown duration, beginning on 15 January 1779.

7

Salzburg and Munich

1779–81

If we accept that Wolfgang hated the return to Salzburg as far as musical prospects were concerned, we might suppose that, at any rate, he would eagerly enjoy the prospect of being welcomed back to the bosom of the family. But in fact he must have slightly nonplussed his father and sister by bringing back with him an extra bosom, his Bäsle. In spite of the sexual jokes in his letters to her, it never appears that there is serious love between them. At most she is the consolatory playmate. The first extant letter she received from him after her return to Augsburg is couched in the same style as the rest, and is far from heart-break. It begins with his addressing her as his little cello by a punning transference of 'Bäsle' into 'Bässchen'—little bass, and contains an ode to her which is a skit on Klopstock's *Ode on Edone*.

To return to a motherless house must have created a sad unease for Wolfgang, which would hardly have been mitigated had there been a silence on that score. But Leopold's grief had already wrenched from him a reproach in a letter to his son which had roundly said that if Wolfgang had not needed his mother's supervision in Paris she would still be alive. Leopold could of course blame others for the comparative ignominy of the return. 'Caesar or nothing' had been his watchword, and Wolfgang had not become a Caesar. But Leopold would have been sufficiently sensitive and introspective to reflect that he had fathered the attempt and thereby the ignominy. But if reproaches and self-reproaches were in the air, the friendships and easy-going ways of Salzburg soothed the buffeted feelings, and we never hear of reproaches from or to Nannerl. From her diary, to which Wolfgang sometimes contributed in quirky style, we sense the affable routine of the life: for Nannerl at least, a daily attendance at mass, often at seven in the morning, and friends helping her to erect her hair, turning the occasion into a coffee-hour; frequent friends were Victoria, a daughter of the deceased organist, Adlgasser, and the almost inseparable 'Katherl', daughter of the Court surgeon,

Gilowsky. Bimberl was still going for walks, and cards, especially picquet and taroc, were often played. Target-shooting on Sundays, of which Wolfgang had been a proxy-member on his journeys, continued with modest stakes, and it was a sure seal of family friendship to be invited there. By this token, Ceccarelli, the castrato, was obviously by now a friend. But what is perhaps most striking about the diary of this period is the frequency and the detail about visits to the theatre. In the winter of 1779–80, the Böhm troupe were in residence, in a frequently changing mélange of comedy, tragedy and ballet, often offering three different entertainments a week. Doubtless most of it was ephemeral stuff. But if we are tempted to dismiss it as beneath a Mozart's attention we must remember that a year later, when another troupe managed by Emanuel Schikaneder was in residence, Wolfgang asked Nannerl for a detailed list and critique of the Salzburg shows to be sent him at Munich, where he might have been supposed to have his head and hands full with his own *Idomeneo*. The stage was Wolfgang's passion; he learnt his trade watching, when not actually working with, professional people. As for the inevitable dross, to watch failures, and know why they fail, is an essential part of theatrical education.

But it was as a church musician that Wolfgang resumed the earning of his daily bread, and in March 1779 he took the opportunity to reassert himself by writing a big Mass in C, K.317, perhaps for the annual service at Plain, near Salzburg, a place of pilgrimage for many, including Nannerl. Its image of the Virgin was supposed to have been miraculously crowned—hence the name 'Coronation' attached to this mass. It does indeed resume the tunefulness of the pre-Paris masses, of which there is a delightful example in the soprano-tenor duet in the Kyrie, with a Schubert-like alternation of major and minor. But though the orchestra is no bigger than in other 'solemn' Salzburg masses the Parisian experience has confirmed the certainty and concentration of its powers of expression. The Credo is marked by a prolonged burst of perpetual motion on the violins, matching the glitter on an illuminated crown. This festive display is transformed, by an unerring sense of the mysterious, into muted modulatory descents accompanying Incarnation and Crucifixion. In the Agnus Dei the soprano soloist uses in triple time the theme we indissolubly associate with the Countess singing 'Dove sono' in *Figaro*. Perhaps Wolfgang's mind momentarily played with the imagined sound of Aloysia's voice here and asked itself, in advance of the Countess, where the beloved moments had gone. But in any case, such re-use would come naturally in the eighteenth century. As far as Wolfgang was concerned, when he composed *Figaro* the writing of masses was a thing of the past, and he was by then perhaps inverting Luther's enquiry why the devil should have all the best tunes.

This thought links the 'Coronation' mass with its successor written in March 1780, K.337, also in C. Here the opening phrase of the Agnus Dei is later used by the Countess in her other famous song, 'Porgi Amor'. But in the mass the music quickly diverges from *Figaro* (if one may put it that way) and is furthermore enriched by three delicious *obbligato* accompaniments, by oboe, bassoon and organ, with a background murmur of muted violins. Such luxuriance restores the balance of euphony disturbed by the Benedictus, in which instead of the usual solo quartet we have an impressive but decidedly craggy four-part *tutti* fugue, which seems designed to exasperate the audience so that it relishes the more the charming Osanna refrain. Wolfgang's return as organist doubtless caused a change in the last three Epistle Sonatas, written in this 1779–80 period. These pieces were a Salzburg speciality, a one-movement, short, extrovert intermezzo in the action of the Mass written for organ and strings with sometimes wind as well. Interesting to the point of flamboyance is K.329 in C, which highlights the organ by giving it specific passage-work for the right hand, as opposed to what occurred in all but three of its fourteen predecessors, the confining of the organ to a filling-in part played from a figured bass, with all the melodic interest elsewhere. A one-movement piece of sturdy design, Wolfgang's third setting of 'Regina Coeli', dates from about this time. This no longer expands details in Italianate leisure; its alternations of *tutti* and *soli* never interrupt its continuous energy.

But the final crown of the Salzburg church music is the pair of settings of Vespers music. In 1779 Wolfgang wrote the *Vesperae solennes de Dominica*, K.321. Though in 1774 he had set the first and last items (*Dixit Dominus* and *Magnificat*, K.193) this was his first composition of the whole set of five psalms and Magnificat which comprise a festal Vespers. But there is nothing tentative about the work, which reads as though the composer had mentally worked his way through a dozen such compositions and was now intent on extracting the last drops of juice from procedures in danger of drying up. For instance, the successive movements involve the juxtaposition of keys only distantly related. The fourth psalm, 'Laudate Pueri', traditionally set in the old contrapuntal church style à la Martini, cannot help admitting a symphony-like transplanting of a more lyrical paragraph adorned with violin trills to humanise it, as it were. The 'Laudate Dominum' is a soprano solo of the purest Italian pedigree, by turns melting and virtuosic, and adorned with an organ part, perhaps for the new official organist. But the work shows a mastery of composition which permits of ever-new solutions of built-in problems. For instance, the doxology 'Gloria Patri' has to end all six successive movements. Liturgically, its function is to subsume all the disparate and originally individual sentiments of the texts with a general hymn of praise, and in the case of the psalms to bring them from their Old Testament milieu into the infinite horizons of Christianity. The idea of a symphony-style recapitulation here is bound to occur to composers of Wolfgang's period, even if the words 'as it was in the beginning' were not there to suggest it. But what to recapitulate, and in what order, and with what preparation—sudden, or spaciously inevitable—and with what enlargements to match 'for ever and ever'? With six different solutions in K.321, and six more the following year, one can only bid the reader 'listen and wonder'.

The corresponding work of 1780, K.339, though called *Vesperae solennes de Confessore*, sets exactly the same words, but with such fecundity that anyone knowing only one of the sets would not be able to imagine how different the other could be. Even in 'Laudate Pueri', with a yet more archaic subject than before, there are surprises, and not just modernisms either, but powerful contrapuntal ingenuities that would have thrilled Martini. The quiet rapture of the soprano solo in 'Laudate Dominum' is exceptional even amongst so many examples. One still hears facile talk about whether such music is 'properly liturgical'. The end of 'Laudate Dominum' surely shows not only imagination but also liturgical insight? When the solo begins there is no reason to suppose that the movement will not continue thus to the end; instead, at the very moment when the soloist sings the last syllable of the psalm, the choir softly recapitulates the main theme to the words 'Gloria Patri' as though all mankind, though properly awed by the beauty it has just heard, cannot forbear to join in. But without the soloist it is not 'all mankind', and so musical and psychological needs are both satisfied when the soloist rejoins the chorus's supportive voices for an 'Amen' which is the final flowering.

Thus all the Salzburg church music for choir and orchestra is completed. Again there is no sign in the music of anything being irksome. Apart from a Kyrie or two, a couple of magnificent torsos and one perfect miniature, there is indeed no further church music of any kind. The logic of the musician's position in the eighteenth century supplies the reason. His situation is that recorded by St Matthew of the would-be labourers in the vineyard: 'Why stand ye here all day idle? Because no man hath hired us.'

In the secular field there is another sonata for violin and piano, K.378 in B flat. The fact that the violinist begins with an accompanimental figure is misleading. There is a complete sharing out of the material which is, furthermore, of a kind to sound well on either instrument. The opening of the slow movement, a spiritualised gavotte, seems to belie this, but the long delay before the violin plays its main theme serves only to enhance it. The apparently easy-going *rondeau*—note Wolfgang's French spelling—suddenly 'goes off the rails' into an exuberant tarantella-like *allegro*, the rails being regained by a touch of cadenza. If any man had hired Wolfgang for another violin concerto this could well have been it, including as it does the traditional interrupted rondeau.

Two master works in the same key—E flat—can be assumed to be of this period though neither score is dated. They both show the rich mingling of the concerto and the symphony as a result of the Mannheim/Paris experience. Had the Sinfonia Concertante for violin, viola and orchestra, K.364, been a Paris work it would probably have had only two movements, like the 'concertante' parts of K.320. The work's title arises from there being more than one soloist, but it has become symphonic. There is a new integration of the orchestra and it is given greater weight in the formal scheme; the wind section—a modest pair each of oboes and horns—plays an essential thematic part, particularly in the outer movements. But the work is also in three movements; if it is to be a demonstration for Salzburg of what Wolfgang had learnt on his travels there is no need to restrict it to the Parisian two. Two movements, to keep a tonal balance, would need to have the same keynote; with a third there can be a contrast of key and a bigger emotional excursion. In the first movement the orchestra deploys a procession of succinct and varied themes, including also a Mannheim-type crescendo; the soloists emerge in imitation of the controlled swelling long note which a singer would call *messa di voce*. It is a measure of the new richness of invention that throughout this movement the solo passages never quote any of the orchestral thematic material ample though it is. At the same time, subtle cross-references in the accompaniment ensure that we sense a thread, with never a hint of mishmash. The slow movement, as in the 'Jenomy' concerto, is in the minor key, with no relaxing prettiness. Indeed, the word 'plaintive' seems too light for its feeling, which the soloists' decorations seem rather to intensify than to palliate. The final *presto* takes on the squareness of a *contredanse*, with regular eight-bar phrases for page after page; the sheer joyousness makes this no defect. The 'emergence' theme of the soloists has a 'Scotch-snap' rhythm—repeated 'short-longs', which Italians are apt to call a 'Lombard' rhythm. We may perhaps in this piece deliberately refer to Scotland, since something very like this subject (in the same key, what is more) occurs in the J.C. Bach sonata, op. 5 no. 4, the third which the Mozarts between them turned into a piano concerto, K.107, and there is every likelihood that Bach was enlivening London audiences with a favourite piece of eighteenth-century local colour.

In some ways a companion for this work, having two soloists and the same key, is the concerto for two pianos, K.365. If, lacking specific information, we envisage the work as primarily for Wolfgang and Nannerl to play, we can imagine the alternations, now plain, now deliciously varied, being spiced with affectionate and humorous family emulation. There are, of course, structural surprises, like the recapitulation in the first movement: in the 'right' key but with the 'wrong' subject. But to pursue such points would simply mean that all future concertos would be individually analysed, for each differs in shape from its peerless companions. In the final rondeau, which incidentally is not interrupted by a change of tempo, there is a curious reference to a scrap of tune not obviously cognate with the rest—a tune which later became the main subject of the rondo in the C major piano concerto, K.467. Perhaps it is a family reference.

The first of the three symphonies Wolfgang wrote in this period—in G, K.318—is an overture in a shape which he must have heard from Grétry in Paris: fast-slow-fast, but with the sections leading into one another. This example, however, is not just a pot-pourri; the second *allegro* resumes and balances the design of the first. If one omitted the central *andante* one could with little alteration make a respectable symphonic first movement out of the remainder. It might have been intended as an overture to some musical play given by Böhm's company. To call it instead of 'Symphony' an 'Overture to an unknown comedy' would be nearer the truth and would get it many more performances. It was certainly used later (1783) in Vienna for an *opera buffa* by Bianchi called *La villanella rapita*. The symphony in B flat, K.319, uses the small pre-Paris orchestra. The *d r f m* motif is heard again in its first movement. There was originally no minuet, but Wolfgang added a perfectly compatible one later in Vienna. The original occasion is unknown, but the last movement in particular brims with carnival spirits in its mixture of tarantella rhythms and quick marches. The bassoon parts in this symphony are becoming much more characteristic. Interspersed with passages of the old 'all-hands-to-the-bass' style, there are frequent telling underlinings of the themes an octave below. The original occasion for the third symphony—in C, K.338—is also unknown, though the score has a date (29 August 1780). Much of the first movement is gaily martial, rather like the seeing-off of Cherubino to the wars at the end of the first act of *Figaro*. In its course Wolfgang quotes the strenuous unisons and the upward-rushing scales of the 'Paris' symphony (a middle, rather than a first, *coup d'archet*). The finale is even more of a tarantella than its predecessor.

There must have been a festal occasion in summer 1779 for the orchestral serenade in D, K.320. The first movement has a good deal of energetic *tutti* writing which is hardly distinguishable from that of a symphony proper. A point of interest is that the 'French' *maestoso* opening is actually recapitulated, that is, the introduction becomes part and parcel of the piece. The first minuet continues with stately pomp, to be suddenly mingled with, as at a general ridotto, by more cheeky, popular elements. In the middle of the piece are two movements—the first actually marked *Concertante*—which obviously revert again to Paris, to the *sinfonia concertante* genre which took the French by storm in the 1770s. To give no fewer than six players—pairs of flutes, oboes and bassoons—the chance to air their individual voices without distending the piece is a touchstone of technique indeed.

The following summer (1780) is the likely date of a Divertimento in D, K.334 (with its March, K.445) for two horns and strings, probably for a family friend Sigmund von Robinig, known to the Mozarts as 'Sigerl'. The jollity of the outer movements is rather lengthy, but the variations in D minor contain unexpected angularities of melody and rhythm and unusual sonorities. The first minuet on the other hand has always been one of Mozart's most popular creations.

Probably begun in the winter of 1779 was a stage-work posthumously published as *Zaïde*. The libretto was by an old family friend, Johann Schachtner, the Salzburg court trumpeter. The manuscript has no overture, but this is not surprising as the work is unfinished, lacking its doubtless happy dénouement; the overture would, in the normal course of things, be written last. The spoken libretto is also lost except for some lead-in cues and the words for alternate declamation and music known as melodrama, which fitfully interested Wolfgang at this time. A gem of this score is the trio at the end of the first act, using the E major tonality which he often associates with the serenity of nature—shining sun, shimmering rainbow—which will be proof against the distant louring of fate. Here the simple tunefulness of German popular song is diversified by cross-rhythms and *coloratura* expansion. This is a musician's delight, but before we decide that it is a case of caviare to the general for the average *Singspiel* audience, we should remind ourselves that the best travelling companies, not to mention the metropolitans of Vienna, possessed singers who could handle the Italian virtuoso style and instrumentalists who could abet them, and it was hardly likely that the managers would transport such appendages out of altruism. *Zaïde* was of course overtaken by *Die Entführung*.

Possibly also for the Böhm troupe Wolfgang turned his attention to 'König Thamos'; he rewrote some music of 1773, and added a good deal more entr'acte music. Certainly Böhm used the music later (c.1785) for a play by Karl Plümicke called *Lanassa*, in which context Wolfgang heard it in Frankfurt in 1790. Incidentally, Böhm also toured, in German, *La finta giardiniera*. In the new 'Thamos' music Leopold wrote above each entr'acte what it represented. For instance, the music which leads into the fourth act is headed: 'The third act ends with the treacherous conspiracy of Mirza and Pheron' and the annotations show where the curtain rises on the fourth act, and where the key-words of the dialogue fit into what is obviously intended as a 'melodrama'. It is a pity that *The Magic Flute* with its definitive statement of the subject-matter and the mise-en-scène has apparently robbed this music of the performance it deserves.

Looking at the matter dispassionately, it is not possible to hold that this last corpus of Salzburg music, of which space does not permit a full catalogue, represents some marked fall in quality or even in quantity. To picture Wolfgang's antipathies as amounting to a plight at this stage seems to be mere romanticising, and in any case plights seem neither to impede nor to stimulate great creators. It was not a full two years' work in any case, for some time in the autumn of 1780 was taken up by the eager composition of parts of *Idomeneo*, the commission from Munich which had been unsparingly cultivated and so long in coming. Now at last Wolfgang could put forward his full strength for the incomparable forces he had known from their Mannheim days, and he could compose in advance in many cases for voices he knew well, so as not to rely on what could be crammed into the hectic running-up period in Munich itself. In Nannerl's diary for 22 August 1780 we read the bald statement: 'in the afternoon father Varesco was with us'. This may refer to a preliminary talk, for Varesco the Salzburg court chaplain was commissioned to make the libretto, out of a French play, Danchet's *Idoménée*. This followed the tendency of the Munich repertoire to look to France, not merely in original subject-matter, but also in the extensive use of chorus and ballet as integral to the drama. Italian ballets, as we have seen, were usually mere intermezzi. The choice of text was perhaps the Elector's, or perhaps that of the Electress, Wolfgang's knitting teacher. In Paris, Wolfgang had an abortive search for an opera libretto; for him the fruit of Mannheim and Paris was Munich. *Idomeneo* is the partly-French opera that never came his way in Paris, and includes the vocal and orchestral resources he had never used in Mannheim. Whoever had chosen the subject, it is quite clear that all concerned—composer, designer (Lorenzo Quaglio), ballet-master (Le Grand)—had to work to a detailed plan which was supervised by the Indendant of the court opera, Joseph Anton Count Seeau, who had held this Munich position under the previous Elector, Maximilian III Joseph. Seeau had thus overseen the staging of *La finta giardiniera*, though not, as *Idomeneo* was to be, at the Residenz-Theater, or 'New Electoral Opera House' as it then was.

This summer of 1780 represents the earliest date, according to the handwriting studies of Wolfgang Plath, to which we must displace from the Paris period four piano sonatas, K.330-33, which include some of the best known. The first, K.330 in C, is bound to look light-weight after the rigours of the A minor sonata, K.310. Its 'beginner's' key, the school-room style of melody for the right hand, and a left-hand accompaniment which is largely one note at a time, all contribute to the easy-going impression. But there are formal subtleties, or at least surprises. Both the outer movements have 'developments' which in fact discuss nothing at all of the previous material, whereas the 'contrasting' middle of the slow movement is bound in with the rest by the closest rhythmical affinities, as the perfect simplicity of its coda helps to make plain.

There are unalloyed pleasures in the much-played A major sonata, K.331. None of its three movements uses the drama of sonata-form design. The first consists of variations on a pastoral, pretty tune which Wolfgang marks *grazioso*. If we may no longer call this work a 'Paris' sonata we can still claim a French style for the tune (incidentally rendering the more incongruous Max Reger's Teutonic and interminable orchestral variations on it). The second movement is an extended minuet, and the last is an *Alla Turca* with the sound of the forte-piano's mechanism imitating what the eighteenth century took for Turkish music.

The two outer movements of the F major sonata, K.332 are both, for all their familiarity, splendid examples of the rich diversity of successive themes which yet hang together by that compositional magic which Leopold called, in a letter to Wolfgang (13 August 1778), *il filo* (the thread). The letter was urging Wolfgang to follow J.C. Bach's example in works that were charming but well-constructed withal. The B flat sonata, K.333, which may even be dated as late as 1784, might have been following just such a prescription. Its opening theme is strongly reminiscent of Bach's sonata op. 18 no. 4, and it ends with a rondo which grows under the fingers from the innocent charm of its opening to the dimensions and style of an unaccompanied concerto, complete with a thoroughgoing cadenza.

Before we go with Wolfgang to Munich on 5 November, there are dates to note and family matters to attend to. After all, though he does not know it, Wolfgang is never to reside in Salzburg again. In Nannerl's diary under 24 September we read in Wolfgang's hand, 'Herr Schikaneder also shot with us.' The future instigator of the *Magic Flute* thus comes into family intimacy only a week after the theatrical company in which he was actor-manager had begun a Salzburg winter season, having doubtless caused much pleasure by giving the family free seats on demand. (The family shoots were air-gun affairs for modest stakes with comic targets supplied by the members in turn.) On that same day, another operatic connection was made, for the family went to a musical comedy by Gottlieb Stephanie, who was the librettist of *Die Entführung* and of *Der Schauspieldirektor*. On 31 October Aloysia Weber was married in Vienna to the actor Joseph Lange, from whom Frau Weber exacted an expensive marriage-settlement. Lange was the first to play Hamlet in Vienna. He was indeed a man of parts, being also the painter of the well-known though unfinished portrait of Wolfgang of a few years later. The first child, Maria Anna Sabina, was born only seven months after the wedding, and the marriage broke up around 1795. Less than a year after that marriage Wolfgang calls Lange a jealous fool and in the same letter confesses that he is not yet indifferent to Aloysia. Perhaps the most useful thing she did for mankind was to evoke seven concert arias from Wolfgang, the last as late as 1788. Significantly, the later ones lack the warmth of feeling of the earlier.

Wolfgang's last Salzburg autumn must have seen the start of the famous family picture by Johann Nepomuk della Croce. The presiding mother in her oval frame was copied; late in the proceedings, from a portrait which Wolfgang had to borrow in Vienna the next year from its painter Rosa Hagenauer-Barducci, a tricky diplomatic achievement. We can date Nannerl's first formal sitting (30 December) because she mentions the erection of her hair in a postscript of a letter to Wolfgang, by now in Munich, dated the previous day. In this she was following the fashion of Marie Antoinette, whose brother Joseph II had in 1777 likened her head of hair to the height of St Stephen's Cathedral in Vienna. The picture is a poor essay in proportion and perspective. The crossed hands of Nannerl and Wolfgang, though an effect founded in fact, are far too near the top of the keyboard for effective sonority; Leopold's violin quite dwarfs him and he would have to stoop without purpose to bring his head down to the same level as his seated, short-statured son. Yet there is something haunting about it—the beleaguered family looking straight down its noses at a world the father has taught it to distrust. The picture has a centre, a portrait by a better artist; the family, however, has none.

There is a puzzle about Wolfgang's leave of absence until 18 December.

Left: An unknown pencil has captured the pert features of Maria Anna Thekla Mozart, the 'Bäsle' ('little cousin')

Right: Aloysia Lange, née Weber, appearing as Zémire in Grétry's opera *Zémire and Azor*, 1784

Theaterplatz, Mannheim: the National Theatre is the building with the pediment on the left

A street scene in Munich with, on the left, the house called 'Sonneck'—'Sun Corner'—where Mozart wrote much of *Idomeneo*

The Mozart family portrait by Johann Nepomuk della Croce, 1780/81, discussed in detail on page 126

This silhouette, dated 1791, shows an ensemble in the service of Prince Oettingen-Wallerstein and offers convincing evidence of the use of the double-bass in wind serenades

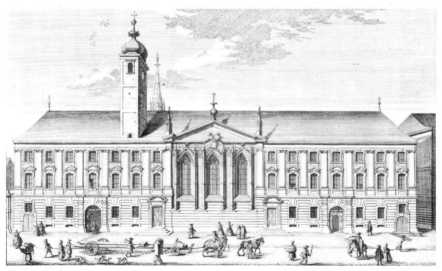

The House of the Teutonic Order in the Singerstrasse, Vienna, where Mozart's final period in the Archbishop's service began

The busy Vienna street 'Der Graben'. The Trattnerhof, which at one time served Mozart both as lodging and concert-room, is the tall building in the right foreground

The Kobenzl Hill, part of a romantic park in the Vienna Woods district laid out by Count Kobenzl, to which Mozart was a frequent visitor in 1781

Either Wolfgang or the Archbishop, or both, must have known that such a final date in any ordinary circumstance would have been too soon. The difference between a technical overstaying and a culpable one was a matter for the Archbishop's judgement, which he did not bring to bear on Wolfgang till the following March. Wolfgang describes his journey to Munich with robust vivacity: 'That post-chaise—those seats—hard as stone. I didn't think I could keep my arse with me all the way from Wasserburg to Munich. It was fiery red; for two whole stages I supported myself on my hands to keep it in the air.' The fact that Varesco was resident in Salzburg had greatly helped the composition that jolted along with Wolfgang. He was no man of the theatre, but competently rendered Danchet's French into the obligatory Italian, and most important, he was a pliant, quick and careful subordinate of the Mozarts, though not without some inevitable grumbles on his part. With Wolfgang in Munich, Leopold became not only the mediary between him and Varesco, but also (luckily for us in the insights they give) the confidant of the composer's thoughts because he could truly understand them. Indeed, he even offered suggestions to Wolfgang, for instance about the accompaniment of the speech by the statue of Neptune: 'Presumably you will have deep wind-instruments to accompany the subterranean voice. How would it be after a short subterranean sound if the instruments *sustained quietly, then began truly to sustain, then made a crescendo to a frightening degree,* then a *decrescendo as the voice began?* and thus a shuddering crescendo *each time the voice leaves off.*' This is just what Wolfgang does do in two of the no fewer than four versions he makes of the passage. Following Gluck's oracular example in *Alceste,* three of these use trombones—for the only time in the opera. But ironically it seems more than likely that the fourth version, for clarinets, bassoons and horns, was used, Count Seeau at last putting his foot down about orchestral expense (three trombones for eight bars).

The crux of the story is the fatal vow, like Jephtha's in Carissimi's and Handel's oratorios, or Agamemnon's in, say, Gluck's *Iphigenia in Aulis,* whereby Idomeneo to save himself from shipwreck promises to sacrifice to Neptune the first living creature he meets, which turns out to be Idamante, his son. It is impossible to encapsulate such things without appearing to mock them. But an opera is not a plot, though it cannot do without one, nor is it a means of conveying information. One can only hope that opera-lovers at least will understand the passion for emotional realism which pervades the correspondence, and of course, the great work itself. There is no discrepancy between such a realism and such a vow, even when as here it is reinforced by the ravages of a sea-monster. With Mozart at the plenitude of his powers we are not 'suspending disbelief'. We are entering, in *Idomeneo*, as indeed in *Così fan tutte*, into a wider, deeper reality than the every-day world during those precious minutes in which the music speaks to us. That those minutes should not be too long is one of Wolfgang's main preoccupations. He is willing to pay heavily for the right decision; for instance, in the last act when the statue has commanded that Idomeneo should abdicate, and Idamante rule with Priam's daughter Ilia as his queen, Electra, consumed with love for Idamante and with rage at the end of her hopes, was to have sung a recitative and aria. Wolfgang completely composed this superb piece of music, then realised that it would have to be sung to a stage-full. He reduced 189 bars in his finest vein to a mere 26, albeit an orchestrated recitative of stunning vehemence.

It was as well that the women singers and the orchestra gave no trouble, for Wolfgang had to take pains with the men. Raaff, as Idomeneo, was an old friend, but his singing powers had to be nursed, and as for his acting, 'he is a statue'. Wolfgang had to teach Idamante his part note by note, calling him his 'molto amato Castrato del Prato'. The splendid orchestra, despite the unprecedented detail and concentration demanded of them, seem to have appreciated the work from the start. The clarinets are still treated as a special sound. They accompany the cathartic abdication 'Oh Creta fortunata! Oh me felice!', where their part is the more noteworthy as the horns are the only other wind instruments here; but the clarinets are then silent to the end of the piece, throughout the last chorus and the whole final ballet. They are much less used than the oboes and are hardly ever added to them. In other words, except in the overture, there is none of the comparatively featureless wind-band writing of the 'Paris' symphony. The clarinets are more like singers themselves, and their characteristic melting timbre has to await the right emotional milieu.

But at this point one must fight off the temptation in respect of all the operas from now on, to write a number-by-number *catalogue passionné*. It must suffice to mention the first number of the harbour scene towards the end of the second act, when Electra and her companions from Argos suppose that they are to sail home from their Cretan captivity on a calm sea. 'Placido e il mar' is in E major, the key of propitious zephyrs (see *Così*) which is quite unused elsewhere in the opera. The lulling motion of the ship at anchor is precisely caught by a combination of barcarolle and berceuse. There is a gentle delight in euphony, with the upper voices in parallel thirds, which reminds one of the gentler side of Berlioz. Needless to say, Neptune will have none of it; there is a fearsome storm, complete with momentary piccolo, and the act ends *pianissimo* with the chorus fleeing in terror—a very different idea from bringing the house down in the Italian manner.

Leopold and Nannerl arrived in time for the final rehearsal which took place on 27 January, Wolfgang's twenty-fifth birthday. The first performance, twice postponed, was on 29 January. It seems that there were only two others, on 3 February and 3 March. The only surviving newspaper report gives an approving sentence on the scenery but no critique of the music.

Unprecedented heights had been trodden, and there was no option but to descend again. But there were two works at least which could well have been begun in order to show the Elector another thing or two. One was the Kyrie in D minor, K.341, which had it been continued to form a complete mass would have been a great creation, uniquely scored as it was for full symphony orchestra, including eight woodwinds and four horns. The other is usually, but not with certainty, assigned to this period, and is one of the most remarkable of all Wolfgang's compositions, which if not completed in Munich before he had to leave, might have been spurred by the splendid wind players to hand there. It is the Serenade in B flat, K.361, for no less than thirteen instruments: two oboes, two clarinets, two basset-horns (a kind of alto clarinet), two bassoons, four French horns and a bass line which is often given to the contra-bassoon, but which is marked *pizzicato* in the second trio of the second minuet. Apart from the difficulty of effectively plucking contra-bassoons, the combination with double-bass is vouched for by such pictoral evidence as the silhouette of Prince Öttingen-Wallerstein's ensemble dated 1791. The introductory *largo* epitomises the two poles of the work—the grand richness of the unparalleled sound in the French-style chordal rhythms for all but the first clarinet, and that instrument's response with contrasting intricacies of sensuous line. The first *adagio* treats the leading oboe, clarinet and basset-horn as though they were one operatic soloist with three colours of voice, singing above gently throbbing harmonies and a constantly moving bass which curiously and perhaps accidentally harks back to *La finta giardiniera*. The quiet harmony, at once undulating and static, towards the end of the fifth variation in the penultimate movement constitutes one of the most delicious sounds in all music. To this post-*Idomeneo* time also belongs the quartet in F, K.370 for oboe and strings. There is no direct evidence, but it is most unlikely to have been written for any other than Friedrich Ramm, the first oboe of the orchestra whom Wolfgang had known since Mannheim days. The virtuosity called for in much of the oboe part would, if it were for another oboist, call for such a talent to be named somewhere. The individual, indeed assertive tone of the oboe makes it impossible to allot it any truly subordinate part. Mozart realises this, of course, and in fact there is no single oboe phrase throughout which is not melodic. Nevertheless, the problem of scoring is solved with such apparent effortlessness that the listener can hardly be aware that there is one, so subtly is the balance of interest maintained between the oboe and the trio of strings. The cross-reference of themes and rhythms are wondrously rich in the first movement, whilst the middle of the rondeau is diversified by an extraordinary passage in which the oboe divides the main beats into twos, fours and eights, whilst the strings continue to divide them into three. This coupled with the soft, high note at the very end certainly represents a vote of confidence in Ramm which *Idomeneo* must have amply justified.

8

Breaking Out in Vienna

1781–83

All too soon came a parting of the ways of an unforeseen duration. On the urgent order of the Archbishop Wolfgang left to rejoin some of his entourage, then in Vienna; Leopold and Nannerl went back to Salzburg. Wolfgang arrived in Vienna on the morning of 16 March 1781 and on that very afternoon had to play at the Archbishop's quarters, the house of the Teutonic Order. This we learn from his letter of the next day, written in Dr Mesmer's garden. He too was quartered in the Teutonic Order's house and dined at noon ('too early for me') below the valets but above the cooks. He had indeed descended from Parnassus. But now we have to deduce Leopold's replies. The last extant letter from him to Wolfgang is that of 22 January, before they met at Munich. The rest were doubtless destroyed after Wolfgang's death by his widow. But this in a sense accidental one-sidedness is curiously appropriate; the physical distance and the chronic shortage of the means to overcome it, coupled with Wolfgang's two drastic decisions both presenting a *fait accompli* to Leopold, between them meant a distancing in the relationship. Whatever his protestations, and despite the much-felt deprivation of a beloved sister, Wolfgang henceforth began to lead his life, for most practical purposes, as though Leopold had never written him another word. If because of this we begin to look at everything through Wolfgang's eyes from now on, this is perhaps as it should be. For us, as opposed to a powerless, proud and grieving father, what matters is what Wolfgang did, not whether it was right or politic to do it.

The Archbishop had to keep his end up in Vienna, and his musicians were one of the means to this end. There was nothing unusual in this, nor in the fact that he regarded their services as his private property, and his alone. For more than four months he had paid Wolfgang a salary (we should certainly have heard about it if he had not) and received nothing for it, unless it were momentary rays of reflected glory, and his position demanded that he should be the source of glory, not the recipient of its reflection. Hence the orders at short notice to play for Prince Galitzin, the Russian Ambassador. Hence the initial refusal, grudgingly countermanded, to allow Wolfgang a public appearance even though for charity—the recently established Society of Musicians which was for the benefit of their widows and orphans—a charity to which all the musicians of note gave their services. This enabled a really large orchestra to be assembled; Wolfgang quotes forty violins in all, ten violas, eight cellos, ten double-basses, six bassoons and the rest of the wind doubled. Wolfgang does not name the symphony of his which these forces played, but said it went *magnifique*. This choice of word and the suitability of the work for such large numbers makes it likely that Vienna thus heard the 'Paris' symphony at Wolfgang's first public appearance there as a grown man. For the promised piano solo he played his variations, K.354, on a tune 'Je suis Lindor' from Baudron's opera setting of Beaumarchais's *Barber of Seville*. The renewed delight in his powers in using forces otherwise out of reach makes it no surprise that on the very next day there is Wolfgang's first mooting of leaving the Archbishop's service, a possibility that doubtless perturbed that other employee of his, who incidentally was currently drawing both their salaries in Salzburg.

But 'last straws' were heaping themselves thick and fast on Wolfgang. On 8 April he was bidden to play a concert to the Archbishop's father, Prince Rudolf Colloredo, together with Brunetti the violinist and Ceccarelli the castrato. They did three of his own pieces. Brunetti played the separate Rondo in C, K.373, a graceful, comparatively easy piece; Ceccarelli sang a recitative and air, K.374, the air also being in a rondo shape and not unlike Brunetti's piece in easy-going style, with traces in its main tune of the famous 'Che faro' in Gluck's *Orfeo*. Brunetti also joined Wolfgang in the sonata in G, K.379, which was composed the previous night between eleven and midnight, only the violin part being written down for the concert, Wolfgang playing the rest out of his head. The piece begins with an unusual *adagio* which has a half-way division and a repeat and which shows every sign of being a complete movement before leading into an abrupt *allegro* in the minor key; then there is a charming set of variations not demanding to play nor to listen to. Either Brunetti was not very skilful or lacked the time to practise—the latter very likely given the circumstances of the composition. But the concert must have been worth something more than Wolfgang's unprintable word for the affair. Wolfgang received nothing. Because of the duty he could not attend a concert at Countess Thun's at which the Emperor was present and two singers received high fees. Wolfgang is by now asking Leopold point-blank whether he should quit the Archbishop and stay in Vienna. In a letter of a week later (18 April) we hear the news that will do as much as anything to tip the balance: the impresario-playwright Gottlieb Stephanie is to give him a new libretto to set, a good one. This is the first hint of *Die Entführung*. The next stage (28 April) is for Wolfgang to suggest that he does indeed return in the Archbishop's service to Salzburg but that Leopold must promise to agree to his returning to Vienna the following spring with or without permission. Obviously Leopold gave no such encouragement, and no silence of his could mean consent.

So on 9 May there is a partly verbatim account of a final altercation with the Archbishop which stings Wolfgang into announcing his quitting of his service. 'Today was my lucky day.' The same letter also mentions old Madame Weber's kindness in giving him a pretty room in her house, the second floor of the building known as the 'Auge Gottes' (God's eye) which fronts on two streets, the Am Peter and the Tuchlauben. But it also transpires that this taking in of Wolfgang by that lady was not an emergency measure caused by the break, but had happened a week before. The combination of the shattering news with the dreaded name of 'Weber' must have elicited a letter from Leopold which to say the least was not supportive. Wolfgang writes from his highest horse on 19 May: 'I must confess I can't find a single trace of my father in your letter—I see a father indeed, but not that best, most loving one, who cares both for his own honour and that of his children—in a word, not my father.' Manhood asserted, he goes on to make it clear that he did not leave the Archbishop from any deliberate wish to be what we would call a freelance, even if he had grasped such a premature conception. He wanted service with honour—like Joseph Haydn's, though he does not mention the name. This was not quite the end of the dealings with the Archbishop. Since Wolfgang was making the issue one of honour it behoved him all the more to have a written resignation accepted, and he made also a point of paying back the allowance for a journey he was not now to undertake. Repeated attempts to do this culminated in a dismissive kick from the Archbishop's Chief Steward, Karl Count Arco, on 8 June. The kick has been felt by Mozart-lovers ever since. But there is something to be said on the other side. Wolfgang's hauteur must have precipitated the kick, and must have seemed doubly insufferable when the delays over the resignation which angered Wolfgang may have had well-meaning motives. It is known that Leopold and Arco had been in correspondence meanwhile and it is not difficult to guess what was said. In fact, the Archbishop never did officially accept the resignation. All this can be counted to his credit and, until the final exasperated moment, to Arco's too. There was never a suggestion that Leopold's own position was in jeopardy, and he died in harness. By their lights the Archbishop and Arco could feel justified in being obstructive.

The beginning of summer was hardly the time, with all the likeliest customers out of town, to launch concerts, to find wealthy piano pupils or to collect subscriptions for published compositions, which were the three ways Wolfgang proposed to use to support himself. But meanwhile there was composition to be done. At the end of July Stephanie gave him the libretto of *Die Entführung aus dem Serail* ('The Abduction from the Harem') and he flung himself into the work, though in fact there were to be delays and the first performance was to be almost a year later, in Stephanie's headquarters, the Burgtheater. The letters to Leopold as often as not begin with rebuttals and reproaches for Leopold's suspicions and worries about money, about the volatility of Wolfgang's character ('never the golden mean') and above all about the menace of Frau Weber's designed gossip, causing a bad-tempered move out from 'God's Eye' to a room in the Graben by the naïve young man who protested that marriage was not for him. But the work on the new opera also led to those remarks from one professional to another which so illuminated the progress of *Idomeneo*. At the start, Wolfgang wants the power of music immediately deployed; the libretto began with a monologue which he asks Stephanie to replace with a little song for the hero Belmonte—easily enough acceded to, since a song to introduce oneself was a very usual feature of such plays. Then, after Osmin's introductory song, the dialogue should be replaced by a duet. Then the character of Osmin must be filled out with more songs to take advantage of his exceptional deep bass, 'especially as he has the public wholly on his side.' But we have a truly Mozartean aesthetic expressed in the remarks about an aria in which Osmin's rage is made to increase until he is beside himself.

Just when the aria seems to be ending there is an *allegro assai* in a totally different time and key . . . but as passions, violent or not, must never be expressed to the point of disgust, and the music, even in the most terrible situations, must never offend the ear but must even then please us, in short must always remain music, I have gone from the key of the aria, F, not to an unrelated key, but to a relative one—but not the nearest relative, D minor, but into the more removed A minor.

The sentence epitomises the ways of genius; we proceed without a full stop from what is dramatically realistic, through an intuitive feeling for what is artistically fitting (expressed with certainty) to the precise technical detail of how the effect is to be made. In spite of all, happy is the father deemed worthy to be the recipient of such things. But suddenly the happy urgency ceased. Not one, but two operas by Gluck—*Iphigenia in Tauris* and *Alceste*—were timed to be in the repertoire in November and December for the state visit of Grand-Duke Paul of Russia, and this ruled out till the next year the staging of *Entführung*.

But Wolfgang also needed three more sonatas for violin and piano to make up the set for which his friend the Countess of Thun was already soliciting subscriptions, and these occupied part of his summer. Two in the same key (F, K.376 and K.377) were by their style and relative easiness designed for shared pleasures at home, rather than the concert hall. The balanced say allotted to each instrument makes for a perhaps unexciting symmetry, and in the composition too one can sense a desire not to distract by ingenuities of recomposition, quite long paragraphs being reproduced later in the movements more or less as they stand. An exception is the set of variations in D minor in K.377, whose mysterious closing *siciliana* must have been a jumping-off point for the corresponding movement in the D minor string quartet, K.421, dated two years later. But to close the set he wrote on a more ambitious scale the Sonata in E flat, K.380. All three movements have something of the concerto about them. The first commands the 'public' interest with big opening gestures and a generous succession of strongly differentiated themes. The second is of the plaintive-*andante* genre which several concertos exhibit, and the final rondo uses the type of breezy 'a-hunting-we-will-go' tune which is featured in the horn concertos and several piano concertos. What is more, considerable agility is required of both players.

For St Theresa's Day, 15 October, Wolfgang wrote the lovely wind serenade in E flat, K.375. The first recipient was the sister-in-law of the Court painter, Joseph Hickel—she being a Theresa—and then the musicians to their gratification played it for two other Theresas that evening. But there was another encore to come; to Wolfgang's delight it was played outside his own lodgings on 31 October, his own name-day. He describes the lovely surprise of that first chord of E flat, heard just as he was about to undress. Well may that chord send a thrill of anticipation down the spines of those who know what is in store—the effortless balance of virtuosity, serenity, counterpoint and variegated colours, all couched in sensuous sound, especially in the work's ultimate form with oboes added to the original sextet of clarinets, horns and bassoons. Nowhere is the kaleidoscope of colour more deftly turned than in the interlocking song of the slow movement.

Meanwhile, on 23 October, Wolfgang wrote the last surviving letter to the Bäsle. There is affection in it, but no jokes. Significantly, though by now he lives in a room in a house in the Graben, he gives the Weber address for the continuation of the correspondence. We have no continuation, but there is an echo of Wolfgang in the Bäsle's subsequent history. An illegitimate child of hers was baptised in Augsburg Cathedral on 22 February 1784. Remembering Wolfgang's signature 'Trazom' she signed the register as 'Trazin'—the wife of Traz, or of the sweet one, Zart. The father, Ludwig Berbier, called himself 'Reiber'. The priest knew the real names and recorded them in the margin.

If we conflate a letter to Leopold (22 December 1781) with one to Nannerl while Leopold was away in Munich (13 February 1782) we can visualise Wolfgang's day in the last year before his marriage. He is awakened by the barber at six a.m. He is fully dressed by seven. He composes till ten; then there are lessons (provided the pupils are in town to receive them). There are only three at this stage, all women. The first Vienna pupil was Countess Rumbeke, who with her cousin Count Kobenzl befriended Wolfgang, taking him for trips out of the city. Second was Frau von Trattner, she at twenty-three being the wife of a husband aged sixty-four. He was a painter to the court, as well as a bookseller and paper manufacturer. When Wolfgang was living in the Graben, to give Frau von Trattner a lesson was only a matter of walking across the square. In 1784 Wolfgang not only lodged in the Trattnerhof with his wife, but held three subscription concerts in its largest room. Frau von Trattner was repaid by the dedication of two of the finest piano solo works, the Fantasia K.475 and the Sonata K.457, both in C minor, published together by Artaria in 1785. The third pupil was Josepha Auernhammer, daughter of a Vienna Councillor. Wolfgang pitilessly records how ugly she is, and how, fruitlessly, she falls in love with him: 'She is as fat as a farm-girl, her sweat makes you feel sick, and she goes about so bare that one is bound to get the message—"*I beg you, do look here*".' Be that as it may, she was a good enough pianist to partner Wolfgang in a concert at home, both in the two-piano concerto K.365, refurbished with clarinets, trumpets and drums, and in a sonata 'in zweien' which almost certainly means the sonata for two pianos in D, K.448. In this unclouded, extrovert piece we can certainly imagine master and pupil rattling along on precisely equal terms.

But we must resume the day with eating either at home or out with friends, it could be as late as three p.m. At any rate there is not usually more work before five or six, and at that hour there might be a concert. But otherwise it would be composition again till about nine. Then it would be seeing Aloysia's sister Constanze Weber and putting up with her mother till coming home at ten-thirty or eleven, then often writing again till one a.m. Even if some of this regimen is recorded to refute charges of laziness, three-quarters of it would be impressive. We know for certain that whatever else Wolfgang could not afford to do, he indulged his passion for the theatre as often as he could.

But now on 15 December, within a year of arrival in Vienna, within five months of sententiously declaring that his talents and matrimony do not mix, Wolfgang tells Leopold of his desire to marry—and, of all people, a Weber, Constanze, a younger sister of Aloysia. Leopold's reactions as he helplessly watches his suspicions borne out, and his son in the toils, can be easily deduced from the letters back to him, now angry, now patiently but too hopefully explaining financial details, now pleading for an understanding backing. As to whose toils he was in, Wolfgang eventually agrees with Leopold's estimate and thoroughly blackens the mother and Aloysia, but the more to highlight the angelic qualities (or at least the suitable ones) of Constanze. She is not ugly, but is far from beautiful. Two little black eyes and a pretty figure constitute such beauty as she has. We can perhaps judge this for ourselves in the portrait painted by her brother-in-law Lange, now in the Hunterian Museum of Glasgow University. Wolfgang persuaded himself that he had got what he wanted—he may indeed really have done so—but it is certain that Madame Weber, a widow with three daughters still to settle, got what *she* wanted, Wolfgang at that stage having cleared the decks for a brilliant career by the parting with Salzburg, in which she obviously gave unambiguous advice. From the time when Wolfgang first accepted her kind lodging he was there to see, but saw nothing. Leopold was in Salzburg, but saw it all. First the gossip linking the lodger with the daughter, then the advice to move out—not to silence the gossip but to fan it and to lend colour to the notion that Wolfgang having compromised the girl was ready to jilt her. Then the interview with her guardian Johann Thorwart, who had a hold over Wolfgang's future as the right-hand man of Prince Rosenberg, the Intendant of the National Theatre. Thorwart exacted from Wolfgang a document binding himself to marry Constanze within three years or else pay her a large annuity. Then Constanze—a crowning touch—tore the document up in her mother's presence when the guardian had gone, expressing the while her perfect trust. Thorwart meanwhile had broken his promise and told Vienna of the transaction. Wolfgang got Constanze to leave her family and lodge with a patroness of his, Baroness von Waldstätten, a move which helped Frau Weber the more, as the Baroness lived apart from her husband and had a light reputation. Threats by the mother to send the police to get her daughter back were the *coup de grâce*. The wedding took place in St Stephen's Cathedral on 4 August 1782. Constanze's witness was Thorwart; Wolfgang's was Franz Gilowsky, brother of Nannerl's beloved Katherl. The wedding feast was given by Baroness von Waldstätten. Not only that but she did her best to reassure Leopold that Constanze was not like the other Webers, and she furthermore invited Leopold to stay with her in Vienna, which quite bowled him over. But the fact remains that Wolfgang married before Leopold's consent arrived—a day later. It is a small point, but not insignificant, that Wolfgang has to try to refute a complaint from Leopold that he was not even told the date of the wedding. On this point Leopold is in the right and Wolfgang in the wrong twice over. We know the date from the marriage-register of St Stephen's.

But meanwhile despite these distractions Wolfgang's Vienna career had been slowly gathering momentum. An influential friend in this was Maria Wilhelmina Countess Thun. Wolfgang called her husband a 'peculiar Cavalier', he being a disciple of Dr Mesmer and himself practising the laying-on of hands and other mysteries. The Countess was nine years older than Wolfgang, and she received the most precious of his musical confidences. It was to her that he played (doubtless on her Stein piano that he praised so highly) extracts from *Idomeneo* soon after his arrival, and he played her most of *Die Entführung*, act by act as it was completed. It was largely following her advice that at his first big public concert ('Akademie') on his own account, on 3 March 1782, he gave parts of *Idomeneo* and a piano concerto which was the K.175 with its new tuneful rondo-finale (K.382).

Mozart as a symphonist was heard on the morning of 26 May in the first of the subscription concerts held for the first time in the pavilion of the royal park called the Augarten on the far side of the Danube canal in Leopoldstadt. The symphony was probably the C major, K.338, and Wolfgang repeated with Josepha Auernhammer the two-piano concerto. But another symphonist was represented there, the librarian of the Imperial library, Gottfried van Swieten, who had until 1777 been the ambassador at the court of Frederick the Great at Potsdam. It was his interest in J.S. Bach and Handel which was shortly to open Wolfgang's ears and eyes to the powerful glories of genuine baroque counterpoint.

But the event which must have convinced the Webers that the forth-coming marriage was a promising one was the first night of *Die Ent-führung* on 16 July at the Burgtheater. Although some critics were cantankerous about the plot, the music had a success, measured in the frequency of subsequent performances, such as no other stage work of Mozart had in Vienna in his lifetime. Indeed Wolfgang had to step in to prevent too frequent an exploitation of the success. The plot is a popular romantic story of the hero with his comic servant rescuing the heroine (with her pert servant-girl) from the clutches—magnanimous at the last moment—of a Pasha and his black, by turns comic and lustful, servant Osmin, the most individual character of them all. We have seen how Wolfgang's musical stagecraft impelled him to lay strong hands on the opening, and it is illuminating to see how the crucial arias in which the characters introduce themselves show infallibly and immediately what sort of people they are. Belmonte, the hero, takes up in his first song the *andante* which interrupted the overture. It was then in the minor, but he sings in the major, clean-limbed and ardent, with a nice top G which he knows how to hold and swell. The song sounds uncomplicated, like Belmonte in fact. Osmin sings a morose serenade with plenty of bottom notes, and a gloomy 'Trallalera' which will amuse both those who are in the know about things Italian, and those who are not. The difference in the women is strongly marked. Constanze's first recitative and aria is like an *adagio* introduction and a first movement of say, a piano sonata with subjects rather than mere tunes, and with runs and trills at the ends of the paragraphs. Blonde must wait till the beginning of Act II to have her say. The first noun she sings is 'Zärtlichkeit' (sweetness) and the music takes a tone which is more tuneful and 'popular' than Constanze's. The lower ranks of the audience immediately feel she is one of them, but then find, to their gratified surprise, that she too can rise to the occasion with scales, the last of which is actually higher than anything Constanze has sung. Needless to say, Constanze is not on the stage to hear this *lèse-majesté*. Mozart the musician has set Mozart the dramatist a problem at the beginning of Constanze's air of defiance, 'Martern aller Arten', by writing a splendid and lengthy concertante of flute, oboe, violin and cello to introduce what is really a rejoinder. No musician would greatly care if this introduction were twice as long as its sixty bars, but it doubtless stayed in the Emperor's head when he allegedly commented: 'Far too many notes, my dear Mozart.' The score contains one of the most brilliant of drinking songs, 'Vivat Bacchus', which Wolfgang mentally dedicated 'to the gentlemen of Vienna'. The joining of German popular comedy and Italian operatic style did not begin with *Die Entführung*, though it has no predecessors to approach it in musical worth. The Italian opera was far too obvious a target for skits for such a combination not to have been used in parody. But questions of established monopolies had in fact caused an Imperial decree that, at the Kärntnertor theatre at least, Italian opera could not be given popular performance unless mixed with German elements. But the *Singspiel* as a developing art-form could never be the same again. As Goethe wryly and admiringly put it, Mozart had 'ruined everything'.

Whilst Wolfgang was trying to follow up the success of *Die Entführung* by making a wind-band arrangement of it in a hurry—lest pirate arrangers should beat him to it—there came a request from Leopold for another Haffner serenade, this time to celebrate the ennoblement of young Siegmund. He 'offered it up—to you, dearest father' and promised to send it by instalments. With the letter of 27 July he sent the first *allegro*, and proposed to send on 31 July the two minuets, the *andante* and the last movement. If time permitted he would send another march—otherwise the old Haffner march would have to do. It is clear from all this that a serenade, not a symphony, was expected at Salzburg, and it was sent, new march included, on 7 August. The tour de force of quick composition was to be matched in performance in the outer movements: 'the first movement must go with real fire and the last as quickly as possible' (dangerous words!). At the beginning of 1783 at Wolfgang's urgent request the music was sent back to Vienna so that he could use it at one of his own concerts. He added to the score the two flutes and two clarinets which presumably Salzburg did not boast. It is as a symphony (K.385) we now have the work, as the score does not include a second minuet; the march is possibly the one catalogued as K.408/2. When Wolfgang got the music back he professed himself happily surprised since in his hurry he had not remembered a note of it. In the first movement the playful-pompous unison opening motif is rarely absent, either in its melodic or rhythmic shape, and in the last we have perhaps an echo of the Parisian trick—another unison motif, but delivered softly, and with an unmistakable reference to what must have been in the forefront of Wolfgang's mind, Osmin's song of short-lived triumph (also in the same key) towards the end of *Die Entführung*.

But this serenade had also, apparently, to compete with another, the great work in C minor for wind octet, K.388 (later arranged for string quintet). For whom it was written is not clear. There may be a clue in a letter of 23 January 1782 listing the possibilities for a 'small permanent income'. Wolfgang mentions the young Prince Lichtenstein (three years younger than himself) who wanted to get together a wind-band, with a view to Wolfgang writing for it. The letter of 27 July apologises for the enclosure of only the first movement of the 'Haffner' because of having to compose a serenade in a hurry. Wolfgang goes on to say that had the serenade not been for wind-band some of it might have been used for Salzburg. If this C minor serenade is really the one he is referring to, the only conceivable movement that would have suited the Salzburg event would have been the *andante*. Something very like its main theme suited, by way of serenade, the two young men in *Così*—and indeed suited the two ladies all too well. Apart from there being no trace of two minuets, the rest of the work in any case diverges enormously from the implications of its title. The first movement uses the language of drama—some would go so far as to call its prevailing mood one of stoic defiance; certainly it amounts to far more than the plaintive or even the sorrowful. Even the last, variation movement only relents from the minor to the major at the last moment, and the minuet makes a learned display of the close imitation called canon both directly and 'by inversion', which is to say that the answering voice follows the leader's tune by singing it upside-down. This is hardly a usual serenading device, especially when Wolfgang blazons his ingenuity with an academic description of what he has done: 'in Canone al rovescio'. If indeed the young Lichtenstein was the recipient of this masterpiece he was paid a surpassing compliment—but we hear no more of the 'small permanent income' from that source in any case.

Throughout 1782 there had arisen a new grist to Mozart's composing mill of incalculable importance. Baron van Swieten, whose private music-makings on Sundays he regularly attended, had introduced to him many masterworks of Handel and Bach which he had obtained on his travels and which were virtually unknown in Vienna. In Bach and Handel Mozart confronted a contrapuntal style in all its living splendour and power, beside which the remnants of the contrapuntal tradition in contemporary 'learned' music must have suddenly seemed dry bones. To integrate the living force of 'baroque' counterpoint into his own style was not only a compositional necessity for Mozart; it was an essential stage in the history of music, without which some of the structures to come, not only his own but Beethoven's, would have had insufficient foundations—with a gap remaining between the new *galant* 'song and dance' style and the force—applied counterpoint—which could have expanded it. As all composers must, Mozart worked his way through this crisis, not just by thinking, but by writing. He would come to grips with Handel by copying out his works for study, and with Bach fugues by his arrangements of them, doubtless for van Swieten, for string trio and string quartet. Significantly, the six for string quartet, from the second book of the '48', are all of the more 'learned' type, with comparatively impersonal subjects designed for the ready showing of contrapuntal devices. Indeed for Wolfgang, and obviously for van Swieten too, a fugue named as such was, like old-fashioned marriage, not to be enterprised, nor taken in hand, unadvisedly, lightly, or wantonly. The works of around 1782 which Wolfgang calls fugues are often incomplete, almost all laboured, and sometimes, like the G minor fugue, K.401, written with an occasional disregard for the dimensions of the human hand. It is obvious that they are not works of art, but wrestling-matches. The wrestling is not (as sometimes with Beethoven) part of the intended artistic experience; it is simply Wolfgang teaching himself, loins girded, by the most efficient means. Trying to increase Leopold's and Nannerl's esteem of Constanze, he attributed to her an interest in fugues, which sounds very implausible. The Fantasia and Fugue in C for piano, K.394, which he wrote ostensibly in this connection, has a certain majestic, though anonymous, momentum in its fugue, but the effect is spoilt by the previous fantasia being such a splendid movement. The flowering of the new experience, and its amazingly quick absorption, comes not here, but in the great Mass in C minor, K.427. It was written to fulfil a vow that when he brought his wife to Salzburg he would have a new mass of his performed there. Discussion of it can wait until they arrive there in 1783. But they really intended to set out for Salzburg in November (letter of the 13th) in spite of Constanze being pregnant; they were held back by terrible weather, during which the mail had not even managed to get through to the first stage with eight horses. The next letter postponed the attempt until the spring, on representations from Vienna friends, which one feels could easily have been overruled by a really hearty invitation from Salzburg.

The mood of 1782 varies between sanguine confidence in the future, whistling in the dark and an occasional frank look at alternatives. A letter of 17 August mentions the possibility of going again to Paris—Wolfgang says he has written to Le Gros—or even to England. 'Lately I have been practising my French and I have already had three English lessons.' By 19 November he is describing himself as an 'Arch-Englishman'. There is even an unfinished fragment of a setting of an ode celebrating Admiral Howe's relief of Gibraltar, begun 'at the request of a Hungarian lady'. The words were by one Michael Denis, who 'restored the lyres of the Bards to his country'. But vicarious patriotism was not enough to get Wolfgang beyond the first fifty-eight bars of indigestible words beginning 'O Calpe!'.

Looking back at the untidy welter of events and experiences in 1782 we can well admire the strength of purpose that ensured that composition still flowed. But before the year's end three other series of works were begun. At intervals in the Mozart correspondence the name of Joseph Leutgeb crops up, first in 1763 as a horn-player in the Salzburg establishment. But he was always willing to exploit his obviously considerable talents elsewhere, and he seems to have been of the character to provoke affectionate hilarity, certainly with Wolfgang, who sometimes amused himself in annotating music intended for Leutgeb with 'encouraging' remarks. There is a fragmentary rondo for horn and orchestra, K.371, dating from Wolfgang's final weeks in the Archbishop's service, but this may not have anything to do with Leutgeb, who later told Wolfgang's widow he knew nothing of it. But Leutgeb was undoubtedly on hand in Vienna at this time, having got himself 'a little snail-shell of a house' and a cheese-factory. The horn quintet in E flat, K.407, was almost certainly written for him as were probably all four of the horn concertos—two attributions are certain—which this work heralded. A German name for the instrument at the time was 'Waldhorn' and its woodland associations are naturally seized upon, both in its dreamy *cantabile* and in the hunting-call tunes in all the concerto finales. The quintet is unusual in using two violas rather than two violins in the quartet of strings so that the solo violin is able to stand away from the lower texture when a dialogue with the horn is required. It also provides a clear example of a partial transplant of the main subject of the middle movement into the finale. One must be cautious about erecting into a conscious artistic experience the sort of cross-references of detail which may be intended to be subconsciously received, but this example is obvious, and therefore intended to be so.

But meanwhile there is another beginning. Written in quick succession beginning in autumn 1782 are the first three (K.414, 413, 415) of the incomparable series of Vienna piano concertos. The *Wiener Zeitung* of 15 January 1783 announced them as being available from April in fair copies for subscribers. To spread the catchment net more widely they were said to be capable of accompaniment by string quartet alone, but though the wind parts are modest, the music is impoverished by their absence. The subscription was not a success, but the *Wiener Zeitung* of 12 January 1785 advertises their printing by Artaria. The title-page makes no mention of the possible reduction in the accompaniment though it still mentions (doubtless only for commercial reasons) the harpsichord as an alternative to the piano. Wolfgang on 28 December 1784 tells Leopold of their intended character: they are 'half way between the too difficult and too easy—they are brilliant, easy to the ear, but naturally not descending to emptiness; here and there the knowledgeable have something for their satisfaction alone, yet so couched that the ignorant must be content without knowing why'. Nothing is certainly known about the first performance of the first two, but Wolfgang definitely used K.415 in C for his own 'Academy' on 23 March. The Emperor Joseph II attended this, and it was presumably in his honour that Wolfgang added trumpets and drums to the score. This work was in any case suitable, as its first movement, like several others, plays with 'trumpet and drum' pomp, even in their absence. The last movement is full of the slightly mocking wit which might have been censored were it verbal, with two *adagio* interruptions instead of the customary central one. It contains an extraordinary wrench of momentary modulation which is over before the chasm has time to yawn, and it finally goes out like a candle with *pianissimo* trumpets and drum-roll. The slow movement of K.414 in A contains a memorial to J.C. Bach, who died on New Year's Day 1783. Wolfgang heard the news some months later. In a letter to Leopold dated 12 April he writes: 'I suppose you have heard that the English Bach is dead? What a loss to the world of music!' Naturally, after the encounter with Johann Sebastian, none of his sons can simply be referred to as 'Bach'. The *andante* of K.414 begins *sotto voce* with a quotation of the solemn tune from J.C. Bach's overture to *La Calamità* with which Wolfgang had interrupted the finale of the piano-duet sonata, K.19d. The tribute of the boy composer has become the tribute of the mature artist. In the concerto it is succeeded by an unmistakable re-use of the main theme of the first movement turned into triple time—the intellectual play behind the popular front. Again, in the final rondeau the gentle tune is of the type which you catch yourself humming when the music has stopped, but underlying the whole movement is pervasive subsidiary material, sometimes unobtrusively made into seemingly effort-less counterpoint. This is what Wolfgang meant when he wrote of pleasing both the knowledgeable and the ignorant. The charm of the melodies in K.414 make it the favourite of the three, but it is ironical that these three immediately published concertos are on the whole decidedly less played than any subsequent ones.

The outburst of creative energy caused by freedom in Vienna—and perhaps by marriage?—encompassed yet more. On the last day of 1782 Wolfgang had completed the first of the set of six string quartets that he was ultimately to dedicate to Haydn. There can be no doubt that this G major quartet, K.387, was from the start envisaged as the first of a set; possibly the impulse to return, after a gap of nine years, to this medium—already beginning to be regarded as the mainstream of chamber music—was emulation of Haydn's set, op. 33 which Artaria had recently published. Certainly Wolfgang offered to sell to the Paris publisher Sieber six new quartets at a time when in all probability only K.387 was finished. He explained to Sieber that the music couldn't be cheap, and the subsequent dedication to Haydn spoke of 'long, laborious fatigue'. We cannot know whether most of this labour went into the achieving of the classical balance of interest and activity, apparently at a stroke. It must suffice to say that the six quartets are all worthy of Haydn, who had by this time of his own op. 33 established such a norm. The minuet of K.387 established a new weightiness for such movements. Wolfgang did not follow Haydn's increasingly frequent excursions in the direction of much faster minuets, which were to become what Beethoven unequi-vocally called 'scherzos'. But he often, as here, gave to the minuet a sonata-form in miniature, involving the notions of well-timed recapitulation and of a restatement (and refurbishing) of at least one secondary subject. The movement which usually claims most attention in K.387 is the final *Molto allegro*. Here the long-note subject—as of a counterpoint exercise—seems, until each instrument has entered, to be becoming just that, but immediately the music breaks off into Italian *opera buffa* style. But at the moment when the main secondary theme is expected there is another learned exposition as if of fugal work. So the high-spirited and audacious mixture is continued, for the long ears as well as the short. But the most donkey-like ears would doubtless, in Wolfgang's judgement, belong to those who were disturbed by the lightning changes of musical costume.

When we realise that in addition to inaugurating these new series Mozart had committed much of the Mass in C minor to paper in 1782, we certainly cannot accuse Constanze of sapping his creative energies. His letter of 28 December to Leopold does show some changes to his bachelor schedule. There is now no six-o'-clock call from the barber, and lessons occupy the whole morning till dining at two. Then follows an hour for digestion, and only after that can he compose, and even then not if he has concerts to give or to attend. But we ought not to let the momentous 1782 pass without rounding out our picture. The same wondrous man who composed K.387 and the Mass in C minor also wrote two canons of which the opening words mean 'lick my arse'. History does not relate the exact occasions for these. The first is written for no fewer than six voices, and both are notated in the soprano clef.

As far as the public were concerned, Wolfgang's greatest success in 1782 was *Die Entführung*. It had been performed in Prague, and in 1783 it was to be heard in Warsaw, Bonn, Frankfurt and Leipzig. Its success caused Count Rosenberg to suggest that Wolfgang looked for an Italian comic opera libretto, as Wolfgang reported to Leopold at the end of 1782. This was indeed a momentous suggestion, but its only immediate effect was a frustrating search and two unfinished attempts. *Figaro*'s moment had not yet come.

The new year brought social events with Wolfgang and Constanze at their centre. In the middle of January they gave a private ball at their lodgings, their landlord, now Raimund Wetzlar, giving them extra rooms for the occasion. It lasted from six till seven, but as Wolfgang explained, 'not for one hour'. The Irish tenor Michael Kelly (who sang in the first performance of *Figaro*) records in his memoirs in 1826: 'Madame Mozart told me, that great as his genius was, he was an enthusiast in dancing, and often said that his taste lay in that art, rather than in music.'

(Incidentally, Kelly is joined by several others in attesting Mozart's love of billiards.) On 3 March the Mozarts and their friends enlivened the company at a masked ball in the Assembly Rooms of the Hofburg with a home-made Harlequinade to which Wolfgang had supplied the music, which survives in a sketchy form as K.446. But between these events falls a shadow, a letter to Baroness von Waldstätten asking for a small loan to pay off a debt. We do not know the outcome.

The name of Aloysia Lange crops up frequently in Wolfgang's concert-life. At the beginning of the year she had sung a specially-written scena and rondo, K.416, at one of the recently instituted 'Dilettante Concerts' in the casino and ball-room known as the 'Mehlgrube'. On 11 March he assisted at her benefit concert in the Burgtheater; she revived 'Non so d'onde viene', K.294, his first composition for her, and Wolfgang's very considerable contribution was the 'Paris' symphony and his own playing of the C major concerto, K.415 and an encored concert-rondo, K.382. Gluck found himself in the next box to the non-performing partners, Lange and Constanze, expressed his admiration of the music and invited both pairs to lunch. The relationship of Gluck and Wolfgang seems throughout to have been one of sincere mutual respect without becoming anything warmer. The biggest concert in several senses was Wolfgang's own on 23 March. The Emperor attended, and what is more, 'against his habit, attended the whole concert', as Cramer's Music Magazine of Hamburg drily put it. This was indeed a tribute as the fare was not niggardly, comprising the whole of the Haffner symphony, two piano concertos, a new set of variations on a popular tune from Gluck's comic opera *The Pilgrims of Mecca*, the two 'sinfonia concertante' movements from K.320, four solo songs (two from Aloysia)—to say nothing of 'a short fugue, because the Emperor was present'. Exactly a week later the Emperor heard a repeat performance of the C major concerto, K.415, with which Wolfgang repaid Therese Teyber for singing at his own benefit.

On 7 May is the first mention of the famous name of Lorenzo da Ponte, whose real name was Emmanuele Conegliano. He had just been appointed by the Emperor, thanks largely to the reigning court-opera composer Salieri, to the post of poet for the Italian opera in Vienna. The mere connection with Salieri persuaded Wolfgang that he himself had little to hope for from da Ponte, but the search for a libretto was still foremost in Wolfgang's mind and he wondered, to Leopold, whether Varesco was too annoyed by their cavalier treatment of him over *Idomeneo* to concoct another libretto, this time comic. But even as he writes thus, his mind is beginning to prescribe: the most essential thing is for the story as a whole to be really comic, but there ought to be two equally

Unfinished oil painting of
Mozart at the keyboard by
Joseph Lange, probably dating
from winter 1782/83

Constanze Mozart, née Weber,
as painted by her brother-in-law
Joseph Lange in 1782

A view of the Upper Belvedere Palace, Vienna, with its symmetrical gargoyle-cataracts and hedged gardens setting an operatic stage for a conversation-piece. Etching of 1785

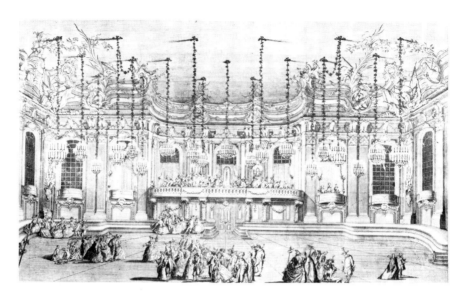

An indoor equivalent, in exuberant
magnificence, to the illustration on
the previous pages: a masked ball in
the Vienna Grand Assembly Hall,
1748

The composer Antonio Salieri
(1750–1825), who as doyen of
Vienna's music epitomized to
Leopold and Wolfgang the Italians'
knack of appropriating the best
musical positions. He was friendly
enough to Wolfgang to conduct his
compositions occasionally

important female parts, one serious and one middling in this respect, but the third female character could be entirely comic. Here again one sees the need for diversifying with real, bigger emotions the potentially featureless foothills of constant comedy. There must be a countess as well as a soubrette. By now Wolfgang has committed himself to bringing Constanze to Salzburg in July, that is, after the birth of the first child. This took place on 17 June with none other than Wolfgang's mother-in-law helping the midwife. The baby boy was put to a wet-nurse although Wolfgang's family conviction was that the oat and barley gruel with which Nannerl and he had begun their days was the best baby-diet. The names were Raimund, after the generous Wetzlar, who had insisted on being a god-parent, and Leopold.

There is a story that the minuet of the D minor string quartet, K.421, was written whilst Constanze was actually giving birth. Be that as it may, this, the second of the 'Haydn' six, certainly seems to have been completed before the journey to Salzburg. The preponderance of the minor key in both the outer movements is bound to lend the work an air at least of sadness, but the main subject of the first movement, delivered *sotto voce* with interior palpitations, hints at a more passionate utterance which comes to the fore in a striking middle section combining mysterious modulations with harshly dissonant imitative entries. It is irresistible to suppose that this first movement inspired that of Haydn's celebrated 'Fifths' quartet in the same key, op. 76 no. 2. The last movement is a set of variations, lending a serious, plaintive air to a *siciliano* tune. The final variation is elongated into a tail-piece by the sudden raising of a repeated-note figure to a disquieting dominance as it occurs on each instrument in turn through a wide range of compass.

It seems likely that we must place in this period another famous string quartet, that in E flat, K.428. The manuscript carries no date, but it hardly seems possible that so substantial a piece could be omitted from Wolfgang's catalogue begun in February 1784. It is indeed described as 'Quartetto IV' on the manuscript, and the third quartet *is* dated: 9 November 1784. But the reordering of the set for publication so that numbers three and four change chronological places could well be a matter of balance between heavier and lighter styles; even the look of the key-signatures might have weighed with Wolfgang, with the quartets in the ultimate order using in succession signatures of one, two and three flats. The opening of K.428 puts a quiet and immediate challenge to the listener: instead of the comparatively straightforward first tunes of previous quartets there is delivered, without harmony, a phrase which goes out of its way to use notes foreign to the scale. The challenge of its intonation has not lessened down the years; the two violins play the selfsame notes for four bars, and an octave away the viola and cello must do the same. These perils survived, how warm is the theme's subsequent harmonisation, which unhesitatingly but with perfect balance uses the modernisms of the classical vocabulary! The same tendency to chromatic harmony informs much of the slow movement, with a superficial resemblance to a *Tristan* motif, though naturally less protracted. A more obvious echo is in Beethoven's first 'Rasumovsky' quartet, whose quirky second movement seems deliberately to play with one of Mozart's ideas. But Mozart can be quirky too; the final movement with its 'popular' main themes and sudden rests and alternations of *forte* and *piano* flatters Haydn's example, as does its shape, hovering like so many of his finales between the symmetrical returns of a rondo and the free excursions of the sonata form.

There were some fears in both Wolfgang's and Constanze's hearts as they journeyed to Salzburg in July. Wolfgang seems genuinely to have thought that the Archbishop might arrest him as a long-prepared outcome of his failure to achieve a written dismissal. Constanze's worries had more basis. She was coming to be inspected by a family who might close ranks as soon as they saw her, a family which knew its Europe and which far outshone her in powers of expression. If the quest for reconciliation made them irreconcilable it would be her fault. Her contributions to letters to Salzburg had been meek and sycophantic postscripts. On 19 July she brought herself to write to Nannerl but this was to set right a ploy which had misfired. Wolfgang had mentioned that they would arrive in September—so as to give Leopold and Nannerl a surprise by arriving a month earlier. But Nannerl's reproaches meant that Constanze had to be let into the secret. Because the relevant page of Nannerl's diary is missing, the exact time of the arrival is not recorded. Their stay seems to have gone well, with a constant stream of visits made and accepted. Nannerl often mentions the theatre, and she can hardly have gone alone. During the visit they could for instance have seen with her both *Romeo and Juliet* and *Hamlet*. They were probably not in time for Nannerl's name-day (26 July) but within its octave, on 31 July, Wolfgang brought her an ice-cream and in the evening a gift of punch and a poem to go with it, signed by himself as 'poet laureate of the marksmen'.

Sessions with Varesco evolved an Italian comedy of sorts, *The Goose of Cairo*. The musical numbers of the first act survive, including a very presentable finale of 461 bars of continuous music, but although the vocal lines seem to have been settled, only one number, a trio, is fully scored. It seems clear that Wolfgang could not find enough interest in the libretto to carry on, and was not willing to face any further long-distance discussion with Varesco once he had returned to Vienna. But there was another reason for this opera to flag then. Wolfgang had received, it appears from da Ponte himself, another comic libretto, *Lo sposo deluso* ('The deluded husband'). But this too, though containing a splendid and completely composed trio, never came to fruition. The list and description of the seven characters and of their relationship to each other augurs well, but the proper working out eludes both composer and librettist. Nevertheless in both these incomplete operas there are hints, at the very least, of the immortal characters to come who seem, though not yet visible, to stand in the way of their precursors.

Constanze's second husband, Georg Nickolaus von Nissen, assembled for her a biography of Wolfgang which she published in 1828. From this we learn that the two remarkable 'Salzburg vacation' pieces, the Duos for violin and viola, K.423/4 were written as an act of friendship to Michael Haydn. The Archbishop was pressing Haydn for the completion of a set of six such duets, but he had only written four and was too ill to do more. Thus there came into being two three-movement works which have obliterated all others of the kind. For us the rise of the professional string quartet has tended to eclipse smaller combinations, but there were plenty of examples at this date of unaccompanied duets for either two violins or violin and viola, for use where, for instance, *chez* Leopold, two rather than three or four string players were gathered together. The problems in writing such duets are obvious: the sound always threatens to be thin, and lacks the normal lower ranges, and the melodic interest ought to be shared, unless the movement in question is to be a serenade-like solo with the second instrument in unrelieved subordination. Only rarely does Mozart put the instruments to the trouble of playing two notes each—double-stopping—in an imitation of a quartet that is bound to become ineffective. The richness is gained instead by the placing of each line so that the implied harmony is clear and warmed by the interplay of vibrant singing melodies. In short, the harmony is achieved by counterpoint. The solution of the balance-of-interest problem is also a contrapuntal one. The viola's tunes will normally be lower than the violin's. To write an accompanying line which sounds just as well above the tune as below calls for a special technique called 'double counterpoint', but too much reliance on this solution would make a very academic effect, and when the tune is in the lower line the skill (and the creative opportunity) must usually lie in the rewriting of the upper line to include new harmonies and turns of phrase. The fact that most listeners are quite unaware of such considerations when listening to these airy and witty pieces is just as much a tribute to Mozart's mastery of counterpoint as its explicit display in the Mass in C minor. Amusingly enough, Mozart's two duos, together with Michael Haydn's four, were dedicated to the Archbishop, as a surviving title-page makes clear. There was no question, incidentally, of Wolfgang's arrest or of any threat to Leopold's continued employment.

But the musical climax of the visit to Salzburg was obviously the C minor Mass. At the beginning of 1783 Wolfgang had told Leopold in rather vague terms about a vow of his to write it as some sort of thank-offering for Constanze. The vow was made, he says, when she was still single, and the mass was intended for Salzburg performance, partly perhaps to reinforce a recognition of her by both family and public—he obviously set little store there on any further recognition of himself. Witness to the promise was 'half a mass' already written (the letter is dated 4 January). In fact what we have is a complete Kyrie, Gloria, Sanctus and Benedictus, together with two movements completely planned but only partially orchestrated carrying the Credo to the end of 'Et incarnatus'. There are two soprano solo parts, sometimes involving notes of equal height and with the second in any case largely outside the normal range of an alto. Constanze certainly sang in it, as we know from Nannerl's diary, where she is the only singer named. How much she sang we do not know. Suffice it to say that if she could sing the presumably preparatory vocal exercises (Solfeggii, K.393) which Wolfgang wrote for her she would at least have taken a creditable part. The diary says that the whole musical establishment was at the performance—at St Peter's, not the cathedral. They would indeed need to be, for the music is outside the usual choral demands, sometimes increasing the usual four parts to five and even eight.

If indeed there was only the one rehearsal mentioned by Nannerl the participants must have been very competent indeed, or the performance poor, for the music far outstrips any previous masses known to them, even of Mozart's, in its alliance of contrapuntal resource with intense feeling—an intensity which welds together the German and Italian elements, the solo charm with the grand apparatus. The harmony is often both massive and surprising, and the counterpoint makes no less rhetorical an effect with its interweaving of as many as three disparate and strongly characterised motifs at once. The traditional set-piece, the 'Cum Sancto Spiritu' fugue, starts with a subject consisting of equal long notes as dry as that of an exercise in Fux's 'Gradus ad Parnassum'. To say that it is treated in ever-closer imitation and also in inversion is, though accurate, to say nothing that Fux could not do, and masterfully at that. But a new dimension is added to the sense of cumulation. The well-timed marking of paragraph-endings with three bars each of sudden *piano*, suddenly elongated to seven such bars, the vortex-like moments of modulation, the final electrifying delivery of the subject in vocal unison—in all these the master of *symphonic* timing is taking a hand. In Mozart's hands the fugue is not merely high rhetoric; it is high drama as well.

The 'Qui tollis' is a compendium of baroque conventions made new. We first hear from the strings the dotted rhythms which are to be the incessant accompaniment. The figure is an imitation of scourging, as Bach and Handel to name no others make plain. By this means Mozart evokes the suffering Lamb of God, and links the vision with, for example, 'Surely He hath borne our griefs' in *Messiah*. Meanwhile the bass line is constantly drooping through falling semitones in the baroque figure of grief, except when it is so to speak sustaining the praying hands lifted upwards in 'suscipe deprecationem' ('receive our prayer'), or forming the solid basis of the throne in 'Qui sedes ad dexteram patris' ('who sittest at the right hand of the Father'). The two four-part choirs, now alternate, now joined, give an overwhelming impression of mankind filling some large canvas with its grief-laden importunities. The trombones twice break away from their traditional choir-doubling role as though marking the tread of the funeral-march-in-advance down the Via Dolorosa. The movement ends *pianissimo*—a touch of the psychological-cum-physical realism mastered in *Idomeneo*.

The 'Et incarnatus' for soprano solo—perhaps not for Constanze—is given a wind *obbligato* of flute, oboe and bassoon, and takes to its furthest length the tradition of melting virtuosity in *siciliano* rhythm. Here again 'conventions' coalesce: the flute hovering like a sacred dove, the prevalence of falling figures for the coming from heaven to earth, the rhythm of countless 'pastoral symphonies', but above all, the human voice welcoming in ineffable tones the newcomer to the human race which is intended never to be the same again.

The pressures of Vienna which under the reforms of Joseph II was emphatically not the home for music of this kind, meant that Mozart never finished this mass, though he did salvage most of the music in the unsuitable form of an Italian oratorio *Davidde penitente* in 1785. The vaguely-formulated vow could not carry him past the pressing necessities of the rest of his life. Whether any other reason is required—the cooling of faith or love—is speculation. But in its unfinished state the work is yet definitive, a peak of musical creation and a vital statement of what can properly be described as a passionate religious sense.

The performance took place on the morning of 26 October—not the 25th which Nannerl writes by a slip of the pen. On 27 October, between other events of the day, she writes 'at 9.30 my brother and sister-in-law departed'. He had another eight years to live, but she never saw him again.

9

The Accolade and *Figaro*

1783–86

On the way back to renew the assault on the Viennese public Wolfgang stayed three weeks in Linz, where he and Constanze were the honoured guests of Count Johann Joseph von Thun-Hohenstein, the father of the Count Thun who with his wife Wilhelmine was amongst Wolfgang's most energetic supporters in Vienna. On 31 October, the day after their arrival, Wolfgang tells Leopold that he is giving a concert four days later and must write a symphony for it. Thus there comes into very sudden being the 'Linz' symphony in C, K.425. It is the first such work to have an *adagio* introduction. Perhaps the nod to the French tradition in the unison dotted-rhythm opening is not by now very remarkable, but it gives way to a wistful dialogue clouded over by the minor key to enhance the emergence into the 'sunlight' of the ensuing *allegro*. This is a device taken to greater lengths in the forthcoming C major string quartet, K.465. After this striking opening the work is energetic, clear and colourful in its outer movements though perhaps lacking in real melodic individuality by Mozartean standards. What is of interest, however, is the way in which the 'clouding' technique of the introduction is allowed to spread into places where we might expect a settling to a straightforward major key. When this happens it is often the bassoon which makes a plaintive contribution in its individual tenor voice. Both of the fast movements carry echoes of *Die Entführung*, as though Wolfgang was showing to the cognoscenti of Linz the fingerprints of what was then his most famous piece.

It is possible that it was not until they arrived at the bereft home that they knew the controversies over how to feed little Raimund were now otiose; he had died on 19 August of intestinal trouble. By the year's end Wolfgang had eased himself back into concert life by appearing in the Burgtheater on 22 December in aid of the 'newly established Society of Musicians' with a piano concerto (we do not know which one) and a recitative and air sung by the tenor Adamsberger, probably K.431, in

160

which the 'passage-work' sometimes featured in concerto arias—for instance, Aloysia's—is eschewed, and the sentiments expressed by a new simplicity of line and a wonderful sense of the sonorities of flutes and bassoons together.

On 9 February 1784 Wolfgang began his own catalogue of works written from then onwards until the end of his life. Not all the works are there, and sometimes there are discrepancies between the dates on the scores and those in the catalogue, but it is an invaluable document, the more so as it quotes the beginnings of the works. The first six works listed, and in particular their dates, show an astonishing burst of creation:

1. Piano Concerto in E flat [K.449]   9 February
2. Piano Concerto in B flat [K.450]   15 March
3. Piano Concerto in D [K.451]   22 March
4. Quintet for Piano and Wind in E flat [K.452]   30 March
5. Piano Concerto in G [K.453]   12 April
6. Sonata for Piano and Violin in B flat [K.454]   21 April

This succession has to be read with another list, sent to Leopold on 3 March, of twenty-two engagements for Wolfgang at public and private concerts between 26 February and 3 April, together with the remark 'Have I not enough to do? I don't think that by this means I'll get out of practice.' The full morning of lessons still obtains. A new name appears, Barbara or Babette Ployer, who was talented and lucky enough to have the first and fifth works on the list written for her. The E flat concerto is the last to describe its wind parts, for a pair each of oboes and horns, as *ad libitum*, and indeed it looks as though Wolfgang also countenanced a string quartet accompaniment. But although there are many more rests in the wind parts than in all subsequent concertos the music is poorer without them, and the scale of the work, if not of its sound, is on a par with its neighbours. The last movement is slightly reminiscent of the original last movement of the D major concerto K.175, which perhaps because of its overtly contrapuntal style Wolfgang had replaced with a lighter rondo to suit Viennese taste. Perhaps he hankered after this 'lost' movement. What he achieved now was a deft display of supporting counterpoint and a catchy tune which bubbles up with new variations at all sorts of other points beyond the expected ones in a rondo. Its final guise is as a gigue which instead of interrupting the movement sweeps it along to an exhilarating end. Although it was written for Babette, Wolfgang also played the concerto on his own account. In three successive weeks he gave K.449, 450 and 451 at his concerts in the large music room in the Trattnerhof, where since January the Mozarts had taken rooms.

Babette's own performance of K.449 at a private concert at home on 23 March probably caused Wolfgang to miss the first public performance of the great thirteen-instrument serenade K.361—or at any rate four movements of it—at a concert given in the Burgtheater by the outstanding clarinettist Anton Stadler. Johann Schink, a theatre critic and man of letters, heard it, detailed its instrumentation, and twice in consecutive sentences called it 'glorious and sublime!'.

In the next piano concerto, K.450, the wind instruments show in the clearest terms that they are not optional by leading out the main theme, and indeed by sharing out two others in alternation with the strings. The audience if it had not seen Wolfgang at the piano might have persuaded itself that it was listening to some sort of *sinfonia concertante*. The way in which the soloist at length asserts his own right, with flourishes and a trill, to present the main theme himself, is part of the comedy-drama of the situation. The Viennese came to the Trattnerhof to be entertained, and many of the turns of phrase echo what they might have heard at an *opera buffa*. One of the phrases harks back to the A major violin concerto, and is made conspicuous by its use at the beginning of the cadenza, perhaps the one moment after the beginning when Wolfgang could have relied on the total attention of his audience. The slow movement is a basic hymn-like tune with increasingly elaborate variations. The original score offers the comparatively rare sight in Mozart of alterations both to the tune and to its elaborations after an 'original' had already been inked in. The tune, which sounds as though it had dropped from heaven, dropped by degrees. The last movement shows passages of crossed hands, and the final page makes explicit on the horns the 'hunting' motif underlying its pastoral gaiety.

The D major concerto, K.451 re-enters the world of trumpets and drums, and the horns assist as if on the parade-ground rather than in the forest. The outer movements do not possess the sheer melodic charm of K.450, but the slow movement has a patch which is interesting because Nannerl found it uninteresting. She had seen the music and tried it out for herself when Wolfgang had sent it home for copying to prevent piracy. The passage, in the piano part, is of a type which occurs fairly often; taken literally it is a succession of long notes with leaps between them which would sound bare, even more so on the instruments of Mozart's day. That they were merely scaffolding for the soloist's improvisation is shown by Wolfgang's example of how to render the passage, sent in answer to her comment. We have it in Nannerl's handwriting, she having herself copied out the piano part. Even if it turned out that this particular filling was her own invention it would scarcely affect the necessity for doing such things, or its value as an example.

We are hardly stepping out of the world of the concerto with the next week's composition, the quintet for piano, oboe, clarinet, horn and bassoon in E flat, K.452. The piano part more often than not shows a concerto-like elaboration, and yet each wind instrument has its idiomatic say with hardly a trace of subordination. In the last movement Mozart makes the concerto ambience explicit by writing for all five players a 'cadenza in tempo', after which they round the piece off in harmony, with no tune as such, thereby calling attention to their rhythm which is exactly that which an ensemble of characters would use on an *opera buffa* stage in quiet self-congratulation at a satisfactory dénouement. For the rest, description is a waste of ink. Let Wolfgang's touching pride and joy suffice: 'It had the greatest applause. It is the best which I have ever composed. How I wish you could have heard it! What a lovely performance!' We do not know who the lucky wind players were.

Also contracted to use the Trattnerhof concert room was a Dutch pianist named Richter. Whether in the face of this competition (or perhaps with Wolfgang's collaboration) his concerts took place is uncertain. He struck Wolfgang as an amiable and modest fellow, and at any rate he evoked a revealing *mot* which Wolfgang retailed to Leopold on 28 April. Richter on hearing Wolfgang exclaimed: 'Good God! how I work and sweat, yet get no applause—but for you it is child's play.' To which Wolfgang replied: 'I had to work hard, in order not to work hard any longer.'

The fanfare rhythm of K.451 opens the G major concerto, K.453, but softly on unaccompanied violins. The onset of the accompaniment in the second bar poses a question which heralds the world of witticism we are embarking on: does the harmony come in 'a bar late' or merely 'a bar later'? It is not necessary to know the answer; the teasing is all. If this theme is a foretaste of the wedding march from *Figaro*, one of the subsequent rich procession of themes is a herald of the *Allegro molto* of the overture to *Don Giovanni*. The whole first movement is one of the blithest examples of the march made into entertainment. On the other hand the *andante* allows both hesitant pauses and cloudings of harmony, the latter leading into extremely distant regions just before the return. The last movement begins as variations on a charming tune with a bird-song connection. At this time Wolfgang briefly kept an account book. On 27 May he bought a starling. He then quotes over the words 'that was beautiful' the opening bars of the variation tune of K.453 with a pause and a sharp not in the original. The dates hardly allow us to suppose that the starling was bought because it already knew the tune, so we must imagine Wolfgang happily teaching it. If the wind players in K.452 behaved towards the end like an *opera buffa* ensemble, the situation towards the end of the concerto is made explicit by Wolfgang writing 'Finale' at the head of the last *presto* section. This is obviously not a 'finale' in the sense of a new final movement but can only refer to the pile-up of the characters at the end of an operatic act. As with Wolfgang's stage-finales the plot is obviously still going on with repeated interruptions of both the build-up and the tune. If the pianist has one partner rather than another in the orchestra it is the joyous flute.

The last beneficiary of this outburst of composition was a violinist, Regina Strinasacchi. She was on a concert tour which had taken her through Italy. Wolfgang not only wrote for her the Sonata in B flat, K.454, but accompanied her at her Vienna concert in the presence of the Emperor. Now at last the pressure of time had caught up with him. He had to play his part of the sonata from memory with his seeming 'part' on the desk consisting of nothing but empty music-paper. But this must have been a true exercise of memory, since the division of the melodies between the instruments, and their frequent contrapuntal dialogues, quite rule out the possibility of a mere extempore accompaniment. The outer movements again from time to time use comic-opera turns of phrase. The *andante* begins as though it is a reversion to the bland and flowery tones of ornate Italian song, perhaps in deference to what came naturally to La Strinasacchi, but as in the companion-pieces of this wonderful spring the harmony is made to veer away into far distances of tonal perspective. These sudden mysteries and poignancies for those who have ears to hear, have their ineffable effect because they are enshrined in entertainment music. The writing of entertainment music, as indeed of almost every note he wrote, was a matter which Mozart took as seriously as any musician who has ever lived. It was left to the next century, with its more self-conscious stance as to what constituted Art, to misunderstand this truism.

As the season subsided for the summer Wolfgang could look back on the 'entertain or perish' campaign with joy and pride. He had been able to list for Leopold no fewer than 176 subscribers to his Trattnerhof concerts, representing a handsome income. The names include princes, barons, counts, a bishop, ambassadors and army officers of high rank. The majority are senior government servants but there are also bankers and merchants. The relative financial comfort certainly permitted a rare event—a move to a larger lodging in September perhaps brought to a head by the birth of a second child, Karl Thomas, who survived to die unmarried in 1858. But the main family· event of the summer was Nannerl's wedding on 23 August to Johann Baptist von Berchtold zu

Sonnenburg, who was resident magistrate and chief administrator of the district based on St Gilgen, at the western end of the Wolfgangsee. He was a widower twice over and fifteen years her senior. What is more Nannerl took over with her husband no less than five step-children. Curiously enough her marriage took her to the very same house that her mother had lived in as a child. There is nothing to show that the marriage was either eventful or unhappy. It lasted until 1801 when von Sonnenburg died and Nannerl returned to Salzburg with her one son, two daughters having died young. It was certainly not the first time that Nannerl's hand had been sought. It is evident from a letter from Wolfgang to Nannerl in 1781 that they then both wanted a Salzburg government official named Franz Armand d'Ippold to succeed. But presumably Leopold objected. In a sense the real attachment in Nannerl's life was to Wolfgang. The Salzburg visit with Constanze and the apparently successful transfer to Vienna probably convinced her that their intimate comradeship could never be the same again. Her heart may have sunk at the thought of more years with a father who felt as bereft as she, and slighted into the bargain. If the marriage seems prosaic there is enough to make it believable, especially for a spinster of thirty-three.

With Nannerl's marriage begins a series of letters from Leopold to her which not only give precious news of Wolfgang's doings—he is almost always called 'my son' or 'your brother'—but which are full of loving solicitude. The first (30 August) has a saddening postscript: 'Hasn't the dog-spirit of Pimpes appeared to you?' In the second Leopold speaks of himself in 'eight rooms in deathly silence. It doesn't matter by day, but by night, whilst I'm writing this letter, it's rather sad. If only I could still hear at least the dog snoring or barking.' On the other hand Wolfgang as usual buffets her with his high-spirited humour. Less than a week before the wedding he says: 'I must write now if my letter is still to greet a Vestal virgin.' He encloses a poem, which ends with advice to say to herself when her husband moodily frowns:

'Lord, Thy will be done by day,
But mine be done by night.'

On the day of the wedding, Wolfgang was in fact attending a performance of Paisiello's opera *Il Re Teodoro*, an Imperial commission at thrice the normal sum. Wolfgang was taken ill in the theatre with an inflammation of the kidney and it was a month before he recovered.

But the inexhaustible welling-up continued. Let us suppose that Wolfgang was on the mend in mid-September. Karl was born on 21 September, the move to the new lodging was on 29 September and the

very next day is the completion date of another piano concerto, K.456 in
B flat. It was most probably the one which was commissioned by the
blind pianist, Maria Theresia von Paradies, then on a concert tour which
included Salzburg, Paris and London. She and her mother are both
shown in Nannerl's diary to have visited the Mozarts during Wolfgang's
and Constanze's Salzburg visit. If the concerto was primarily intended
for use in Paris the plaintive ariette-like theme of the central variation
movement would be the most familiar ground. As in the other movements,
but particularly in this one, Mozart shows his trust in the wind players'
artistry both as individuals and as a seven-part band. The first movement
with its playful-martial themes and the rondo with its blithe jollity are
as Viennese as all the others. But this summary sentence must not convey
any hint of routine, for wit abounds. The opening march begins *piano*—no
longer a surprise, perhaps—but it is never played *forte*. Its main paragraphs end with a constant succession of trumpet-calls—but there are no
trumpets in the score. There are passages in the last movement where
the main beat is simultaneously divided into twos and into threes, not in
an agony of expressionist self-doubt but out of sheer *joie de vivre*.

But hard on the heels of this 'sweetness and light' comes a remarkable
piano sonata dedicated to Therese von Trattner, that in C minor, K.457.
Whereas its beginning might be thought of as merely a 'Mannheim'
gesture in a minor key, the continual interruption of would-be lyricism
by abrupt reversions to the opening gesture, and in particular the
reversion in the last movement to an utterance which is, if anything,
harsher and more abrupt takes this sonata (in the view of nineteenth-
century critics) far down the road towards Beethoven. The work of
Beethoven for which this sonata is obviously the jumping-off point is the
sonata in C minor (the same key), op. 13 known as the 'Pathétique'. The
slow movements have clear correspondences in the rondo shape and in
the borrowing by Beethoven for his main subject of the opening of one
of Mozart's. But if we take matters further we are in danger of denying
Mozart the right to primacy in the use of vehemence as an artistic means.
In any case Beethoven in his last movement—an easy-going rondo—shies
away from Mozart's almost attitudinising drama. It is interesting to
wonder whether Therese was surprised by this music, or whether she
had an inside knowledge of this obverse side of the public entertainer.
The same question is raised by the yet more remarkable Fantasia K.475,
dated the following year (25 May) as to its written-down form. Wolfgang
endorsed the Fantasia as an introduction to the sonata by having them
published thus by Artaria in 1785. Its apparently groping modulations,
undertaken without preamble, can hardly be heard without a shivering
premonition of 'Oro supplex et acclinis' in the Requiem. Whether in any

sense Wolfgang was on his knees as he wrote this gaunt and fateful music we cannot know. We can only wonder at the Protean qualities that throw up the sonata in the midst of such apparently joyful companions.

It was still *Die Entführung* which kept Wolfgang's name before the public at large. The Böhm company did it—badly, it appears—in Cologne; a company headed by Schikaneder and Hubert Kumpf began a three-month season at the Kärntnertor with it, in the presence of the Emperor, and Leopold, who otherwise only knew it from the score, at last had the pleasure of hearing it performed in Salzburg by Ludwig Schmidt's company. Two successive letters to Nannerl in November are full of pride not only in Wolfgang's work—the full houses, the applause, the twice-encored drinking song—but also in the performances, which he is quick to agree without real evidence were superior to the Viennese ones. The weekly written chatter on all sorts of subjects which the letters to Nannerl contain quickly efface the impression of the introverted father mouldering in his eight rooms. The theatre is frequently mentioned; it was after all just across the square, and Leopold was a Mozart.

The impulse to continue the set of quartets for Haydn returned—if indeed it was ever lost—and the next entry in Wolfgang's catalogue after the C minor Sonata is the B flat quartet, K.458 dated 9 November. It is somewhat lighter than its predecessors, as Leopold noted, and is sometimes called the 'Hunt' because of the style of the opening bars, but in comparison with the rondos of the horn concertos this is a misnomer. There is, however, something of the country air about the tune which arrives out of nowhere in the first movement at a place where something more rigorous in the line of development could be expected. Another surprise is the length of coda-peroration which this not very argumentative movement permits itself. The slow movement is of linked sweetness, but not long drawn out, and the combination of badinage and counterpoint in the final movement sounds like an affectionate parody of Haydn.

But with another concert-season to prepare for, yet another piano concerto is completed on 11 December, the F major, K.459. Yet again does it begin quietly with a march rhythm, but the number and diversity of the ensuing themes is if possible richer still. Wolfgang's catalogue mentions trumpets and drums but there is no trace of any such parts and it is possibly a mere slip of the pen. It is far more likely that at this stage Mozart would make a point of *not* having them to play the martial rhythms which permeate so much of the ever-changing texture. The central *allegretto* contains some blissful simplicities and treats the wind with special love. But it is the final rondo which most distinguishes this work from its fellows. Its tunes are of a calculated naïvety, but they are interspersed with bouts of extended and brilliant counterpoint. Had the work been a quartet, or a symphony, one might have spoken of his taking a leaf out of Haydn's book, but here Wolfgang possesses the book in his own right.

On 14 December, Wolfgang embarked on a membership which, in contrast to Haydn, he took seriously for the rest of his life. He was admitted to the first grade, apprenticeship, in the 'Zur Wohltätigkeit' ('Beneficence') lodge of the Freemasons. Many of his patrons and friends and the publishers Torricella and Artaria were masons, but if there were any initial self-interest it is as nothing compared with such a declaration of faith as *The Magic Flute*. In Bavaria, nearby, the Elector had recently suppressed the order altogether. In Vienna the Emperor Joseph II turned out to be ambivalent in his attitude. His fanatical and authoritarian belief in Reason led him to an anti-clerical stance which the Pope's personal remonstrances could not alter. He dispossessed the Jesuits, to use their property for education, and was determined that the church should not vie with the secular state. Wolfgang shared his father's hatred of obscurantism and superstition, yet on any ordinary reckoning was a pious, indeed deeply religious man. One man's article of faith is another man's superstition, but he seems whole-heartedly to have accepted the fundamentals of Catholicism as consistent with a war on superstition. The enthronement of Reason was not for him the dethronement of God. But Joseph II, having in effect subordinated church to state, was not happy with another powerful society within the state, and he never became a mason himself. Wolfgang may have been contemplating the step for some time, for 1783 is the probable date for a fine (but unfortunately incomplete) hymn to the sun for accompanied male chorus 'Dir, Seele des Welt-alls', K.429. Here the Masonic Trinity of Reason, Wisdom and Nature is reflected in the three voice-parts and in the three flats of the key-signature of E flat, the predominant key of *The Magic Flute*, whose solemn choruses are unmistakably prefigured here.

So the calendar turns to 1785, the year of the culmination of Leopold's life in hearing the accolade of Haydn. As though mid-January were some self-imposed deadline Wolfgang's catalogue records the last two quartets of the set within a few days of each other. The quartet in A, K.464, dated 10 January is perhaps the most mellifluous and graceful of them all, yet it is also a *tour de force* of composition. The effort which Wolfgang claims went into the writing of the quartets must in this case have gone into apparently effortless counterpoint, particularly in the first movement where every recurrence of material and every transition is re-thought and discussed in a tireless instrumental conversation. Doubtless this 'dialoguing' was learnt from Haydn's op. 33 set, which their composer claimed as representing a new style; but whereas Haydn's dialogues build up from the manipulation of short motifs Mozart's in this quartet are more flowing in their effect. Haydn's tendency to economise in the number of different subjects used is obviously imitated here—one might almost say taken to its logical conclusion. For instance the minuet (as opposed to the trio) extends for 72 bars, every single one of which can be referred to the music of the first eight. The same impulse towards the single-theme movement is evident in the choice of variation form for the *andante*, notable for the overflowing into other intruments, by way of coda, of the rather Beethovenish drum-like motif of the cello in the last variation. Beethoven did indeed copy this quartet out to study, and commentators have seen some similarities between it and his own A major quartet, op. 18 no. 5, written a dozen or so years later. But Beethoven in his last movement is wise enough not to court the comparison with Mozart's economy of themes, for here K.464 offers a formal feat of inexplicable perfection; an analysis of its materials could derive almost the whole of its 262 bars from motifs that would hardly occupy a dozen bars in the writing out, and yet the music sounds as though its ever-new rearrangements could go smoothly on for ever. Eventually the work goes out like a candle, but even then the sympathetic listener gets the feeling that it is still miraculously going on somewhere out of ear-shot.

Four days later the last of the Haydn set of quartets is recorded in the catalogue, the C major, K.465. The psychological effect of deciding to write in C major, and consequently without a key-signature, is compounded by acoustics, for the C is powerfully reinforced by being the bottom, most sonorous note, of both cello and viola. One might almost describe the two instruments as being built in C. This untrammelled, unclouded sonority marks not only the end of these 'Haydn' quartets but also the end of the symphonic oeuvre in the 'Jupiter'. But perhaps Haydn sums it all up in *The Creation*: God said 'Let there be light', and there was Light; and what could the light be except the massively vibrant chord of C, on hearing which, at his last public appearance, Haydn was so overcome that he could only point to heaven and say 'It came from thence'. But massiveness is not a function of a string quartet, and K.465, uniquely among the mature quartets of Mozart, begins with an extended *adagio* introduction. It carries further the 'clouding' found in the introduction to the 'Linz' Symphony, also in C, but the initial impression of the quartet is not merely clouded, but almost groping, with the viola and first violin beginning on contradictory notes, albeit with perfectly logical harmony. The object is *not* to rouse romantic emotions and then disappoint them, but to have us ultimately enjoy the light. Nothing of Mozart's intended for the public ear could remotely correspond to the earth being 'without form and void'. This introduction may best be likened to the next stage in the creation process: 'and the Spirit of God moved upon the face of the waters'. But to nickname the quartet 'The Dissonance' on this account is entirely to misread it. One might as well call the sun 'the fog'. The sunny tune when it does come is blithe and unstrenuous, but either the tune itself or its rhythm peerlessly binds together the whole, though after the extreme thematic economy of the previous quartet Mozart allows himself other themes of different character. One of them left its mark on Beethoven again—in the first movement of the Piano Sonata op. 14 no. 1, a work which significantly enough he also wrote for string quartet. In the slow movement an early reprise, after only 44 bars, leads us to expect something short and sweet; instead, Mozart elicits new beauties from the material, and when at length we fancy ourselves at home he even adds a simple but ineffable closing theme which we have never heard before. Of the last movement we can say that without losing his own individuality Mozart is addressing Haydn in Haydn's last-movement language, using brisk dance-like subjects, markedly instru-mental with hardly a vestige of the vocalist, and teasing us with sudden *fortes* and silences and with asymmetrical phrases. The message would be abundantly clear to Haydn: 'I understand what you understand; we can speak to each other over the heads of those who have not travelled thus far.' Yet there could be nothing more purely Mozartean—unless it were Schubertian—than one of the end-of-paragraph themes which steals in from what is suddenly miles away, harmonically speaking.

On the very next day, 15 January, Wolfgang got some friends together and played at any rate some of the set to Haydn—who was not yet the dedicatee. According to a letter from Leopold to Nannerl 'he performed his six quartets for his dear friend Haydn and has sold them to Artaria for a hundred ducats'. If indeed all six were performed it would have been a long sitting, with the parts of the last one barely dry, let alone practised. We can however surmise the eagerness and joy of the occasion, whether it was a case of Haydn being sent for because the task was done, or of the set being finished because Haydn was due the next day.

By now Leopold had been invited to Vienna, to hear amongst other things the season of Lent concerts which Wolfgang was giving in the Mehlgrube Casino. Leopold surely needed little persuasion to join Wolfgang on the high-tide of success. The two seasons 1784–85 were arguably the highest that the tide ever rose for Wolfgang in Vienna. Leopold even managed a cheap means of getting to Vienna. One of his boarder violin-pupils, Heinrich Marchand, was the son of a theatre manager in Munich, and by making the considerable detour to that city he was able to escort Heinrich to Vienna in Marchand's own chaise. He set out from Salzburg on 28 January, allowing himself a pleasurable week of theatregoing in Munich. Nannerl and her family kept the Salzburg house warm for him in his absence, literally, since a letter from Leopold assured them that he was leaving plenty of firewood for them—and wine for that matter. But before Leopold's arrival in Vienna there was a significant happening in its theatre world. Only a year after its first production in Paris, the Schikaneder-Kumpf Company announced Beaumarchais's play *Le Mariage de Figaro* for 3 February in the Kärntnertor theatre in a German translation by Johann Rautenstrauch. But Joseph II noted that the piece 'contains much that is objectionable', and at the last moment the performance was banned, though the text was allowed to be published. With a sharp eye for business the Viennese paper *Wienerblättchen* lost no time in serialising some of what Vienna was missing on the stage, and the translator in a foreword dedicated the book to the memory of the two hundred ducats he had lost by the ban. Nor is this the only whimsicality: under Cherubino's picture—if indeed it be his—on the title-page are words to the effect that 'printed follies only acquire worth when their circulation is hindered'. It was indeed a curious half-way attitude of the Emperor's in the face of an overt attack on 'tyranny' by Beaumarchais. In another field, of church music, we witness the same perhaps deliberate stance mid-way between conservatism and root-and-branch reform. A decree of 1786 reads: 'Loud choral singing, having been proved medically to constitute a serious danger to health, should therefore be replaced by quiet singing, or better still by spoken prayer.' No wonder that Mozart contributed nothing to Viennese church music at this time!

On 10 February, the day before Leopold arrived, Constanze may well have busied herself in seeing that their spacious lodgings looked at their cleanest and most impressive. As usual Wolfgang can have been of little domestic use on this day, the finishing date of the composition of the Piano Concerto in D minor, K.466, to be played by him at the first of the 'Mehlgrube' concerts the next day. Indeed Leopold tells us that Wolfgang did not have a chance to try out the last movement for himself, being wholly occupied with seeing that the parts were made ready correctly, a process that was still going on when Leopold arrived at midday on 11 February. When he has time to write to Nannerl Leopold comments with delight and pride first (in spite of all else that has already happened) on the size and expense of the quarters, and next on the means of paying for them, the subscription concert attended by great numbers of the aristocracy. 'The concert was incomparable and the orchestra played splendidly.' He calls K.466 'a new and very fine concerto'; not on the face of it a surprising or unjustified remark. But it is applied to Wolfgang's first concerto in a minor key, and the only one whose opening subject does not lend itself to humming, its quiet syncopations being more palpitation than tune. Indeed it was thanks to the predominant passion of this work, which only veers into D major at the end of the rondo, that it remained in the nineteenth-century concert repertoire, Beethoven's utterances in the minor key having meanwhile given most of Mozart's music a 'Dresden china' look in comparison. Perhaps Leopold, pitch-forked into a glittering occasion on the day that he ended a horribly uncomfortable journey, was simply overwhelmed, and perhaps even some days later he was not recollecting in tranquillity. But at the end of the letter he mentions another performance of the concerto—'the new big ("grosses") concerto'—which Wolfgang played *magnifique*, with again no comment on its tempestuous nature. Perhaps our surprise is a measure of our own vestiges of Romanticism. Could it be that, just as the audiences of Dowland and of his Italian contemporaries loved the pleasures of a theatrical lament, Wolfgang saw merely a stimulus to his audience, as well as to his own imagination, by this sudden change of posture in the 'theatrical' world of the concerto? Its successor, in trumpet-and-drums C major, K.467, is obviously no whit inferior as a work of art. Perhaps Wolfgang, by something like conscious calculation, used the theatrical 'darkness' of K.466 to enhance the 'light' of K.467, giving them the same relationship as the introduction of the C major quartet to the rest of that work. After all, for better or worse, these concertos had to be talking-points as well as entertainments. Even the middle movement of K.466, entitled 'Romance', has its charming tunefulness interrupted by a 'storm' which apart from occasional string chords commits the accompaniment to the wind band with the tenor range of the bassoon well to the fore (provided the pianist lets him be heard). After the first *tutti* of the final rondo the trumpets are very sparingly used, to enhance the effect of the delicious quiet two-bar phrase, at last in the major key, with which they help seal the closing moments.

After such a first day Leopold might have expected a relaxation, perhaps in the company of his five-months-old grandson, Karl Thomas. But instead the supreme excitement was to come—a visit from Haydn so that he could hear (probably) three of the six quartets. Indeed it could be that Leopold had a part to practise, for it seems likely from his letter that he and Wolfgang took two of the parts, the other players being two brothers who were fellow-masons with Wolfgang, the Barons Tinti. But the performance, and even the pieces themselves, must have been as nothing compared with the words from Haydn which Leopold quoted to Nannerl: 'I tell you before God, as an honest man, that your son is the greatest composer that I know, in person or by name: he has taste, and added to that the greatest knowledge of composition.' At that marvellous moment all the self-subordination, the huge journeys, the forethought, the agonisings, the well-intentioned recriminations—all were justified by the words spoken by the only man living who was qualified to utter them. Artaria's publication of the quartets, arbitrarily described as Opus X, came out on 17 September, their title-page putting the revered Haydn's name first and at least in equal size with Mozart's.

But Leopold's pleasures were occurring with intoxicating frequency. On the day after the performance of the 'Haydn' quartets he went to hear Wolfgang play in a concert in the presence of the Emperor. The occasion was a benefit for the Italian singer Luisa Laschi, who was to be the original Countess in *Figaro* and who also sang Zerlina in the first Vienna performance of *Don Giovanni*. The concerto Wolfgang played was almost certainly K.456 in B flat. Whilst Leopold the man was dazzled by the beauty of the Princess of Wurtemberg two boxes away, Leopold the musician was moved to tears of delight at hearing so clearly the interplay of the instruments. Nor did he neglect to tell Nannerl how the Emperor had waved his hat and called out 'Bravo, Mozart!' as Wolfgang left the platform. So it continued, with Wolfgang in constant action in benefit concerts and private concerts. Nor were the delights only musical. Some sort of rapprochement was sealed by a luncheon at Frau Weber's where 'the roast was a fine plump pheasant'. A Friday lunch which included Christian Cannabich's son Karl and a priest gave no heed to the fast-day and included pheasant, oysters, glacé fruits 'and (I must not forget to mention this) several bottles of champagne'.

Although his Mehlgrube subscription series was still under way Wolfgang profited handsomely by giving a concert on his own account in the Burgtheater on 10 March, at which he introduced the C major concerto, K.467. Typically, the trumpets, horns and drums are heard for the first time not as a loud beginning but as a soft tail-piece to the opening phrases. Though there is as great a number and variety of themes as ever before, the whole is closely knit by the military motif of the opening bars. When at the year's end Leopold received a copy of the score in Salzburg he commented on the difficulty of the passage-work and on the unusual harmonies it implies, 'which do not fit unless one hears all the instruments playing together'. But it is hard to imagine the slow movement being found abstruse. Its repeated chords and rising bass and indeed its very key link it with the slow movement derived from Schobert in the pastiche-concerto K.39 of many years before, but such details are as nothing compared with the lovely melody which soars above them. The final rondo has much the same vivacious and fleet-footed wit as the final movement of the C major quartet, and a point of real similarity in one of its chordal subjects. Three days later the same Burgtheater resounded to the music of the Mass in C minor, recast and with some additions to form an oratorio, *Davidde penitente* (K.469) given, with a new symphony by Haydn, at a concert for the benefit of the Society of Musicians. Truly the Mozart cup was running over at this time.

Aloysia and her husband Lange were hosts to the Mozarts on 19 March (another rapprochement for Leopold) and Lange made a drawing of Leopold, whose loss is the more regrettable when one sees the fine though unfinished oil portrait he made of Wolfgang. Soon before the end of this memorable visit Leopold was admitted as an apprentice Mason to the same lodge as Wolfgang, and indeed on 16 August was promoted to the second grade, that of 'Journeyman'. This was the occasion of a charming gavotte-like song, K.468, usually called 'Gesellenreise'. The giddy promotion continued: a week later Leopold became a 'master', and probably the last music which he heard in Vienna was Wolfgang's cantata *Die Maurerfreude* ('The Masons' Joy'), K.471, performed in honour of Ignaz von Born, master of the 'Concord' lodge. Though the Emperor maintained at best an 'arm's-length' attitude to Freemasonry, he did reward Born for a metallurgical discovery and make him a Knight of the Realm. Wolfgang's cantata consisted chiefly of an elaborate and shapely aria for the tenor Valentin Adamberger. The transition by recitative to the final *Molto allegro* uses again the triplets and rising arpeggio bass of the slow movement of K.467 to the words 'Take this crown'. The soloist is joined at the end by three-part male choir in the more usual simple communal style of a brotherhood not given to rivalries in musical skills.

The next day, doubtless well content both with his exhilarating experiences and with the prospect of relaxing from them at home, Leopold left Vienna, with Heinrich Marchand again, accompanied as far as Purkersdorf by Wolfgang and Constanze. He would not see them or Vienna again. But soon he was able to exert his paternal love in another direction. Nannerl came back to the Salzburg house and had a son, baptised Leopoldus Alois Pantaleon (no less), on 27 July. Doubtless feeling that the stepchildren were enough for her to handle, she left baby Leopold with the doting grandfather who surrounded him with nursing care and called him the 'Prince of Asturias'. Only an outbreak of thrush in September caused severe anxieties, culminating in the Will of God being mentioned. Meanwhile Leopold had to endure long silences from Wolfgang—nothing for instance between letters arriving on 17 September and 11 November. In the latter he begs forgiveness, being up to the eyes in his opera *Le Nozze di Figaro.* It is obviously time to rejoin him in Vienna.

Thanks to these silences we do not know the precise time at which Wolfgang and da Ponte started their work. They had met two years before, but then da Ponte was working with Salieri. How fortunate that by now Salieri reckoned that he would rather cut off his fingers than set another line of da Ponte! The attractions of *Figaro* as a possible opera were obvious: it had been banned as a play in Vienna, and the French censors had given it the best possible publicity before allowing it in Paris. What is more, Paisiello's opera *The Barber of Seville* had remained successfully in the Viennese repertoire since 1783, so that a sequel to that story, with Figaro common to both tales, was obviously a good commercial proposition. But further censorship had to be avoided. This was mainly achieved by the sort of alteration which to a thinking musician-dramatist would be inevitable anyway, the omission of Figaro's tirade against tyranny in Beaumarchais's fifth act. In its place we have a short diatribe against fickleness, cuckoldry making for better music than politics, especially with the sprightly symbolism of French *horns* supplying what Figaro declines to say ('il resto nol dico'). The writing must have been mainly done in six weeks—the figure given in da Ponte's memoirs—starting in mid-October. It seems that rather than compose the work straight through Mozart set similar kinds of numbers in groups according to their basic emotional character, possibly because that was how da Ponte supplied them, for his memoirs certainly speak of the composition being a hand-to-hand business with Wolfgang setting the words as he received them.

Yet, as ever, there were other things to be done, not only lessons in the afternoons after a morning's composition, but indeed other compositions. But first, amongst other songs, the summer of 1785 brought forth 'Das Veilchen' ('The Violet'), a famous and charming piece almost always mentioned as the forerunner of the art-song (as opposed to an aria on the one hand and a mere ditty on the other) which is nowadays called a *Lied* and is associated primarily with Schubert. The poem of 'Das Veilchen' is by Goethe and like his 'Heidenröslein' (set by Schubert) is an ageless cautionary tale in folk-song language. But whereas Schubert sets 'Heidenröslein' strophically, that is with the same tune for each verse, Mozart drives a musical coach and horses through Goethe's strophes whose correspondances and near-correspondances are the very essence of the poetry. There are no musical repetitions at all, until an astonishing one at the close, where after the end of Goethe's poem one line is repeated and one, 'Das arme Veilchen!', ('the poor violet') is presumably Wolfgang's invention. No wonder Goethe looked on song-composers with some suspicion.

A new genre for Mozart was broached by the quartet in G minor, K.478 completed on 16 October. The instruments are piano, violin, viola and cello. Though the piano is not overbearing, the idioms of the piano concerto are much in evidence. Except for some telling moments of imitation the strings are usually playing all at once, to provide a balance to the sonority of the piano. But they do not lose their individuality; indeed the viola with a *cantabile* exploitation in the slow movement of its higher as well as its lower range shows itself to be truly emancipated from any subordination lingering on from mid-century. This quartet arose from a commission for a set of three from the publisher-composer Franz Anton Hoffmeister. Although Wolfgang wrote two such works Nissen tells us that Hoffmeister negotiated a relinquishment of the contract because the public found the first one too difficult. The difficulty may have been instrumental, for each part has taxing moments, and the first movement has something of the severity of demeanour (and one of the motifs) to be found later in the last movement of the 40th symphony. But listeners who persevered until the rondo would surely have found it on a par with the gaiety of the happiest of the concerto finales, not least at the very Haydnesque joke of the loud false cadence just before the end.

What is more disturbing than editorial cold feet is the letter sent by Wolfgang to Hoffmeister on 20 November asking for either a loan or an advance: 'I take my refuge with you, and ask you to assist me with some money, which I very much need at this moment.' That this should be the case hardly six months after the end of a most successful season is a worrying puzzle. If we are unwilling to ascribe the whole embarrassment merely to domestic extravagance we might suppose that Wolfgang, 'up to the eyes in *Figaro*', needed to buy time by dropping pupils. A pupil whom he certainly did not drop was Thomas Attwood, a young Englishman learning composition with him from the summer of 1785. Wolfgang the 'Arch-Englander' was obviously Attwood's friend as well as his teacher, exercising his English upon him, and, from the evidence of the considerable body of surviving corrected exercises, being a much more sympathetic and realistic teacher than he was to the wretched daughter of the Duc de Guines. When Attwood returned to London in 1787 he became organist of St Paul's Cathedral and a creditable composer of church music in an unassuming melodious style. The aspect of Mozart that he was best able to assimilate was the tuneful chorus-work of the Masonic music of this period. In Attwood's hands such choruses became simplicities rather than solemn simplicities, but their craftsmanship stood out in a comparatively slipshod milieu.

A Masonic work which though short is decidedly not simple also momentarily interrupted *Figaro*, the Masonic Funeral Music, K.477 which was used on 17 November to commemorate the Duke of Mecklenburg-Strelitz and Franz Esterházy of Galantha. It is a purely instrumental piece but featuring the plaintive alto-clarinet sound of the basset-horn—either one or three, since Mozart wrote the latter alternative if a pair of ordinary horns were not used. The basset-horns were in vogue in the Lodges at this time; for instance, at a concert at the 'Crowned Hope' on 15 December 'two hon. Brothers David and Spenger' played a concerto on the instrument. Wolfgang also added another optional and infrequent visitor to his scores, a contra-bassoon. The effect of this work is a noble solemnity, neither grief-stricken nor terror-struck at death. An unmistakable allusion to Catholicism occupies the middle of the piece, a psalm-tone allotted to the unusual sound of two oboes and a clarinet in unison. This may be a reference to the Psalm quotation in the Introit of a Requiem Mass: 'Thou O God art praised in Sion . . . unto Thee shall all flesh come.' But if it is, it is a simpler version of the chant current until recently. Also before the year's end Wolfgang contributed two splendid numbers—a quartet and trio, K.479 and 480, to an opera otherwise by Francesco Bianchi called *La Villanella rapita*. Since these additions would certainly hold their own in *Figaro* they might be supposed to have overwhelmed Bianchi, not that the audiences, still less the theatre-managers, cared a jot for such discrepancies.

Dated 12 December in Wolfgang's catalogue is a sonata for piano and violin in E flat, K.481. Nothing is known of the occasion; it may merely have been for speculative publication. Hoffmeister did indeed print it soon afterwards, and from certain easy-going features of style and construction one could suppose that Wolfgang, like Hoffmeister, was intent on its avoiding the misfortunes of the G minor piano quartet. There was a great deal more substance in the next week's entry, a piano concerto in E flat, K.482. As Leopold retailed to Nannerl, Wolfgang had written on 28 December to say that he had hurriedly given three subscription concerts, with 120 subscribers. The only work mentioned was this one, of which, unusually, he had to repeat the *andante*, a series of richly-wrought variations basically in the minor key, but with most euphonious serenade-like passages for wind band alone, which sound all the sweeter for the fact that this score (for the first time in the concertos) uses clarinets instead of oboes. The 'hunting' rondo is interrupted by another serenade, mainly for clarinets and bassoons, given the slightly demonstrative mark of *Andantino cantabile*. The whole work seems a

miraculous expression of purest joy, no less a miracle for being achieved
again in the next concerto.

The year 1786 began with overwork taking its toll in headaches and
stomach-cramps. Nevertheless, on a command from the Emperor, Wolfgang wrote the overture and the four musical numbers of a one-act
entertainment called *Der Schauspieldirektor* ('The Theatre Manager').
The occasion was a fête given by the Emperor in the Orangerie at
Schönbrunn Palace on 7 February in honour of Archduchess Marie-
Christine, Governor-General of the Austrian Netherlands, and of Duke
Albert of Sachsen-Teschen. As the Orangerie was a hot-house it was
possible to make there a spring in winter. After dinner, 'of 82 covers'
according to the Protocollum Aulicum, the company repaired first to one
end of the hall for the German entertainment (Wolfgang's piece) then
to the other stage for Salieri's *opera buffa, Prima la musica, e poi le
parole*. Given two mettlesome sopranos, the music of *Der Schauspieldirektor* is very funny, as the rival *prime donne* Madame Herz and
Mademoiselle Silberklang climb ever higher in a ferocious contest of
agility before the stunned and pleading impresario. In the spoken part
is an interesting light on the late-eighteenth-century view of Shakespeare.
An actress offering parts like Zaire, Alzira, Cleopatra and Rodogüne is
told by the impresario: 'That is all over with! Corneille, Racine, Voltaire,
these fathers of true tragedy, these are all thrown behind the stove . . .
Shakespearianism rules . . . a tragedy without clowns, lunatics, thunder-
storms and ghosts is just insipid twaddle.'

The next piano concerto, in A, K.488 also uses clarinets instead of
oboes. Interestingly enough Wolfgang, when offering this work amongst
others to the Prince von Fürstenberg of Donaueschingen, through the
good offices of his old friend Sebastian Winter, suggested that if clarinets
were not to hand they could be replaced by a violin and viola respectively.
No mention was made of oboes which obviously would have been to
hand, and which could play most of the clarinet music without altering
its pitch. The slightly unusual key—clarinets up to this point being more
often associated with flat keys—lends the music brightness as well as
euphony. The first movement makes a witty point by what one might
almost describe as a deliberate disappointment. The opening orchestral
tutti is 66 bars only; the piano emerges and spends only ten bars longer
on an exposition covering much the same ground. It signals the end of
the section with the conventional trill; the orchestra sets in again, and we
feel cheated of the 'new tune' which Mozart has taught us to expect in
the 'solo' exposition. There is a short silence, and suddenly there is the
new tune, occurring in the 'wrong' place—the beginning of the development—and announced by the wrong people—the orchestra. The slow

movement is one of the comparatively few to be marked unequivocally *adagio*. Thus what looks like a *siciliano* becomes a good deal more poignant than dance-like, although there is a serenade-like relief in the middle with characteristic low arpeggios on the second clarinet.

An event in March which must have aroused old musical loves was a concert performance, conducted by Wolfgang, of *Idomeneo* in the private theatre of Prince Auersperg's Palace, of which the leading proponents were Wolfgang's friends Countess Hortense Hatzfeld, who sang Electra, and her husband Count August Hatzfeld who played the violin, and for whom Wolfgang had written a concerto-like *obbligato* in a new air for this performance, 'Non temer', K.490. On this mainly amateur occasion Idamante's part was sung by a tenor, Pulini, instead of a castrato. But instead of merely transposing his music down Wolfgang rewrote the part in all the places where the change of octave mattered. The love-duet from act three was drastically reworked, as K.489, to the exclusion of those passages whose effect chiefly lay in the voluptuous singing of thirds in the treble register, which of course was no longer possible with the man a tenor. Mozart in this respect showed how much pitch meant to him—in contrast to some Handel conductors who change the octave of one of the lovers without facing, or apparently even noticing, the musical consequences. He was about to present to the world an *opera buffa* which is quite unrivalled—except by two other such works of his—and yet he may still have felt that if only fate had allowed it, here in *opera seria* was his really fulfilling métier.

But there is still another piano concerto to come, K.491 in C minor. This was Mozart's largest such score, the only one to contain both oboes and clarinets, as well as trumpets and drums. But to this amplitude is added a corresponding richness of form. The first orchestral *tutti* is 99 bars long and as usual full of materials though linked by insistent rhythms. Unusually one can see from the original score that this *tutti* was rearranged to achieve a more spacious effect as Wolfgang realised the magnitude of his design. For when the soloist emerges he hardly states any of these previous materials at all. Instead he embarks on a rich diversity of new themes in an exposition lasting no fewer than another 166 bars before the orchestral *tutti* returns. Thus it is that the recapitulation is seen more clearly and comprehensively than ever before to be not merely a restatement but a reconciliation of what the orchestra and soloist had previously said separately. The quiet ending of the first movement, yet with every instrument playing, must have made its mark on Beethoven's piano concerto in the same key. In contrast to this rigorous drama there is a slow movement which could well have been entitled 'Romance'. Its theme, treated as a rondo, is not so much naïve as of a distilled simplicity. The contrasting episodes use the woodwind with wonderful richness and individuality, the oboes taking the lead in the minor, the clarinets in the major. The rondo shape having been used up, so to speak, the last movement is a set of variations, mainly in the minor key and with march rhythms never absent long. All the greater then is the brightness of the C major variation—typically not the last—led again by the woodwind with a prominent part for the (magic) flute. One can only marvel at the creative energy which irresistibly throws up such a work at the moment when one would have thought the pressures of the imminent *Figaro* were at their most distracting.

By such accounts as we have, *Figaro* differed from Mozart's previous operas in having a librettist who thoroughly understood his job and a cast who believed in the work. Among them were two from the British Isles, Nancy Storace as Susanna and Michael Kelly who doubled as Don Basilio and Don Curzio. Nancy, whose original names were Ann Selina, was to all intents and purposes an English singer, the daughter of an Italian double-bass player who had settled successively in Dublin and London and whose original name was Sorace; he possibly changed it to avoid its literal and bawdy pronunciation by the English and Irish. Nancy and her brother Stephen both studied music in Venice in their youth, she as a singer, he as a composer. In 1784 they were both in Vienna, she as a star at the Imperial Theatre at an unheard-of fee, he as an opera composer, his *Gli sposi malcontenti* being produced on 1 June 1785. Whilst in Vienna Nancy married a violinist named John Abraham Fisher who so mistreated her that the Emperor banished him from Austria. She also banished him in as much as she never let it be known in her subsequent career that she was anything but a spinster, which is how she described herself in her will. Michael Kelly, sometimes written by Wolfgang as 'Occhely', had been trained in Naples and had been in Vienna since 1783. His racy and not very accurate memoirs made the most of the Mozart connection, but were published much later, in 1826.

The autograph score of the overture originally broke off just before the reprise of the opening to come to a pause which led to an *Andante con moto* in D minor in *siciliano* rhythm; there is visible one bar of an oboe solo with *pizzicato* accompaniment, then the whole diversion is crossed out. Such an interruption occurs in the overture to *Die Entführung* and there the slower material turns out to refer to the first song in the opera. Here there is no such reference, and the overture would have been written far too late for any such corresponding song to be added. The aborted tune, as far as one can tell from one bar, is nearest in style to the last movement of the D minor quartet, itself perhaps an echo of the last movement of Haydn's op. 33 no. 5. But it is also like Pedrillo's serenade in *Die Entführung*. We can only suppose that Wolfgang finding himself at last on the brink of a proper *opera buffa* was willing to follow a traditional fast-slow-fast pattern like his 'symphony' in G, K.318, but that pressure of time (and a sense that *Figaro* was long enough already?) caused him to change his mind, and indeed to be content that the overture should not even have a development section at all. As for what follows, the incomparable tunes do not need description but hearing, and of course seeing them performed. But the crucial difference, after which routine will never again suffice, is that the singers are, with every bar they sing, characters. We are not taking from stock a pert serving-maid and categorising her as, say, a soubrette. She is Susanna. No acting, no choice of words by a skilful librettist, will go more than a little way towards this end, and they are quite powerless to redeem characterless music. The characters are rounded human beings; we can imagine ourselves, whether we are men or women, as being such diverse creations as the Count, Figaro or that potential Don Juan, Cherubino. Even a character like Marcellina, whose stage origins were probably a male actor dressed as a dame, is no longer simply a figure of fun. In *Figaro* we smile, and even laugh, but we do not laugh *at* the characters.

Much of the characterisation is done in ensembles rather than in arias. Susanna for example sings only two solos in the entire opera, the second of them—the famous 'Deh vieni'—being the last number before the finale. There are only four arias in the first act, three in the second, two in the third and four and a half in the fourth, the half being the unfinished lament of Barbarina over a lost pin. The tradition of finales which build up to a stage-full was already in being. Da Ponte himself writes wryly and amusingly of the style. 'In the finale it is a dogma of theatrical theology that all the singers should appear, even if there were three hundred of them, by ones, by twos, by threes . . . by sixties . . . if the plot of the play does not allow of it, the poet must find some way of making the plot allow of it, in defiance of his better judgement, of his reason, or of all the Aristotles on earth.' In *Figaro* there are two long finales but they are not mere accumulations of noise and speed. The action continues throughout them until the last moment and they are held together in long spans by manipulations of motifs and of keys—by symphonic writing, in fact. A superb example of a symphonic shaping of a continuing elaborate action is the sextet in act three, which Kelly says was Wolfgang's favourite number. Before it begins, Figaro has been sentenced to marry Dr Bartolo's 'housekeeper' Marcellina because he cannot pay a money debt he is alleged to owe her. The Count and his henchman Don Curzio have now, it seems, finally thwarted the marriage of Figaro and Susanna. But Figaro desperately claims noble parentage and by a birthmark is shown, to general surprise, to be Marcellina's son. Marcellina caps this by thereupon introducing Figaro to his father, Dr Bartolo, with which lovely revelation the sextet begins. The first subject, so to speak, consists of the successive embraces of Figaro by mother and father. Its musico-dramatic consequence consists of confused and thwarted mutterings by the Count and Curzio. The embraces resume, to 'happy families' music by the trio counterpointed by the indignant duet, making a quintet. The sixth, Susanna, enters with a symphonic change of key and a purse to buy off the judgement, whereupon the 'happy families plus foiled duet' music restarts in Susanna's key. Enraged at his embrace of Marcellina, Susanna boxes Figaro's ear. Now the sextet is complete and sings together, but divided three and three as to the kind of music, because Susanna has made a trio of the anti-Figaro duet. Now the needs of musical form and of the action are made to coincide by the orchestra taking up the 'first subject' whilst Marcellina announces, and the rest confirm, who is the mother by identical question and answer passed round the stage: 'Sua madre? Sua madre!' The laughter caused by this must be evoked again, by the same procedure for the father. The feeling, before it does so, that this is going to happen makes it the funnier—and of course the repetition is a *musical* requirement as well. The difference lies in the life-like fact that Figaro rather than the abashed Bartolo initiates the announcement. To make assurance trebly sure, Figaro reintroduces both mother and father to Susanna. Now comes the moment of greatest musical richness; the happy family is now a balanced quartet with Susanna, as the leading lady she has always threatened to be, floating on top, whilst the punctuations of the Count and Curzio, sometimes with inflexions of the minor key, make it clear that they are living to fight another day.

For obvious reasons such a description, which involves the omission of many beauties and aptnesses, must serve for the whole by way of example. But the crucial fact is that the description can be made in *musical* terms, as opposed to a mere cataloguing of comic dramatic action. To hit these musico-dramatic nails on the head time after time in a long opera is an achievement which at the end of the day one cannot explain, only thankfully record.

Curiously enough, the words 'Così fan tutte' ('thus do all women') occur in da Ponte's libretto of *Figaro*. The Count describes to the disreputable music-master Don Basilio how on a previous occasion he uncovered the hiding-place of Cherubino caught in the same room with Barbarina, Susanna's cousin. He illustrates his action by removing the

cover of a chair—and there is Cherubino caught again, compromising Susanna. The moment is caught for us in the engraving by Liénard from the Kehl first edition of this play (1785). At this moment there are low thirds from the pair of bassoons—a Sibelius effect—and the decrepit Don Basilio, a moment ago flayed by Susanna's tongue for his slanders of her virtue, has his precious moment: 'Così fan tutte,' he remarks with a glee which mounts with high-pitched reiteration.

Often quoted though it is, there is place for Kelly's account of the opera's reception, especially by the performers, at the first full rehearsal.

All present were roused to enthusiasm, and when Benucci came to the fine passage [in Figaro's song which closes act 1] 'Cherubino, alla vittoria, alla gloria militar', which he gave with stentorian lungs, the effect was electric, for the whole of the performers on the stage, and those in the orchestra, as if actuated by one feeling of delight, vociferated 'Bravo! Bravo, Maestro! Viva, viva, grande Mozart!' Those in the orchestra I thought would never have ceased applauding, by beating the bows of their violins against the music desks ... I shall never forget his little animated countenance when lighted up with the glowing rays of genius.

The first performance, due on 28 April, was eventually given on 1 May at the Vienna Burgtheater. It was a considerable, though not overwhelming, success. Wolfgang directed it, and the second two days later, but after that he handed over to Joseph Weigl, a competent young man of only twenty. After the third performance the Emperor had to step in to stop encores of pieces except solos. The little duet between Susanna and Cherubino which ends with the latter jumping out of the window into the garden took the fancy with two encores and was the main cause of the decree. But the Vienna performances did not survive the year's end. The 18th of December saw the last of only nine in all until the revival in August 1789. But before the end of 1786 it was also being played in Prague, and a glowing review attributes the success partly to the free use of wind instruments affording grateful opportunities to the excellent Bohemian players, and it ends with a rumour that Wolfgang himself is to attend. And indeed he and Constanze did arrive in Prague on 11 January 1787. The reason for the Vienna eclipse was simple and doubtless seemed to most people perfectly natural: a composer named Martín y Soler had an enormous success with *Una cosa rara*.

10

To Prague and *Don Giovanni*

1786–88

Vienna had received from Wolfgang an incomparable series of piano concertos and now *Figaro*. As its performances were unmistakably petering out he was entitled to feel despair. If such an unparalleled outpouring, designed expressly to please, had left him still without any assured means of income, such as a recognition from the Emperor amounting to more than shouts of 'Bravo!', he must have wondered what more he had to do. On 18 October there was another mouth to feed, Johann Thomas Leopold. We know from a letter of Leopold to Nannerl in November that Wolfgang was seriously thinking of another concert tour through Germany to England, an idea doubtless encouraged by the Storaces, Kelly and Attwood. We do not know in what terms Wolfgang wrote to his father nor how Leopold replied; but the way he relates the matter to Nannerl seems curiously scornful and ungracious. He had never told Wolfgang that he was caring for Nannerl's child. But Wolfgang got to know of it, and had proposed that Leopold should take Karl and the new baby in during their journey. 'Not at all a bad arrangement! They could go off and travel—they might even die—or remain in England—and I should have to run after them with the children. As for the money which he offers me . . . Basta!' Had Wolfgang waited till mid-November before broaching the scheme, there would have been only one child to arrange for; Johann died of suffocation on 15 November.

The next work after *Figaro* in Wolfgang's catalogue is the second of the commercially ill-fated piano quartets, K.493 in E flat, dated 3 June 1786. The public, if that is not too large a word when a virtually unknown genre is in question, would have found this perhaps more approachable than the G minor. The mood is sunny throughout, except for touches of mysterious harmony in the serenade-like *larghetto*, but the pianist needs something of the dexterity the concertos demand. Perhaps the most remarkable passage of composition is the development section of the first movement—51 bars sustaining our interest through modulation and scoring whilst being built almost entirely on one two-bar motif not very remarkable in itself. If Wolfgang was already care-worn he yet writes music for the care-worn.

At this time one of his piano pupils was Franziska von Jacquin, daughter of a distinguished botanist Professor Nikolaus Joseph von Jacquin. Wolfgang, as letters show, was on terms of close friendship with her brother Gottfried. It is likely that the three trios of 1786 were all first heard in their family circle. Two of them, K.496 in G and K.502 in B flat, were for the standard combination of piano, violin and cello. This category, as the many such works of Haydn confirm, still had a tendency to treat the cello part as a reinforcement of the bass of the keyboard, a relic of the practice in baroque sonatas of helping the harpsichord bass with a string instrument. The cello in these two works sometimes escapes this role by taking part in imitative dialogues or by sustaining interior notes as though it were a horn in an orchestra. The music is cheerful and undemanding, for the listener at any rate. But the slow movement of K.496 seems to be the germ for the serenade-trio in *Don Giovanni* and momentarily explores deeper harmonic waters. The Trio in E flat, K.498 is another matter. It is written for a combina-tion—piano, clarinet and viola—so unprecedented as to make it certain that it was for a domestic occasion, a party at which the performers had engaged to be present, let us say Franziska, Anton Stadler and Wolfgang. This is borne out by the nickname of the piece—'Kegelstatt' ('Skittle-alley'). The sequence of the three movements is also unusual. It begins in an intimate manner far removed from the public concert, with an *andante*; but in fact its basic shape is that of the first movement of a sonata. Having begun, in a sense, with the slow movement, Mozart writes a Menuetto which unusually is a centrepiece. It takes on a certain spacious air, with a trio in the minor key requiring some energetic viola runs which the clarinet is spared. The menuetto allows itself a final coda in which the trio momentarily figures again with a witty effect. Even the final Rondeau goes no faster than *allegretto*, which however might have been just as well for Franziska, who had to enliven its pervasive lyricism with flashes of concerto-work.

Four hands at one piano is ostensibly an even more domestic affair, and as he wrote the duet sonata in F, K.497 (dated 1 August) Wolfgang must have thought nostalgically of the journeys and performances with Nannerl. But from its spacious introduction onwards the work is in his richest concert vein, with plentiful but interlocked themes in the first movement, the tail of one sometimes serving as the head of another. The rhythm of Figaro's 'Il resto nol dico' is insistently and wittily used in the central section, even turning itself into a new tune. Beautifully dialogued music in all three movements ensures that the 'secondo' player has opportunities to shine. But the splendours of this piece must not hide the jewels of the next duet, the *Andante with Five Variations*, K.501, dated 4 November. Most of the piano-solo sets of variations are, comparatively speaking, pot-boilers, to popular tunes of the day. This set has an original tune, with a kink in the rhythm of its second part. The felicity of its scoring, with every note counting, is a continual delight. There is none of the automatic duplication of sound that can be so wearisome when the number of hands is duplicated. Happy is the household where such a piece can be often played.

For more obviously public use, and indeed published by Hoffmeister within a month of its completion, is the String Quartet in D, K.499, dated 19 August. This is a single piece, apparently never intended as one of a set, and what occasioned it is not known. Perhaps it was intended as a substitute for the third piano quartet originally owed to Hoffmeister. The first movement is perhaps the finest example amongst the quartets of the combination of seemingly effortless charm and gentleness with a rigour of construction which permits of no wasted bar. The piece is less drastically monothematic than the A major quartet; however, the main theme not only monopolises the development in every-varying keys, but also serves as the connecting thread in most of the transitions. Perhaps most charmingly of all, when a new tune makes a statement the first tune is used to complete it. The *joie d'esprit* of composition flows over into the minuet, where both the reprises, in the trio especially, are adorned with imitative voices, decorating the already decorative. The *adagio* of the slow movement does not so much betoken increased depth of thought; rather does it give room for a rich elaboration of its song. The spirit of the Italian operatic aria is still there, but the detail of the lower voices ensures a classical balance even though the prima donna, so to speak, makes no attempt to hide the cadentrial trills which show who is mistress. The last movement is more direct in style, with a Haydnesque abruptness of phrase.

We know nothing certain about the occasion of the Piano Concerto in C, K.503, catalogued on 4 December. A letter of Leopold's to Nannerl mentions four Advent-academies which Wolfgang was to give, and presumably the work was a feature of one of them, if they were given. The scarce mention of Wolfgang at this period in Leopold's correspondence is not because the latter is sparse. Indeed Leopold's frequent letters to Nannerl are not only full of the liveliest domestic detail, but they also offer to the social historian a fascinating feel of the Salzburg town-life of the time. Domestically, little Leopold never fails of a mention; as often as not he is given a sentence to himself to make the reassuring beginning—'Little Leopold is, thank God, well!' There are a spate of orders from St Gilgen for household requirements and haberdashery, and accounts rendered for them. Balancing these there are frequent acknowledgements by Leopold of fish from the Wolfgangsee. There is news of summer storms and flooding in the town, and night watches to protect the bridge from débris, of what the Archbishop is doing, or suspected of doing, of marriages, scandals and deaths, and above all of the theatre.

But whatever the circumstances of its creation, the C major concerto, K.503, stands apart from its fellows. The mark of *maestoso* given to its first movement has a significance beyond mere mood. More than in any other concerto it makes its effect by spacious architecture, using keys rather than tunes as the basis of the drama, and pervasive rhythms and contrapuntal combinations as the taut but seemingly unbreakable connecting thread. It is as though the entertainment-salon has acquired a disconcerting Olympian dimension, though it would be dangerous to suggest that this is the deliberate reaction of a composer who, having exerted himself to the full in one direction apparently in vain, sets out on another tack without taking further pains to ingratiate himself. So far K.466 has been the only unhummable opening concerto-subject—unhummable but certainly not unmemorable. The user of such crude methods of musical aesthetics would not find the beginning of this concerto unhummable, simply not worth humming. But the purpose of the loud and impersonal first six bars is to throw into relief the sudden quiet of the next two, which contain a little motif. The next eight bars—six loud, two quiet—are the exact, symmetrical and harmonically unremarkable answer to the first eight. In fact, from what we have been led to expect in previous concertos the only remarkable thing about this opening is its unremarkability. But the sixteenth bar doesn't bring these Augustan formalities to a close; without a break the two quiet bars are replayed in C minor instead of C major. The light of common day has suddenly darkened, an effect which could not be achieved by thematic busy-ness or by extraneous harmonic colouring. This passage is about C major suddenly becoming C minor. With the unerring judgement of a Beethoven, Mozart has decided that this is *all* that these first eighteen bars shall be 'about'. Of course there are tunes later on, but since the interest lies in what happens to them in different keys and scorings, they are less frequent and initially more four-square than in the previous concertos. One of the things that happens accords with what the seventeenth bar implanted: their passing in and out of major and minor in quick succession. Commentators have noted the many-voiced but smooth counterpoint just before the recapitulation. Indeed on the basis of the first two movements we could well call this the 'Jupiter' piano concerto.

The last movement is not, however, a contrapuntal display piece, but a bland rondo with the soloist almost continuously employed, and indeed some of his continuous passage-work reads like a cadenza in strict time with orchestral accompaniment.

Catalogued two days later (on 6 December) is the Symphony in D, K.504, known as the 'Prague', because it had its first performance there on 19 January 1787. It is not known when *Figaro* was first performed in Prague; the *Prager Oberpostamtszeitung* of 12 December 1786 says that the opera 'has been given several times here with unlimited applause' and goes on to hint that the composer might come to see the piece. The opera would have had to have proved itself there before Wolfgang would think of coming, and it is doubtful whether the situation could have clarified itself in time for the symphony to be composed for Prague. It is just possible, since Wolfgang had not dismissed even now the thought of going to London, that had things turned out otherwise we should now be calling it his 'London' symphony. It could of course have merely been composed for the Vienna winter concert season. At all events the work has the right to stand on the same pedestal as the three final symphonies of 1788. The introduction thrillingly regains for us the new spaciousness of thought established in the previous concerto. Its first fifteen bars would serve as a very adequate opening, starting with a conventional call to attention, then employing a variety of short expectant phrases such as Haydn might use to usher in a quiet opening of the *allegro*. But at the moment (bar 16) when this might occur there is instead a continuation of the introduction by a loud chord in the minor key. Indeed there is not so much a mere continuation as a piling up of different loud chords and their soft aftermaths. By the time the *allegro* sets in we have spent at least twice as much time as we expected, and have had a foretaste of the dramatic argumentativeness which is to be such a feature of the movement. The *allegro* begins not with a "first subject" but with a whole nexus of short subjects; in the first eight bars we hear premonitions of the overtures of *Don Giovanni* (repeated syncopations) and *The Magic Flute* (repeated quavers) and of the 'Jupiter' Symphony (falling scales on the woodwind). There is indeed a gracefully-singing second subject, but it is imbued with the deliberate pathos of slipping in and out of the minor key, the bassoons with their very individual voices counterpointing the strings in this effect. But significantly enough this theme is confined to its allotted space in exposition and recapitulation. The rest of the movement—not only the traditional 'development'—is given over with unceasing energy to new combinations of the 'nexus'. Unusually we have a glimpse into the workshop, as Mozart left sketches of some of this work. The *andante* is a relaxation only to the extent that it offers a profuse succession of short, captivating themes. But here too the music includes the development section proper to sonata form, a section which Mozart often in effect omits in a slow movement to avoid disproportionate length. But here the instantaneous rendering of the melodic *mot juste* which was achieved in *Figaro* ensures a clarity and punctuality which renders inexcusable any omission of the repeat of the exposition. There is in any case time for it as the symphony has no minuet. Some commentators have suggested that the ethos of the work is too serious to allow a movement of a dance-like character. Simply put like this, the argument prompts the question why there is a minuet in the 40th Symphony in G minor. But the three movements which we do have show an obsessive interest in symphonic argument, and Mozart may have felt that he did not want to write either a minuet not couched in sonata form or one which used the form, but 'writ small'. On the other hand he might well have felt that the triple-time rhythms of the *andante* were already similar to a slow minuet, and that he didn't want to embark upon the alien course of writing a fast minuet. The two encores to Susanna's duet with Cherubino must have been in his mind for the opening subject for the final movement; here again the second tune is for relief, given twice only, and the first subject is all-pervasive. The development starts by apparently referring to the introduction's technique of loud chord and quiet aftermath, and this gives a striking indication of the overflow of such development out of its 'proper' section by occurring shortly afterwards in an entirely unexpected excursion between first and second subjects in the recapitulation. This sense of overflowing energy is of course enhanced by playing both repeats in a movement which is after all marked *presto*.

By now a Prague newspaper of 12 December was circulating a rumour that Mozart was to come to see *Figaro* there for himself. The highly successful performances were put on in the ordinary course of events by the theatre Intendant, Bondini, a process which involved no contract or payment to the composer. But the prospect of hearing *Figaro* again (when Vienna had no such prospect to offer) was irresistible, and the Mozarts arrived in Prague on 11 January 1787. But before the journey there is another work to be catalogued, under the date of 27 December. Wolfgang calls it '*Scena con Rondo* with piano solo. For Mad:selle Storace and me'. There is a long distance to go from this remark to the supposition that Wolfgang was in love with Nancy. That the words—a reworking of a scene from *Idomeneo*—are an expression of love beautifully set hardly constitutes an exceptional situation in his concert arias, though the *concertante* but not overbearing piano part certainly does. But even if some flutterings there were, it could have been a case of Wolfgang loving Susanna and fancying he loved her embodiment, a situation in which Debussy found himself *vis-à-vis* his first Mélisande, Mary Garden. By all accounts, Nancy was captivating in comic opera, but the formidable voice-taster Charles Burney wrote in his *General History of Music* that 'in airs of tenderness, sorrow, or supplication, there is always a reason to lament the deficiency of natural sweetness', alluding to 'a certain crack and roughness'. It is very probable that Nancy included the piece in her farewell concert on 23 February 1787 at the Kärtnertor. It is usually called 'Ch'io mi scordi di te?' ('How could I ever forget you!'), K.505.

The joy at being appreciated, indeed fêted, shines through the letter sent from Prague to Gottfried von Jacquin on 15 January 1787. The jokes and exaggerations are of a kind not seen since pre-Vienna days. Almost immediately on their arrival old Count Thun, last seen at Linz, installed them in his very substantial palace. In the guest room, which Wolfgang calls a 'caritatis camera' a good piano has been brought in, 'which you can imagine is not left unused'. The very first evening 'I drove with Count Canal to the so-called Bretfeld ball'—no mention of Constanze!—'where the cream of Prague beauty is wont to assemble . . . I did not dance or flirt; my tiredness and inborn bashfulness forbade it, but I looked on with complete contentment to see these people delightedly jumping about to *Figaro* arranged into quadrilles and waltzes. For here nothing is talked of except *Figaro*; nothing is played, blown, sung or whistled but *Figaro*.' Yet, characteristically, before the end of the letter homesickness for Vienna, and especially for the Jacquin family sets in. The English trip is still clearly in Wolfgang's mind, since he speaks of the possibility of forgoing their happy comradeship for a long time, 'perhaps for ever'. The reason why he did not go doubtless lies partly in an exchange of letters, now lost, with Leopold, who must have pointed out the folly of arriving at the end of a season instead of its beginning, with no certain commission and, crucially, no money. Meanwhile in Prague Wolfgang had heard one performance of *Figaro* and personally directed another and between these engagements had given on his own account a concert which included the 'Prague' Symphony and some extemporised variations, presumably bringing the house down—if that were not done already—with an improvisation on Figaro's song 'Non più andrai'. As a memento of the honorific balls Wolfgang was able to catalogue on 6 February *Six German Dances* for orchestra, K.509, but in his pocket he had the final irresistible argument against going to England—a contract from the Prague impresario Bondini, whose company were the heroes of *Figaro*, to write another opera for the following autumn. Thus it was that Wolfgang was not of the party that reported their arrival in Salzburg to Leopold on the evening of 26 February. They were Nancy Storace, her mother and brother, an un-named travelling companion, Michael Kelly, and 'a little Englishman called Attwood'. Nancy sang to the Archbishop, Leopold rushed the party through some sight-seeing and they set off, to be lost to these pages, with two four-horse carriages and what appeared to the experienced Leopold to be a staggering amount of luggage.

By Wolfgang's standard there might be said to be a slightly fallow period on his return to Vienna; he catalogued only five works of sonata dimensions before the appearance of *Don Giovanni* under 28 October. But the next entry after the German Dances, though on a smaller scale, is one of his most poetic pieces, the Rondo in A minor, K.511, for piano solo. It was immediately published by Hoffmeister in a miscellaneous collection. Its mood of pathos and even resignation is quite unprecedented in a literature where a rondo is something to be cheerfully rattled off. The ornamentations of the theme's recurrences seem not so much to decorate it as to deepen it, and the brief episode in the major key begins by using the tail-piece of the previous section, a device we shall shortly hear again. There follow two orchestrally accompanied airs for friends—one for Johann Fischer, the first Osmin, treating again the favourite words 'Non so d'onde viene' (K.512), and the second for Gottfried von Jacquin (K.513).

Wolfgang's last extant letter to Leopold is dated 4 April. Early in it he writes as in the old days, as one professional to another, confidentially discussing the playing and composition of the oboist Johann Christian Fischer, incidentally Gainsborough's son-in-law. 'Each ritornel lasts a quarter of an hour—then the hero appears—heaves up one leaden foot after the other—and stamps them on to the ground in turn—his tone is entirely nasal—and his held notes like the tremulant on an organ.' But then he suddenly hears that Leopold is seriously ill. 'I need not tell you how I long to get some comforting news from you . . . death is the true goal of our life . . . his image is no longer terrifying to me, but rather it is calming and consoling! I never go to bed without thinking—young as I am—that I may not see the next day.' These are indeed the sentiments of the *Masonic Funeral Music*.

But as though to point the disjunction of emotions and creativity one of the most cloudless, serene works is catalogued two weeks later, the String Quintet in C, K.515. Here the expansiveness which seems to be induced by the key of C major results in a first movement of no less than 368 bars, excluding the repeat, which makes it, according to Charles Rosen, 'the largest sonata *allegro* before Beethoven'. To all intents and purposes Mozart here broaches for himself a new genre of chamber

music, the immature and stylistically uncertain K.174 of some 14 years
back having no successor. Again the work has no direct occasion that we
know of. It was offered twice on subscription but with insufficient takers.
The first movement opens with a broad dialogue which makes the listener
think there is no other possible layout of instruments than top and bottom
in dialogue, and three playing pulsating chords in between. There is a
momentary silence to enable the subject to begin again in the minor key.
When a modulation does come it sounds Schubertian in its suddenness
and also in its resolution back to the serenity of C major. It is when this
happens that the listener realises that the architecture of this tone-temple
is on a larger scale than he had supposed. The *andante* combines
simplicity of form with richness of content, and employs the first viola
in stretches of dialogue with the first violin in which Wolfgang may have
mentally harked back to Michael Haydn's example. The last movement
is a synthesis of jollity and learnedness. The contrapuntal passages are
rationed to what the mood and the tunes will bear, with no feeling of a
prepared demonstration.

The last extant letter of Leopold is to Nannerl, dated 10 and 11 May.
She had for some time previously been nursing him in Salzburg. Little
Leopold is still well, he himself is not worse, and various family
transactions are as firmly dealt with as ever. His last words about
Wolfgang are: 'Your brother now lives at 224 Landstrasse. He gives no
reason—not a word! But unfortunately I can guess.' The urban projecting
window was exchanged for rooms in a suburb. At least the fatherly love
had no more disappointments to bear. He died on Whitmonday, 28 May,
of a congestion of the spleen according to Joseph Barisani, his
doctor—though an obituary mentioned consumption. According to the
diary of Dominikus Hagenauer, now the abbot of St Peter's monastery,
Salzburg, 'he was a man of wit and wisdom who could have rendered
good service to the State quite apart from music'. Perhaps the Common-
wealth of music knows what it owes to this remarkable and good man.

Before he knew of his father's death Wolfgang had catalogued one of
his most powerful works, the string quintet in G minor, K.516. It sounds
as to most of its length as though it were a deliberately calculated obverse
to the preceding C major quintet, with a falling chromatic theme instead
of confidently striding arpeggios, with an opening seventeen bars of trio
texture, now upper now lower, instead of a minimum of four instruments
at a time, and above all the psychological difference between C major
and G minor which by now is quite unmistakable. But here too the music
is in no hurry to move from its home key. Indeed beginning still in G
minor there is a theme with yearning accented leaps which vies with the
first in memorability and constructive power. So closely and persistently

are these two—or at least their rhythms—interwoven that the music seems neither to have nor to need a 'second subject proper'. The main part of the menuetto is still in G minor and is interrupted by strident eleven-note chords on the third beat followed by silences on the first. The 'consolatory' trio begins by taking the tail-phrase of the menuetto and beginning with it in the major. The slow movement uses mutes throughout, not so much to prettify already beautiful sounds as to give a sense of remoteness, as of a distant haven 'if thou canst get but thither'. Surprisingly there follows an *adagio* in G minor which extends for nearly 40 bars before turning into a major-key movement at last, with a blithe and child-like main theme but also patches of energetic counterpoint. This 'happy ending' has worried some Romantic souls who feel that the clouds either ought not to have cleared at all, or at least not like this. But one feels they are trailing late-nineteenth-century clouds about with them. Interestingly enough, there is a sketch of a theme for this last *allegro* which is still in G minor. What is more, it has the unmistakable outlines of the first theme of the famous G minor symphony, K.550, for which we must wait one more year.

By the end of May Wolfgang heard of his father's death. 'You can guess the state I am in!', he wrote to his friend Gottfried. In the next few months he had completed the ticklish business of agreeing his share of the modest estate with his sister and her husband. But he must certainly by now have been composing to da Ponte's libretto of *Don Giovanni*. There are as usual other compositions completed before the decks are finally cleared. Apart from half a dozen songs there is another, exceedingly cheerful, piano duet sonata in C, K.521, which Gottfried is told to require his sister to practise.

In mid-June Wolfgang even felt compelled to write a piece for two horns and strings entitled *A Musical Joke*, K.522. This is a skit not only on incompetent composition—helpless repetitions of banal material, disproportion of all kinds, grammatical gaffes—but also on bad playing, with horns making a hopeless mess of a tune in thirds in the menuetto, and the first violin ending a ludicrously empty cadenza *in altissimo* and very sharp. We do not know who received it, or whether he was supposed to enjoy it. It was for a time in Schubert's possession.

On 10 August the catalogue records one of Mozart's most famous works, which he describes as 'Eine Kleine NachtMusick' (a little serenade). From the list of movements—and from the fact that the third page of the manuscript has been torn out—it is clear that the work originally contained the usual two minuets, the first of which is lost. The work (K.525) is scored for strings alone, but from the lie of the bass in relationship to the viola part in various places it is clear that what Mozart means by 'Bassi' is cello *and* double-bass, so that a string quartet is a makeshift. One can hardly suppose that Wolfgang would lightly interrupt his operatic labours even for such happy ideas as these without some specific object, but we do not know what it was. It is by now difficult to imagine a world in which such a shapely and appealing melody as that of the Romance did not exist. But there are also formal sophistications underlying the clear textures. The last movement calls itself a Rondo—on the manuscript that is; the catalogue says 'finale'—but a closer look shows that the first recurrence of the main theme is in the 'wrong' key. We could as logically think of the movement as in sonata-form with the themes recapitulated in reverse order. Whatever the occasion it did not evoke reach-me-down music; indeed it seems typical of Mozart that having previously written almost nothing for what we should call string chamber orchestra he should suddenly produce this peerless piece.

Similarly, we know nothing of the genesis of the big Sonata for Piano and Violin in A, K.526, dated 24 August. But it was published by Hoffmeister within a month, so that it might have been a speculation. Both the outer movements are extrovert, even dashing. The first movement could well have been a finale in another context, and indeed the fast scales call to mind the last movement of the A major symphony K.201. There is a true equilibrium of instruments here. The *andante* is a very individual creation; for much of the time the pulse of the music is quietly but irresistibly maintained in a tread of octaves, against which there are spurts of melody, sometimes whimsical, never long maintained but rising to extraordinary heights of expression at climactic points. The final *presto* has a *moto perpetuo* main subject which the piano bears the brunt of at the beginning; indeed the movement bears all the marks, except orchestration, of an ebullient concerto-rondo, with cascading scales for both instruments relating it to the first movement. With this large-scale and demanding 'concert' piece Mozart takes his leave of the violin sonata, which by now we can truly call by that name. (The sonata in F, K.547 of a year later is by Wolfgang's own ambiguous description 'a little piano sonata, for beginners with a violin'.)

Da Ponte tells us in his memoirs that he had a busy summer, making three libretti at once, working for Mozart at night, in the morning for Martín, and in the afternoon for Salieri, who wanted only an 'Italianisation' for Vienna of an opera he had already set, unsuccessfully, in Paris. Da Ponte says that Mozart left the choice of subject to him. He turned to the evergreen play of the loves, blasphemies and punishment of Don Juan, an entertainment which combined the vicarious pleasure, for both sexes, of witnessing seductions with the moral satisfaction of the spectacular fate of the sinner who had provided the evening's delights. Shadwell's *Libertine* with Purcell's help had used the subject in England, and it served no less a person than Molière in France, but it was in Italy (although the original of the story was reputedly Spanish) that the legend was most popular in Mozart's day, being handled by anything from harlequinades to opera. In that very year, 1787, it was given in Venice as an entertainment called *Il capriccio dramatico*, with words by Giovanni Bertati and music by Giuseppe Gazzaniga. The introductory part depicts a manager and a troupe in their usual predicament of facing bankruptcy; there follows a trial run in the shape of a one-act opera—the salvation of them all. Da Ponte took Bertati's libretto as his basis, but recast it so as to amend the inherent dramatic weakness of there being a mere succession of women until the time is ripe for the statue of a murdered father to come to dinner and drag Don Juan to hell. We thus have less than the sum total of characters to be found in all the various versions of the story, but developed and made to last through the action of the play. There are three women: Donna Anna, whose father the Commendatore is killed by Don Giovanni at the beginning of the play, returning as the statue at the end; Donna Elvira, a cast-off love who humanly veers between a thirst for revenge and rekindled love; and Zerlina, a peasant girl. Curiously enough we do not see Don Giovanni successful with any of them in the course of Mozart/da Ponte, though a strong school of thought can imagine Anna's fate during the *allegro* part of the overture. Anna's lover is a somewhat ineffectual Don, Ottavio, to whom she is on the whole remote. Masetto is the guardian of Zerlina, understandably truculent since he does not regard an unscheduled party at Don Giovanni's as suitable for their wedding-day. Elvira is unwillingly and incongruously paired with the comic manservant Leporello from time to time. She is a butt, yet though she may be fooled she has a foolishness that springs from a human weakness which makes her the most interesting and sympathetic character of the three women.

As in *Figaro* there is an admixture of wholly serious characters and music, but the opera is unequivocally called a Dramma Giocoso. It is not, in spite of the awesome aspects of the dénouement, a serious tale larded with comic relief, but a comedy taken seriously as ever by Mozart. It was written after all for an audience in Prague, which did not need winning over.

If they expected another *Figaro* they must have been surprised from the very start, and from that moment they were carried without a break straight into the action by a piece of music which Wolfgang called Introduzione. In less than two hundred bars the Introduzione leads from a comic servant's song to a horrifying murder, but this is all in orchestrated continuous music, with no recitative, and what is more by its motifs and keys it is a musical shape, not merely an accompaniment to a string of events. Whatever the subsequent delights of the evening we cannot forget that 'God is not mocked: for whatsoever a man soweth, that shall he also reap'. Music is *par excellence* the art which allows a D minor sown in the overture to be reaped at the end of the evening.

But to return to that overture, it begins *andante* with two loud chords. Shaw rivets them in the mind with a stage-direction in *Man and Superman*: 'Two great chords rolling on syncopated waves of sound break forth—D minor and its dominant: a sound of dreadful joy to all musicians'; it is only after some striking tremblings and palpitations with *crescendo* rising scales leading to a *piano* descent, that the music suddenly turns, *molto allegro*, into the more usual bustle of *opera buffa*. This preliminary *frisson* is intended to remain in the back of the mind till the dreaded statue is revealed at Don Giovanni's door, with the first chord louder and dissonant. The overture helps us plunge into the swift movement of the action by not coming to a formal stop before the curtain rises. (At least this seems to have been the case in Prague, but puzzlingly enough there is a page in Mozart's own hand which does give it a full-stop ending, which, if it was used at all, belongs to the later Vienna performances.)

As the curtain rises Leporello is pacing up and down as a sentry whilst his master is about his business in Donna Anna's house. Where we might expect the middle section of his solo Donna Anna and Don Giovanni appear, she grasping him by the arm lest he escape, and he hiding his face lest she recognise him. Leporello makes this a trio by gabbling in the darkness. Anna's father appears bringing the music back to the fateful D minor of the beginning of the overture; they fight and Don Giovanni mortally wounds the father. The trio that follows so impressed Beethoven that he noted it down with a reminder of the triplet accompaniment which became a feature of the first movement of the so-called 'Moonlight' Sonata. The last utterances of the dying man are at the furthest remove from moonlight, and their darkness is increased by the *sotto voce* comments of Don Giovanni and Leporello making an all-low-voice trio. The key is F minor (still with undertones of horror in the eighteenth-century scheme of things); Leporello having begun in F major, this gives a tonal balance, but one which shows the evening to have gone sour indeed; and both symmetry and drama are also served by Don Giovanni's first phrase softly echoing the most florid phrase of Anna's previous outburst.

Every bar of the rest of the work seems to impel comment. We must let one number suffice as an example of musical characterisation and wit; it is perhaps the most famous of them all, the duet between Don Giovanni and Zerlina 'Là ci darem la mano' in which he proposes 'nuptials' if she will but go with him. Let it first be said that the tune has an immortal charm that no words can describe or illuminate. But if Don Giovanni were addressing it to someone on his own social plane it could well be more ornate, and he might then give the lady the benefit of an orchestral introduction instead of leading straight in on the heels of the recitative. He delivers his opening proposal in a straightforward symmetrical eight bars; her uncertainties elongate her reply to ten. The pleas and the replies come nearer now, first at intervals of two bars, then of one, except where Zerlina's wobblings are reflected in her line. Then at last, in a new dancing tempo, the voices are together, singing hand in hand, so to speak, exactly as in another sphere Bach treats Christ and his bride the Church. They prepare to go off to the strains of countryside music, the stationary bass of baroque pastoral symphonies alternating with a *pizzicato* accompaniment to a country dance. In one of the best jokes of the libretto da Ponte makes them agree to 'assuage the pangs of an innocent love'. But no sooner is the innocence mentioned than Mozart contradicts it by a chromatic sinuous phrase on the strings—the snake which lurks in the grass of the proposed Eden. Such orchestral comments, with the pit momentarily contradicting the stage, are too sophisticated for Zerlina. What does stop her in her tracks is a truly Handelian aria from Elvira who suddenly appears, to deliver herself of 'Ah fuggi il traditor'. Zerlina would never in her life have been urged to 'flee the traitor' in the full panoply of *opera seria*. As ever, our reactions are potentially contradictory, but all conducive to pleasure. The incongruity of Elvira's address is funny; it is a splendid song with a ringing climax; we have fellow-feelings with Elvira and do not want to laugh at her. Mozart takes just 45 bars to accomplish all this.

The finale of the first act culminates in Don Giovanni's party, intended by him for the seduction of Zerlina, attended by the serious characters, Anna, Elvira and Ottavio, in masks in an attempt to identify the murderer. This involved Mozart in a *tour de force* of combining three dances in different times and rhythms, a task for which a sketch survives, since it took even him a little sorting out. (Incidentally, before the entry of the masquers, keen-eared *Figaro*-lovers can detect a quotation of the tune of 'Non più andrai'.) The three dances are a minuet for the upper classes, a *contredanse* into which Don Giovanni leads Zerlina, preparatory to misleading her, and a waltz which Leporello forces Masetto to join. As the violins of the second and third dances successively join in, Mozart even accommodates to the rest of the music their tuning with the bow, a final pluck of the tuned strings and a tiny flourish. His observation is as pointed as ever. There are also memorials of Leopold here. The rhythm and repeated notes of the first bar of the minuet appear in the fourth of the twelve duos which Leopold added as a supplement to the Paris (1770) edition of the *Violinschule*, and the three preliminary grace-note sparrow-like cheeps with which the waltz begins come also in the 'Teutscher Tanz' of Leopold's famous *Musical Sleigh-ride*.

The abortive dance at the end of act 1 is matched by the fateful supper at the end of act 2, and before the guest of honour arrives there are again three band-pieces though mercifully not combined. Don Giovanni, convinced that his supper is to be for one, begins it to the strains of the act 1 finale of Martìn y Soler's very recent success *Una cosa rara*. Leporello identifies it, and on being asked what he thinks of it says drily that it is suitable for Don Giovanni's merits. The next piece is an aria 'Come un' agnello' from Sarti's *Due litiganti*, obviously another favourite, but it is the third which must have struck home in Prague—the beloved 'Non più andrai' from *Figaro*. At this Leporello remarks 'I know this all too well' and eventually joins in with the tune to words praising the cook. But there can be no stop to music or action. Elvira rushes in, desperately beseeching a last repentance from Don Giovanni. Mocked for her pains with toasts to women and wine she goes out, screams and re-enters to flee elsewhere. Leporello, sent to investigate, cries out off-stage; he re-enters, knees knocking; there are knocks at the door, Don Giovanni impatiently opens it himself and the statue is there. A further refusal of repentance—flames and subterranean voices—Don Giovanni is consigned to hell and the music momentarily stops.

There too did the libretto end for the Vienna first performance (17 May 1788), and there does exist in Mozart's hand a high chord for the three women, Ottavio and Leporello two bars after Don Giovanni's final cry. But it is equally certain that it was also his hand which crossed the chord out. It may be doubted whether anything so chancy musically and so inexplicable dramatically can have survived a rehearsal. To think of ending with the descent to hell must have involved Mozart either in a momentary loss of confidence in the power of his music or in a disillusioned compliance with his Vienna colleagues who had already caused alterations for the worse to the original Prague score. The power of the music in the catastrophe is of course what presents the risk of anticlimax, a risk which merely to read a résumé of the remainder does nothing to dispel: the cast re-enters with policemen, Leporello explains, the characters in their various typical ways announce what their own future intentions are—Ottavio and Anna to a further year's Anna-imposed self-denial, Masetto and Zerlina to dine together, Leporello to an inn to find a better master. They unite in a final chorus pointing out the advantages of being good. But the power of the music to spread the balm and to exhilarate us all in the final jolly admonitions is all-sufficient. What is more, an art-work flawed by a burst frame—however mighty the expression of the bursting—is contrary not only to eighteenth-century aesthetics but to what Mozart would know as music's function. To leave the theatre with nothing more than a shriek in our ears *might* induce us to work out our own salvation. But we should not be helped by the memory that the human beings on the stage had shown no resilience, and that the music had abdicated from that reconciliation which magically springs from the endeavours which reinforce the humanity on both sides of the curtain.

The Mozarts arrived in Prague on 4 October, staying at the 'Three Lions' inn, though they were also from time to time guests at the Villa Bertramka, the home of the Duscheks. With the first performance due on 14 October it was a great, if misguided, compliment by Mozart to the Prague forces that he should have thought ten days of rehearsals long enough. In the event the first performance was on 29 October. But *Don Giovanni* had been intended to honour a royal wedding. The Archduchess Maria Theresia, accompanied by her brother, the Archduke Franz, was on her way through Prague to meet her husband Prince Antony Clemens in Dresden, to whom she was already married by proxy. What was offered instead of *Don Giovanni* on 14 October was a gala performance of *Figaro*, which however the royal guests did not hear the whole of, with an early start in prospect the next day. *Don Giovanni* thus lost its royal patronage but it seems very likely that it had another distinguished and appropriate member of its first-night audience, Giacomo Casanova. Mozart received three cheers at the beginning and the end, and in spite of the difficulties and expense, as the *Prager Oberpostamtszeitung* put it: 'everyone strained every nerve to thank Mozart by rewarding him with a good performance.' Mozart conducted for his own benefit the fourth performance in six days on 3 November.

While he was still in Prague his friend and hostess the singer Josepha Duschek made Mozart write her a *scena*, 'Bella mia fiamma—Resta, o cara', K.528. There is a story that she shut him up in Villa Bertramka till he had finished it, and that he for his part would not finally give it her without her singing it at sight. There may be some foundation for this in the music, which twice employs demanding successions of taxing intervals, illustrating torment of spirit. Nor was the faithful Gottfried von Jacquin forgotten; he sent enough reminders to be at last rewarded with a charming short song 'Das Traumbild' ('The Dream-picture'), K.530. He could have regarded it as a form of thanks for looking after the Mozarts' dog, Katherl.

On 15 November, probably just before the Mozarts arrived back in

Vienna, Gluck had died. The reforms he sought in his mature operas—a greater dramatic realism, abolition of ornamental reprises in airs, continuities of action sustained by continuities of music—may be said to have been independently carried out by Mozart, in *Idomeneo*, and (though in the *opera buffa* field) in *Don Giovanni*. Gluck had been 'Kammermusicus' (court composer) at 2,000 gulden a year. From 1 December Mozart succeeded him at 800. Equally frustrating was the fact that only dances for balls—such as the *Six German Dances*, K.536—were seemingly required of him. Hence a *mot* attributed to him on the occasion of a tax return: 'Too much for what I do; too little for what I could do.' Some time in December the Mozarts had moved back from the Landstrasse into Vienna. On 27 December their fourth child, Theresia, was born, but she lived only six months.

No extant letters survive from the first five months of 1788, nor is there much activity in concerts. Wolfgang served Baron van Swieten's interest in older music by conducting some performances of C.P.E. Bach's 'Resurrection' Cantata. In the composition catalogue, before the new numbers for the Vienna *Don Giovanni* the only sizeable work is the Piano Concerto in D, K.537, often called the 'Coronation', a name not very appropriate as it was not the only concerto Mozart performed at the coronation festivities at Frankfurt in 1790 and it was obviously not written for them. It was presumably written for Lent-academies, but we have no record of them. For all the brightness of both outer movements and the charming theme of the middle one the music reads sadly to those who love its predecessors. It is as though Mozart was deliberately courting a more superficial taste. Apart from a few plunges of key in the last movement, surprises are minimal, but of course all is clear and effective. The solo part is more than usually fragmentary—for quite long stretches there is no authentic part for the left hand. Similarly 'heartless' is the last of the concert-arias written for Aloysia: 'Ah si in ciel . . .', K.538. Again, effectiveness seems to be his furthest aim, though perhaps it is a commentary on the final flickering of what Aloysia had once meant to him. Something altogether truer in its feeling is the Adagio in B minor for piano, K.540, its restrained pathos being at the furthest remove from the public glitter of K.537.

That *Don Giovanni* was ultimately performed in Vienna is to the credit of Joseph II, who cut through intrigues and delays by positively ordering its production, which took place on 7 May. Had Leopold still been alive one can imagine the correspondence about the matter, particularly centring on Salieri who did not relish such redoubtable opposition. Francesco Morella as Ottavio evidently could not manage the runs in 'Il mio tesoro' and Mozart instead wrote for him the simpler but equally beautiful love-song 'Dalla sua pace'. As the two songs are not a straight-forward substitution but are in different acts greedy musicians, producer and tenor permitting, can nowadays have both. Caterina Cavalieri as Elvira, so far from needing any simplification of her music, insisted on an addition in the second act, the very fine 'Mi tradi'. When we are allowed to hear it nowadays, we feel that Elvira has deserved this one opportunity to extend herself. In a crude sense these arias 'hold up the action' but it is the duet for Zerlina and Leporello 'Per queste tue manine', added for Vienna, whose comic action seems a time-wasting irrelevance.

The Emperor, being away at the front in the war against the Turks, had not by 16 May heard the opera, but this did not prevent him from declaring to Count Rosenberg: 'Mozart's music is certainly too difficult for the singers.' He must have been echoing a widespread view. The work had fifteen Vienna performances, all in 1788, but was never again given there in Mozart's lifetime. There was one aftermath: for the singer who had played the title-role, Francesco Albertarelli, he wrote a comic air, 'Un bacio di mano', K.541, to be inserted in Anfossi's opera *Le gelosie fortunate*. In it, one of the subsidiary subjects of the 'Jupiter' appears to words to the effect that 'you are a simpleton, my dear Pompeo; you must study the ways of the world.' Obviously sublimity cannot always depend on subject-matter.

11

Debts and Death

1788–91

In June begins the first of a series of letters asking money of a brother Mason, Michael Puchberg, who was a keen musician and the well-to-do proprietor of a textile firm. Puchberg has already figured twice in the Mozart documents: it was to him that Wolfgang asked his brother-in-law to send the bill of exchange representing his share of Leopold's estate (as Wolfgang was leaving for Prague) and it was to him that the public was directed to apply when subscriptions were solicited on 2 April 1788 for copies of the previous year's string quintets. In fact these subscriptions never amounted to enough to proceed. The extant begging letters, almost too painful to read, amount to twenty between June 1788 and Mozart's death. As Puchberg noted on them the amounts he lent, we know that their minimum total represented a considerable sum of 1,415 florins, probably with other unknown small loans amounting to twice the annual honorarium as Kammermusicus. As a 'security' in the first instance Mozart mentions 'my concerts in the Casino' due to begin 'next week'. But it does not appear that the concerts were given, and one can imagine the state of mind of a family man realising, with a week to go, that the Vienna public for such things was indeed deserting him. Perhaps at this stage they were merely postponed, in his mind. For nothing can alter the glorious fact that in these circumstances he wrote the last three symphonies, K.543 in E flat, K.550 in G minor and K.551 in C, finished respectively on 26 June, 25 July and 10 August. The loss of little Theresia, the move to yet another lodging, the loss of pride—all had no obvious effect on the astounding upsurge of creative energy, even though during the trilogy of the symphonies Wolfgang had been pawning belongings to keep the family alive.

The E flat symphony, like the piano concerto K.482, employs the euphony of clarinets substituted for oboes. For the last time in a Mozart symphony there is a slow introduction. The reference back to the dotted rhythms of the French opera overture is unmistakable. 'Unmistakable', one writes, but one despairs of hearing the up-beat semiquavers played at half their written length, so that the attention is commanded in proper eighteenth-century style. Whereas to the style-conscious such an opening hints at a semblance, at any rate, of a fugue to follow, the ensuing *allegro* begins instead with one of Mozart's blandest tunes to be followed at the *tutti* by a jubilant enhancement on all the violins of the leaps from one end of the compass to another of an operatic heroine. In the light of history we cannot help seeing, albeit on a smaller scale, the coming 'Eroica' in the confident stride and abundant material of this movement. 'Slow movement' gives a false idea of the next, an *andante con moto* with the kind of tune, at once rounded out and sharply edged, favoured by Haydn. The alternate tune is more a gentle contrapuntal dialogue—like the equivalent place in the slow movement of the C major quartet. The famous minuet mingles the stately rhythms of trumpet and drums with the bucolic hurdy-gurdy effect of clarinets in the soprano and bottom end of their registers. The finale again uses a Haydnesque theme, and indeed uses his technique in redeploying it, or an extension of it, at the place where one expects a new subject. But the dialogue in the development section is pursued with, if possible, a more strenuous exploration of distant keys than even Haydn would normally commit himself to. The end is made by abruptly flinging the beginning of the subject into the air, so to speak.

The Symphony in G minor, K.550, is the instrumental culmination of the series of works in this, for Mozart, special key. Like the earlier symphony in G minor, K.183, it insists on remaining in that key even in the final movement, with the slow movement the only one in a major key (E flat). The famous opening theme, over palpitating violas, uses in fact the same rhythm, but to greatly different effect, as that of Cherubino's first air in *Figaro* in which he declares he does not understand the emotions which flutter him. Here lies one of the keys to the poignancy of this work to us. It is still couched in the Italianate rhythms of *opera buffa*; we cannot but think of it as suffusing with tears a language intended for entertainment. We may be at some remove from Mozart in this reaction but we cannot help being conditioned by two hundred subsequent years of musical expression. The *andante* has overlapping contrapuntal dialogue as one of its main elements, but the continual variety of theme, harmony and timbre is held together by constant cross-references—an all-sufficient unobtrusive thread. Both the minuet and the last movement use propulsive dissonant counterpoint, nowhere more so than in the latter's development section which begins with the most drastic of lurches into far distant tonal regions in a manner which even Beethoven did not exceed. The original scoring of the symphony uses oboes to the exclusion of clarinets. But as soon as there were clarinets available Mozart rescored the wind parts to admit them. H.C. Robbins Landon in his edition of the last three symphonies for the New Mozart Edition suggests that this 'clarinet' version could have been played at the Tonkünstler Society's concerts on 16 and 17 April 1791. Salieri conducted, and the clarinets in the orchestra were named—Mozart's friend Anton Stadler and his younger brother Johann. In the *tuttis* the clarinets reinforce the wind sound, but in the solo wind passages it is by no means a case of equal shares between oboe and clarinet. The great majority of oboe solos are given to the clarinet; in the slow movement this is the case with every single oboe solo however short. The only places where the oboes wholly retain their own is in the recapitulation of the first movement where the second-subject material stays in the minor key, and in the trio of the minuet, whose key (G major) would mean awkward fingerings or a change of instrument if the clarinets were admitted. But here the momentary pastoral style would hardly admit the 'boudoir' or serenade-like associations of the clarinet.

Robbins Landon also quotes the source of the nickname 'Jupiter' for the last symphony. It is found in the travel diaries of the famous London publisher Vincent Novello and his wife Mary. They visited Constanze on 7 August 1829 and recorded: 'Mozart's son said he considered the Finale to his father's sinfonia in C—which Salomon christened the Jupiter—to be the highest triumph of instrumental composition.' (Be it noted that this was said after the deaths of both Beethoven and Schubert.) The name appears in an Edinburgh Music Festival programme of 1819. This name-giver was Johann Salomon who was responsible for Haydn's two London visits and might indeed have been responsible for Mozart's too if an invitation in December 1790 had been accepted. Again the key of C major seems to induce both a monumentality and a spacious reluctance to move quickly afield. The opening of the symphony—masculine trumpets, drums and unisons alternating with 'feminine' pleadings on the strings—could have been written by any symphonist in the preceding twenty years. But as the scoring and the counterpoint take over the thread becomes apparent—this time the first bar of the first 'pleading'. But there is a surprise in this exposition: after a silence to emphasise a deliberate discontinuity the tune for Albertarelli strikes up, and surprisingly dominates much of the development. It looks the least likely candidate for such a task before Mozart lays his masterly hand on it. The *Andante cantabile* is the apotheosis of the ornate song which bewitched Mozart since his Italian days. To the beauty of sound of the muted violins is added the woodwind counterpoint featured in so many concertos, but added to this is a new rhythmic dimension sometimes highlighted by unexpected harmony—the exploitation of two-bar stretches of triple time so that the accents fall thus: 1̲ 2 3̲ 4 5̲ 6, instead of 1̲ 2 3 4̲ 5 6. (Visually a very poor substitute for hearing it.) The last symphonic minuet is one of the stateliest, and its trio uses the witticism of beginning its phrases with the harmonic cadence which usually ends such things. The last movement's first theme is the *d r f m* subject. Its long equal notes are an indication that contrapuntal artifice is to come, but as in the G major quartet the music proceeds in sonata shape without ever being a fugue. Nevertheless in the coda there are indeed no fewer than five themes simultaneously building a web of clear and apparently effortless counterpoint. All the journeys have seemingly come home to the irresistible conclusion of the last two symphonies. But this may be mere sentimentality. There might have been another post-'Jupiter' marvel. Certainly, had the series ended with the G minor symphony it would have been difficult to envisage the 'Jupiter'.

But this year which snatches artistic victory from the jaws of financial defeat also contains no fewer than four trios. The first in the unusual key of E major, K.542, is probably the one referred to in a letter to Puchberg dated 17 June: 'P.S. When shall we have another little music-making at your house?—I have written a new trio!' This one is catalogued four days before the E flat symphony to which it is unmistakably a sister-work as to its first two movements. There is of course no 'full-orchestra' introduction, but the triple time, the shapes, the succession and sometimes the actual notes of the symphony's themes (allowing for the different key) are all to be seen in the first movement, and the same obtains to a large extent in the *Andante grazioso*. The last movement however is far from Haydnesque. There is quite a long sketch—more than 60 bars—of a dance-like opening but then Mozart settles for a rondo-shaped movement, not unlike the end of the 'Kegelstatt' trio in which a lyrical main theme is diversified by the stretches of more virtuosic writing for the violin and, particularly, the piano. The cello is not trusted to that extent—it never was, by Mozart—but nevertheless it has a good deal more independence than in previous trios, and is allotted characteristic sounds.

A far less ruminative impression is given by the cheerful Trio in C, K.548 dated just eleven days before the G minor symphony. But the clarity and genial ease of the work hides subtle craftsmanship in the derivation and development of short motifs to consolidate the design. This is especially true of the final *allegro*. A rondo-like structure is usually clarified by having at least three distinct themes; this uses only one, and its derivatives. It may be the movement which Mozart was looking for in the abandoned sketch for the previous trio.

The third trio, dated 27 September, differs from the others in using violin, viola and cello. The catalogue calls it a Divertimento of six movements. It is Mozart's first and only complete string trio, but as far as mastery of the medium goes he might have written a dozen by way of preparation. There is in fact a sizeable sketch of the beginning of another string trio in G, K.Anh.66, consisting of an exposition and the beginning of a development, but it is impossible to say whether it was written before or after the completed trio, or why its seemingly promising material was discarded. As with all the other major instrumental works of 1788, we do not know what occasioned this piece, but it cannot have been without nostalgia that Mozart addressed himself to this isolated final instance of a suite-like entertainment-music more associated, in his output, with Salzburg than with Vienna. There are as usual two minuets, the second remarkable for a high tune on the viola (Wolfgang's excursion?). The slow movement proper comes second, the only one in 1788 incidentally to be marked *adagio*, the others, including those of the symphonies, being all *andantes* of some sort. Here we meet again the Italian aria style, but deliberately using the whole of the violin's compass to point the difference between instrumental and vocal resource. The touches of modulation in the harmony cannot but strike us as 'romantic'. But as in the other movements there is plenty of counterpoint as well, since unrelieved harmony would simply make the listener feel there is one instrument missing for its proper rendering.

With the Trio in G, K.564, Mozart reverts to piano, violin and cello. It is a light-weight conclusion to the series, particularly in the innocent central variations, but given an undemanding situation it has, inevitably, workmanship and charm.

With no letters after August we are left without first-hand information about the rest of the troubled year. But from other sources we learn that Mozart reorchestrated for van Swieten and his Society of Noblemen Handel's *Acis and Galatea*. He conducted a performance of it himself for his own benefit probably in November. This was the first of four such Handel rearrangements, of which the *Messiah* is the most famous. At the year's end the Emperor after a long absence at the Turkish war heard the last of the Vienna performances of *Don Giovanni*, but there is nothing to show whether he thought better of his prejudgement.

Early in 1789 one of Mozart's many moves brought the family back to the Inner City. The house, called 'Mother of God', was in the Judenplatz next-door to his lodgings of April 1783, in what by contrast must have seemed carefree days. We know from an anonymous inscription on a word-book of *Messiah* that Mozart conducted his arrangement of it at Count Johann Esterházy's on 6 March. Interestingly enough for students of performance practice, the choir numbered twelve—though they were doubtless professionals. The first extant letter of the year, later in March, is another request for a loan, this time addressed to Franz Hofdemel, who was shortly to join Mozart's Lodge. Hofdemel was a government official who sprang to notoriety just after Mozart's death by assaulting his wife and committing suicide. Mozart needed the loan to finance a journey, though the travelling itself would be free. He was to be company for the music-loving Prince Karl Lichnowsky travelling to Prague, Dresden, Leipzig and Berlin, leaving Vienna on 8 April. The letters back to Constanze are worded in tones of intimate infatuation, calling her 'little rascal', 'pointy-nose', 'little bagatelle', 'little mouse', and 'stru! stri!'. But there is a serious note: 'I beg you to have regard in your conduct not only for *your honour and mine*, but also for *appearances*. Do not be angry at this request. You should love me all the more for valuing honour.'

The musical news from Prague was that Domenico Guardasoni, the manager of the National Theatre, had 'virtually arranged to give me 200 ducats next autumn for an opera'. This may have entailed the first consideration of *La clemenza di Tito*, Metastasio's famous and much-set libretto which Mozart ultimately gave in Prague in 1791. In Dresden Mozart profitably played at the court his new concerto in D, K.537, and in Leipzig on what must have been a reverential occasion he played Bach's organ in the Thomaskirche. The prince and Mozart then made an excursion to Potsdam where the King of Prussia was in residence. Whether a royal hearing was achieved at this time is not known, several letters being lost covering this stage in the journey. But there was one by-product; to ingratiate himself Mozart wrote piano variations on a favourite theme of the king's, a minuet by his director of chamber music, Jean Pierre Duport—at least, at this time he wrote six of the nine variations eventually published (K.573). On the return visit to Leipzig Mozart gave in the Gewandhaus a concert for his own benefit with the collaboration of Josepha Duschek. It turned out not to be a benefit as far as money was concerned, and Wolfgang blamed the prince for the fruitless detour. There could have been no complaints as to the sufficiency of the entertainment. Apart from Madame Duschek's two big scenas, there were two symphonies, and Mozart played not only two concertos (K.456 and 503) but the C minor fantasia (K.475) and a set of variations.

On the evening of his arrival in Berlin he heard *Die Entführung* at the National Theatre. He also played at court at the invitation of the queen, and received there a request to compose 'six easy keyboard sonatas' for the king's eldest daughter Princess Friederike and six string quartets for the king, who was an accomplished cellist. Arriving back in Vienna on 4 June Mozart immediately took the first steps towards fulfilling this, and the first of the quartets, in D, K.575 was completed in that month. It is perhaps unsafe to use the word 'commission' for these Prussian pieces. If it were a proper contract it was never fulfilled, and the three quartet scores did not carry a dedication and were published 'for a pittance' in the ordinary way. But at least at this stage K.575 had the king very much in mind. He is mentioned in the catalogue, and the cello is offered grateful moments of primacy in all the movements. Though perhaps even here there is a witticism in the opening. The royal participant begins with eight bars' rest; it may be supposed that he is being kept in reserve for an elegant reply, but instead his first contribution is seventeen *sotto voce* Ds below the viola's complementary melody. The spring-like clarity and freshness of the whole work strikes us immediately; as so often in the late works, what on analysis seem sophisticated procedures—for instance the treatment of scales in the first movement—also sound to the ear to be purely instinctive. If there is a labour here, the listeners are spared it. The slow movement, the simplest in style of all the mature quartets, breathes again the youthful air of Italy. There is a sketch for the last movement of eight bars of a gavotte-like theme entitled 'Rondeaux', but this gives place to a theme still destined for a rondo-shape but capable of much more discussion, though never losing the poised sweetness which is the main characteristic of the quartet.

Within a month a terrible letter has to be written or rather wrenched out of Mozart to Puchberg. It begins:

God! I am in a position that I wouldn't wish for my worst enemy; and if you my best friend and brother forsake me, then I, *unlucky and blameless*, with my poor sick wife and my child am lost. When I was last with you I wanted to pour out my heart to you—but I didn't have the heart for it!—and indeed I would still not have the courage—I can only dare to write it—and tremble even whilst writing—and I would not even dare to write—if I did not know that you understand me, and that you know my circumstances and that you are wholly convinced of my *innocence* as far as my unhappy, most distressing situation is concerned. O God! instead of thanks I come with new requests!—instead of repayments new entreaties.

It is hardly bearable to think that the same mind which organised the first 'Prussian' Quartet could be driven to such a desperate virtually unpunctuated outpouring. There were two immediate causes: Constanze had a severe foot infection which the family physician, Dr Thomas

Closset, said should have treatment at the sulphur springs at Baden, some seventeen miles away; but a stunning blow because of its implications is also mentioned in the letter: 'I decided to give subscription-concerts at home . . . I sent the list round fourteen days ago, and there stands the single name *Swieten!*' The postscript begins: 'O God!—I can hardly bring myself to send this letter!—and yet I must!'

In the same month as this letter (July) is catalogued the first, and only, one of the 'Prussian' Piano Sonatas, in D, K.576. But though it is as cheerful as the quartet it could by no means fit the prescription of 'easy'. The first movement makes great play of close imitations between the two hands, their contradictory accents complicating already demanding fingerwork, and the whirling accompaniments to the tune of the last movement lead one to suppose that the princess is either forgotten or being unduly flattered. Two letters in August show that Constanze has gone to Baden for her cure. But the main worry is not her foot, but the freedom of her behaviour towards a man hidden in the letters as N.N. Jealousy is added to the other anxieties. Mozart visited Baden, but could not stay long because of the forthcoming revival of *Figaro* which entailed two new numbers for Adriana Ferrarese, singing Susanna. It hardly seems possible, but one of these, the rondo 'Al desio di chi t'adora' (K.577), was actually a replacement for 'Deh Vieni'. The first performance of the new production was on 29 August, and it led to a commission from the Emperor of a new opera with da Ponte again as librettist, the subject, said to have some basis in recent fact, to be 'Così fan tutte'.

But just before opera composition must have begun in earnest the catalogue includes, on 29 September, one of the best loved of all Mozart's works, the Clarinet Quintet in A, K.581, which he called in a subsequent letter 'Stadler's quintet'. Anton Stadler was not only the leading Viennese clarinettist but an inveterate experimenter with instruments, and there is nowadays little doubt that in an original version this piece was written for his basset-clarinet, an instrument which added four notes to the bottom of the ordinary clarinet's range. The original manuscript was in Stadler's possession and possibly later in Puchberg's, but has long been lost, and the early printed editions keep to the compass of the ordinary clarinet so as not to hinder wide circulation. Although this is the only complete clarinet quintet of Mozart's two frustrating torsos must be mentioned: a quintet for clarinet—or perhaps basset-horn—in B flat (K.Anh.91) which is a first movement completely scored up till three bars beyond the exposition, where it breaks off; and what would have been an elaborate piece, unique in its sound, a quintet in F (K.Anh.90) for clarinet and basset-horn—probably for the Stadler brothers—with violin, viola and cello. This goes as far as the repeat mark at the end of the exposition and most of it is fully scored.

When the queen of the woodwind shares the stage with a string quartet the problems of sharing the musical interest in the classical manner are obvious. To avoid the immediate subordination of the strings Mozart gives them the first statements of all three main themes in the first movement's exposition. In the second of these we have a beautiful example of the 'voluntary variation'. Over a *pizzicato* bass the violin announces a shapely melody, beginning with two parabolic curves. Structurally it would be perfectly possible for the clarinet at its entry to repeat the melody as it stood, and it would also be aesthetically effective, as though to say 'now this is how it should sound'. This is indeed how it sounds for a moment, but in the first curve we find the clouding into the minor (marked *dolce*) which is a feature of the late Mozart style, and to cap this the second curve is altered by a leap to its top note and an enhanced fall from it. Nor is this all, for when this melody is recapitulated the clarinet does not merely go into the minor—we expect that—but it alters the shape and phrasing of the first curve, and enhances the second by beginning it much lower. With the slow movement the clarinet comes into its incomparable own as a singing instrument, the violins being muted to make way for it. Peculiarly touching is the after-melody, when the formal design has been completed and the clarinet sinks slowly through a chromatic scale. In the last movement the same effect is employed to cloud the last variation twice, but just far enough away from the end not to disturb its serene happiness.

On 16 November the Mozarts' fifth child, Anna Maria, was born but only survived an hour, giving presumably hardly any pause to the writing of the opera. The last event of the year was a 'little opera rehearsal' on 31 December to which Mozart invited Haydn and Puchberg. They were also invited to go with him to the Burgtheater to hear the first instrumental rehearsal which took place on 21 January 1790, with the first performance on the 26th, just five days later.

Both *Così fan tutte* and *Die Zauberflöte* show in the highest degree the power of great music to transcend the weaknesses and inconsistencies of mankind, not by glossing over them with some magical make-believe which shuts our eyes to them for the moment, but by deepening and beautifying their presentation so that we feel not just sympathy but love for the humanity shared with us by our brothers and sisters on the stage. To say that we can be better men for seeing *Così* well performed may well seem a tall claim on a mere résumé of the plot. For succinctness and clarity one cannot improve on Dent in his book *Mozart's Operas*.

Ferrando and Guglielmo are two young Neapolitan officers engaged to be married to two young ladies, Fiordiligi and her sister Dorabella. A cynical old bachelor, Don Alfonso by name, persuades the young men to put their mistresses' constancy to the test. They pretend to be called away from Naples on duty, but return that very afternoon disguised as Albanian noblemen. Don Alfonso, with the help of Despina, the ladies' maid, persuades the two sisters to receive them. The strangers make violent love to them, and after some opposition each succeeds in winning the heart of his friend's betrothed. The affair proceeds, in fact, with such rapidity that a notary is called in that very evening to witness the marriage contract. Suddenly Don Alfonso announces the return of the soldiers; the Albanians vanish, and the terrified ladies are obliged to make confession to their original lovers. It is needless to say, however, that all ends happily.

Some mere readers of the above might well think that to enshrine such flippancy in a notoriously expensive art-form was an indication that the French revolution of the previous year had not come a moment too soon. Mozart never mentions the French revolution. Looked at in another way, here we have an ideal *opera buffa* plot—economical and symmetrical. It is less labyrinthine than *Figaro*, less ramshackle than parts of *Don Giovanni* and employs two pairs of enchanting puppets, a puppet-master and an accomplice, the maid Despina who is also disguised as Dr Mesmer and as the notary. One uses the word 'puppet', and certainly in the initial stages of the wager the young men act out the demanded insincerity. The serenade which the 'Albanians' arrange in the second act is in one sense part of the campaign, and looking at the score we see how efficiently the task is done by the two men—or rather by Mozart. Everything is impeccably there: the soft endearments of the wind-band with clarinets on top, the shapely joint song mainly in thirds, and the taking up of the entreaty by the chorus as the men enchained in garlands advance upon the astonished women. The parody, with its unmistakable echoes of the slow movement of the C minor serenade (K.388), is absolute; there may even be a verbal joke for the *cognoscenti* in da Ponte's first line which makes the men call on the *winds* to second them. Yet the transporting beauty of the music makes of the parody something real, rendering it entirely credible that both pairs shall fall in love with the 'wrong' person. Indeed there is enough love generated on the stage at this moment to embrace a dozen wrong persons. At the first protestations of the 'Albanians' Fiordiligi draws herself up to her full height and compares herself and her faithfulness to a rock unmoved by the tempest. Here again we have the most exact parody of the larger-than-life way such sentiments are offered in *opera seria*—pompous dotted rhythms, huge leaps of compass (in one place amounting to two octaves and a semitone in the course of two bars) and pyrotechnics to stun and shame the doubters.

With our minds we see that this is both funny and engineered. It is funny because incongruous; it would be hard to think of anyone less rock-like than Fiordiligi unless it were her younger sister Dorabella. It is engineered, to make the fall the greater from this height. Yet, as Mozart knew, to bring the house down with *bravura* singing of this kind is task enough for any singer. The notes must ring with whole-hearted conviction. Any attempt to make them sound insincere is not only impracticable but undesirable. For with our emotions we are recognising that side of us that would like to be rock-like in similar circumstances. When Fiordiligi finally capitulates she sings 'Ah non son, non son più forte' ('I have no more strength') to the exact rhythm of Cherubino's first song and of the opening of the great G minor symphony, but the music does not then break off into self-disgust; on the contrary it melts into the purest expression of delight. There is an affectionate personal parody but it is a topical reference: when the two suitors appear to have taken poison in desperation at unrequited love, Despina is introduced by Alfonso as a doctor whose first utterance is a greeting in Latin to the sisters including—a nice touch—mistakes in her memorisation resulting in two non-words, 'bones puelles'. She produces a large magnet ascribed to Mesmer, the famous exponent of 'animal magnetism' in whose garden *Bastien und Bastienne* had long ago been performed. Woodwind trills represent the resuscitation.

Così fan tutte is the final flowering of the *opera buffa*. Beethoven is said to have declared the libretto to be quite unsuitable. But to agree that Beethoven would never have set it is merely to recognise that the nineteenth-century operatic canvases were on the whole painted with broader brushes. In a sense the universality that Wagner sought had already been achieved by Mozart, except that there was virtually no-one able to heed him.

After *Così* there are no more entries in the catalogue till the second of the 'Prussian' Quartets in May. But it is possible that even at this time Mozart was doing preliminary work on *La clemenza di Tito* as a result of his meeting with Guardasoni in Prague. But another possible reason for some inactivity falls like a shadow on one of the begging letters to Puchberg: 'my head is completely bandaged up because of rheumatic pains.' Rheumatic fever is now fairly generally accepted to be the cause of Mozart's death. At this period he was occupied, perhaps with Puchberg's help, in attempting to find a better position at court. Joseph II had died on 20 February, to be succeeded by his brother Leopold II, Grand Duke of Tuscany. There is extant a partial draft of a letter to Archduke Franz, Leopold II's eldest son, asking for his assistance in putting before the new Emperor a request for the post of second Kapellmeister, Salieri being the first, and also suggesting that Mozart could give some lessons for the royal family. Whether the letter was ultimately sent is unknown, but in any case neither objective was gained, although there was indeed a direct petition to the Emperor. In a letter to Puchberg of 17 May there is for the first time a direct reference to circumstances affecting composition, explaining that the grief and worry of being in debt 'has prevented me all this time from finishing my quartets'. Nevertheless the second, in B flat K.589, and the third, in F, K.590, were catalogued in May and June respectively. In the first two movements of K.589 the melodies are as graceful as ever but the texture is sometimes thinner, though whether the economy of notes springs from flagging energy or from a deliberate conviction is an impossible and irrelevant question. On the other hand the minuet and its trio are elaborately worked, whereas the last movement makes up in assiduous contrapuntal work for its brevity. For this movement there is also a sketch of an opening of markedly different character containing one of the most charming tunes that Mozart ever discarded. The last quartet, K.590, in its first two movements at least, strikes a more enigmatic note; small motifs are discussed quietly and in shifting keys to the exclusion for the time being of any melodic interest, creating surprising tensions. Similarly the slow movement is dominated by a persistent rhythm rather than anything overtly melodic, and its withdrawn, mysterious air is emphasised by the long stretches marked *piano*. The last movement uses a Haydnesque theme and an almost excessive display of counterpoint which with a fast speed and teasing cross-rhythms make this parting shot very difficult to realise in convincing performance.

On 23 September Mozart and the violinist Franz Hofer, husband of Constanze's eldest sister Josepha, set out on a journey to Frankfurt-on-Main, timed to be there for the coronation of Leopold II. It was the merest speculation, counting on concerts in crowded and festival circumstances. Salieri was of the entourage; Mozart was an onlooker. The inn at Regensburg treated them angelically, Nuremberg was a 'hateful' town, Würzburg was a beautiful, imposing city. As usual on a journey Mozart's spirits rose as he was able to tell himself and Constanze of the money he would make to clear their debts and then—the joy of working. But at other times he feels cold and empty, but whether absolutely so, or only for lack of Constanze he does not say. In another letter from Frankfurt (3 October) he says that he has decided, on account of the money, to write 'the Adagio for the clock-maker'. The clock-maker was Count Joseph Deym (now calling himself Müller) who owned a museum of wax-works and mechanical toys of which the current centrepiece was a mausoleum in honour of the recently-deceased Austrian hero Fieldmarshal Loudon. By means of a barrel-organ funeral music was to be played. Mozart grudgingly wrote three pieces. 'I compose a bit every day—but I have to break off from time to time with boredom. If it were for a large instrument and would sound like an organ piece it might give me some fun. But as it is the organ consists only of little pipes, too high in pitch and childish for my taste.' Be that as it may, the organ repertoire is enriched by the Adagio-Allegro-Adagio, K.594, with its Handelian centrepiece, the Andante K.616, and the big fantasia, as it is usually called, K.608, which with its exhilarating fugal writing makes it indisputably the finest piece of barrel-organ music in the world.

But as to concerts in Frankfurt, two were planned and only one given—in the Municipal Playhouse on 15 October. It was not well attended, according to the diary of Count Ludwig von Bentheim-Steinfurt. It began at eleven a.m. and the intervals between the pieces were so long that the planned final symphony—or part of a symphony—was not given, it being nearly two p.m. with 'everybody sighing for dinner'. There were two singers, a Madame Schick of Mainz who had sung the soprano solo in Righini's Missa Solemnis at the Coronation itself, and the old Salzburg friend Ceccarelli. The only works which can certainly be identified were the two concertos played by Mozart, the F major K.459 and the latest, in D major, K.537. The orchestra was 'rather weak with five or six violins but otherwise very accurate'. It was in all probability all that could be afforded, for there must have been more players available. As to other recognitions of Mozart there had been a disappointment already. A performance in his honour of *Don Giovanni* by the visiting Mainz theatre company was not given, a piece by Dittersdorf being substituted, though the Böhm company gave *Die Entführung* whilst Mozart was in Frankfurt.

The day after the concert Mozart went by the market-boat down to Mainz nearby, and received a 'meagre' recompense there from a concert at the palace. This was his furthest point from Vienna. His perplexity of mind can be read in a letter to Constanze from Frankfurt dated 8 October:

There is a struggle between my longing to see and embrace you again and my desire to bring home a large amount of money. I have often thought of going *further afield*, but whenever I tried to persuade myself to decide on it, the thought always returned of how bitterly I should regret it if I were to separate myself from my darling wife for *such an uncertain prospect, perhaps to no purpose at all.*

Without money the journey could not be continued; without a journey the money could not be made. Further, how could the money in any case be made, if the world did not apparently care enough for either the piano concertos or the operas? On the inevitable way home there was a last visit to beloved Mannheim, where he found *Figaro* in German in the last stages of preparation for its first performances there. There amongst friends he heard the opera for the last time as far as we know. At Munich he played at the Elector Karl Theodor's court at a concert in honour of King Ferdinand IV of Naples and Sicily. When he arrived back in Vienna it was to his last lodging in the Rauhensteingasse whither the family had moved in his absence.

The last major work of the year was the String Quintet in D, K.593. When Artaria published this work in 1793 he described it as composed 'for a Hungarian Amateur'. The final string quintet, in E flat, K.614, was published with it and the pair were announced in the *Wiener Zeitung* of 18 May 1793 as being the outcome of the very active encouragement of a music-lover. Commentators have suggested that both these references may be to Johann Tost, a violinist who had distinguished himself under Haydn in Prince Nicholas Esterházy's orchestra before leaving the profession, marrying and becoming a prosperous merchant. Haydn did indeed write for him twelve string quartets, those with opus numbers 54, 55 and 64. The op. 64 set were written in this year, 1790. The connection is hypothetical and it is assumed that the Hungarian Amateur and the active encourager were one and the same person. What does suggest a connection with Tost and Haydn is the resemblance of some motifs in the first movement of Mozart's D major quintet to Haydn's in the famous 'Lark' quartet, the fifth of the op. 64 set. These might be coincidental, albeit there are three of them and the key is the same. But the key of K.614 and of the last of op. 64 is also the same—E flat—and the main themes of both finales, with Haydn's beloved fast-polka rhythm, are astonishingly alike. Since Haydn and Puchberg were sufficiently intimate to be asked privately and exclusively to Mozart's rehearsals it is very plausible that Haydn suggested to Tost that he should do Mozart the good turn of a commission, and that Haydn himself was the 'active encourager'. He would have had time to do this before he left Vienna in mid-December with Salomon for the first of his triumphal visits to London.

The D major quintet is typical of the last works in having subjects which are announced with a disarming simplicity only to be enlivened by the most dexterous and clear contrapuntal writing. The first movement also, and most unusually, reverts to the slow introduction by way of coda. Even the *menuetto* makes conspicuous use of close imitation, and the final *allegro* alternates a drone-like static bass, as in some rustic dance, with vivacious counterpoints tumbling over one another.

The first work of the fateful year 1791 is catalogued on 5 January. It is the last of the piano concertos, in B flat K.595, with which Mozart took his farewell to the world of the public concert, not playing it for his own benefit, but for that of a clarinettist Joseph Bähr. If the previous 'Coronation' concerto showed itself uncertain, even superficial in its aim, this final one has all the richness and variety of themes of the great predecessors, but with a greater tendency to the harmonic inflections of the minor key and if possible a still more exquisite, though not preponderant, use of the wind instruments, here reduced to one flute and a pair each of oboes, bassoons and horns. The quiet opening theme of the strings is twice interrupted by unison fanfares in the wind. (It seems impossible at this stage for a fanfare to *introduce* anything.) But the effect of these interruptions is also to make these opening phrase-lengths irregular. There is an unmistakable re-use of one of the 'Jupiter's phrases in the course of the opening procession of themes, as also of some figuration from the last movement of the great G minor symphony. The main new theme introduced by the piano is in the minor key almost throughout. The subsequent *tutti* appears to be cheerfully confirming the end of the exposition in the expected way, but suddenly gives the effect of disintegration to lead into a perfectly wrought development traversing a wide range of keys in ever-new dialogue between soloist and orchestra, an achievement of unparalleled succinctness and beauty in the concertos. The *larghetto* uses a *romanza*-style tune; it is diversified by beautiful but undemonstrative colouring by the wind. The final *allegro* is again a mixture of child-like jolly tunes with sophisticated scoring. The main subject, or at least its first phrase, features in the very next entry in the catalogue on 14 January, K.596. It is the first of three songs contributed to a collection 'for children and for children's friends' published in the spring.

But although we cannot avoid a sense of nostalgic farewell in hearing the last piano concerto we are sufficiently warned against reading a sense of autumn into its concluding spring-song by the wholly spring-like felicities of the last string quintet, in E flat, K.614, dated 12 April. There exist, probably from this period, sketched beginnings of two other quintets in the same key of E flat, one in triple time and the other in march time. But the eventual beginning of K.614 is a vivacious horn-call on the two violas. We again see what had long been the norm with Haydn, the use throughout the first movement of, in effect, one theme and its derivatives, though with all the variety which counterpoint and the permutations of five instruments afford. The recurrent theme of the *andante* is not unlike that of the slow movement of *Eine kleine Nachtmusik* in its popular gavotte style. But it does not have even the slight storm of the latter, being more concerned with varied reprises. The trio of the minuet is a sophistication of the type of German dance which Mozart supplied by the dozen as Kammermusicus. The last movement has some hurtling counterpoint, but as a final witticism uses the old 'learned' effect of turning the tune upside-down, not however in the course of a display, but with the simplest possible harmonies.

On 16 April and repeated the next day one of the big concerts of the Musicians' Society with nearly 200 taking part was conducted by Salieri. 'A Grand Symphony composed by Herr Mozart' was announced, and it could have been the great G minor. On 26 April Josepha Duschek sang in a concert in Prague in which one of the items was 'A Rondo by Herr Mozart with basset-horn obbligato'. The only surviving piece which fits this description is Vitellia's rondo from *La clemenza di Tito*, which adds to the likelihood that some work had been done on the opera already, though in fact the final libretto as arranged from Metastasio by Caterino Mazzolà, the court poet at Dresden, was only delivered to Mozart in mid-July. But by now, although precise dates are not available, two other commissions must have been under way, Schikaneder's for *Die Zauberflöte* and Count Walsegg zu Stuppach's for a Requiem in memory of his wife—though this latter was following his custom of an anonymous commission, made through an 'unknown, grey messenger', as Mozart described him.

But even now Mozart was able to supply an occasional piece, the Adagio and Rondo, dated 23 May, for glass-harmonica, with flute, oboe, viola and cello, K.617. This was written for a blind virtuoso, Maria Anna (or Marianne) Kirchgessner to play at her Akademie at the Kärtnertor theatre on 19 August. There is nothing routine or patronising about this music, and the modulations in the rondo would tax even a sighted performer. Mozart knew the instrument, it will be remembered, from trying it himself at Dr Mesmer's. On 4 June Constanze (taking Karl with her) went back to Baden for further treatment, leaving her husband to composition in Vienna, alleviated by occasional visits to her. On one such visit another piece of church music was at long last composed, for the priest there had taken an interest in performing such Mozart music as he could. He was rewarded not only with the intimacy of joking letters—'this is the most stupid letter I've written in my life—but it's just right for you'—but also by the exquisite motet 'Ave verum corpus', K.618, to which Mozart gave the direction *'sotto voce'* to both voices and strings. In mid-July Mozart took his wife and child back to Vienna, and on 26 July Constanze gave birth to their sixth child, Franz Xaver Wolfgang, who survived and indeed turned out to be a musician.

By now the authorities in Prague had at last decided to mark the coronation of Leopold II as King of Bohemia by commissioning from Mozart a new opera. The Mozarts, his pupil Süssmayr and Anton Stadler travelled together, arriving in Prague on 28 August. Mazzolà was praised by Mozart for making Metastasio's stately and much-set libretto into a 'true opera'. This consisted of reducing it by about a third and diversifying the baroque succession of solo arias with pieces for ensemble. It may be that Süssmayr wrote the music for the recitatives to save time, but the story that the whole opera was written and rehearsed in eighteen days is unsubstantiated. Indeed modern research into the paper used shows that more was composed in Vienna than in Prague. The arias that remain from Metastasio's libretto show the traditional *da capo* for a repeat of the opening words, but in no single case does Mozart treat them as a *da capo* aria in the strict sense. The traditional shape in baroque times would be to treat the first part of the poem as a complete unit coming to rest in the home key, then supply a contrasting, shorter middle section, then direct the performers, matching the layout of the words, to restart *da capo*, leaving to them such variations as seemed appropriate to an otherwise identical repeat, which consequently was not written out. A procedure like this which necessitates a full-stop in the home key not far short of the half-way point is alien to the sonata style, and consequently to Mozart's. It will be noted that even Elvira's 'Ah fuggi il traditor' is not a *da capo* aria.

When she had heard the first performance on 6 September the Empress was gracious enough to call it 'una porcheria tedesca' ('German hogwash'), and the work had in general a luke-warm reception. This could well have been caused, and accentuated, by there having been a festival performance of *Don Giovanni* only four days before, attended by the Emperor. But if there is a weakness it is not the mere fact that this is an *opera seria*, but rather that time and perhaps energy did not permit a proper appraisal of what befitted aria and what recitative respectively, thus lending a somewhat arbitrary quality to the choice which does not seem always to match the dramatic situation—not, perhaps, that the Bohemians were likely to find much drama in displays of royal moderation announced beforehand in the title. But taken on its own terms the music can be truly powerful, as in Sesto's famous extended air 'Parto, ma tu ben mio' with *concertante* basset-clarinet—or tender, as in a love-duet for soprano and castrato 'Ah perdona' which won such approval as there was. Here the music has the unaffected natural ease of two minor characters who are not at that juncture required to express themselves singly. But what are perhaps the most interesting numbers both involve the chorus. In the finale of the first act the Roman Capitol burns in a

An advertisement from the 'Mausoleum' of Field-marshal Loudon for which Mozart supplied barrel-organ music (see pages 217–8)

LIEDERSAMMLUNG

FÜR

KINDER UND KINDERFREUNDE

AM CLAVIER·

FRÜHLINGSLIEDER.

WIEN,

GEDRUCKT BEY IGNAZ ALBERTI, K. K. PRIV. BUCHDRUCKER. MDCCXCI.

Title-page of the 'Spring' section of a song collection 'for children and friends of children' to which Mozart contributed three songs (K.596–8). One of them, 'Komm', lieber Mai', begins in the same way as the last movement of the last piano concerto

The church at Baden for which Mozart wrote the motet 'Ave verum corpus'. The journeys to and from Vienna would take him through the gate to the left

The Vienna suburb of Wieden, c.1790. The large building in the centre is the so-called Freihaus, in one of whose courtyards was the 'Magic Flute' theatre—the Freihaus-theater or Theatre 'auf der Wieden'

The only known picture of the interior of the
Freihaus-theater: an engraving for publicity,
1791. The scene is from *Der Stein der Weisen*.
The actor-manager Schikaneder wrote this
libretto, and it is very likely that he is the
solitary figure commanding the audience

Below left: An engraving by Ignaz Alberti
forming the frontispiece of the original libretto
of *Die Zauberflöte*

Below right: A costume design for Papageno
from the same source (see page 228)

Some bars from the Introit of the
Requiem, in Mozart's hand

St Stephen's Cathedral, Vienna: an
engraving of 1792. Here Constanze
and Wolfgang were married—
and also Aloysia and Lange. In the
Crucifix Chapel (centre of picture)
Wolfgang's body was blessed

treacherous attempt on Titus's life, and a distant chorus first dissonantly punctuate the sentiments of the principal characters in the foreground, then gradually complement on equal terms their cries of outraged sadness. Their other striking use is in a homage to Tito rendered *sotto voce*, not as a muted sentiment, but to convey amid the jealousies and intrigues of the principals the precious feeling of peace that Titus's reign gives them. The quiet harmonies of clarinets—doubtless Stadler again—and bassoons lend much to this effect of an inward, still happiness evoked again in *Die Zauberflöte*.

So the last journey ended with the Mozarts and Süssmayr returning to Vienna in mid-September. Stadler had stayed behind to give a concert on his own account. *Die Zauberflöte* is entered in the catalogue under July with a list of the cast and the date of the first performance (30 September), leaving only two instrumental pieces, the overture and the march of the priests, to be included, with just two days to spare, on 28 September.

La clemenza di Tito was in every sense a Court opera. *Die Zauberflöte* was a suburban opera. It was to be played in a suburban theatre 'on the Wieden'. It was like all such popular entertainments to be in German with spoken dialogue, and Schikaneder the actor-manager was to guarantee the winning over of the audience by undertaking the principal comic part of Papageno the bird-catcher, the dimensions of which he could make to measure since he was the librettist. The ingredients of the plot were to tickle the latest fancy: fairy magic, transformation-scenes, a whole menagerie of animals, a captive princess in danger, a threat of a fate worse than death, a handsome rescuer and above all, in the tradition of the *commedia dell'arte*, a comedian to be the human go-between linking the audience with these fantasies. The opera contained all these, but to them were added Schikaneder's masterstroke, the revelation to the audience of the secret mysteries, affording a spectacle both awesome and stunning, of Freemasonry. Some of these fairy-tale elements are those of a traditional English pantomime. *Die Zauberflöte* is a pantomime which becomes sublime, the sublimity being brought about by Mozart. But its effect is made by the journey from the one level to the other, for that indeed is its subject-matter—the journey with all its surprises, pleasant, unpleasant and sometimes inexplicable, from the dark enslavement by basic appetites and superstition to the golden freedom of self-mastery and wisdom.

As in *Don Giovanni*, Mozart plunges us into the action with a substantial piece of continuous music which he calls 'Introduction'. The hero Tamino enters pursued by a serpent, having used his last arrow. He cries for help and unheroically faints as three veiled ladies magically

appear with silver wands, slay the serpent, cast admiring glances on
Tamino and vie with each other for the task of remaining to guard him
whilst the others go to tell their mistress of the arrival in her kingdom
of one who could restore her former peace. But they leave together, whilst
Tamino recovers to be encountered by Papageno—the embodiment of
basic but not wicked humanity. His is the most authentic of the pictures
of the *mise-en-scène*, since he is an illustration in the original publication
of the libretto. His entrance-song with the pan-pipes is the epitome of
all such popular songs of the time, with identical verses and the blunt,
simple tune that goes straight—as it must if it is to do its task—to the
affections and memories of the audience. Tamino, given by the returning
ladies the portrait of their queen's lost daughter, Pamina, falls in love
with it. The song is properly an aria, composed in one sweep of music,
but though it establishes Tamino as a serious character it speaks the
simpler musical language of which there are several hints in *La clemenza
di Tito*, enabling him to keep contact with the audience directly but
without sacrificing art. The Queen of the Night is another matter. She
appears, to thunder and a transformation scene which rends the moun-
tains, to sing a recitative starting in the big Italian style, which turns to
the simple sorrowing of a mother lamenting her daughter, but which
reverts to fierce *bravura* reaching other-worldly heights as she bids
Tamino find and rescue Pamina. As this formidable part was taken by
Mozart's sister-in-law Madame Hofer there is no reason to suppose she
could not perform it—else it would have been written otherwise. Apart
from this apparition and this aria we might imagine ourselves witnessing
another romantic rescue-opera like *Die Entführung*, and when we first
see Pamina she is being lustfully menaced by a black man whose very
name, Monostatos, seems to indicate a one-track mind. Then the surprises
begin, and we find that Pamina is being detained by a noble priest
Sarastro whose chariot is drawn by six lions. We may well ask why such
a creature as Monostatos is in his entourage at all. The short, box-office
answer is that Osmin was a tremendous success in *Die Entführung*. The
philosophical answer is that the trial of being with Monostatos is part
of Sarastro's educational apparatus, and that he is also a symbol; he is
black not because his skin is black, but because he is original unregenerate
matter, resistant to even the first step in alchemy which might refine him
from black to gold.

So the second act sees the lovers purified by trials, of silence which
Pamina misinterprets and which Tamino is bound not to explain, and
then ultimately of passing though fire and water to the strains, not of
orchestral imitation of the horrors, but of the magic flute accompanied
by soft wind instruments with trombones and drums. Papageno has been

proved unfitted for such sublimities but he has been given a consolation prize, a Papagena who in true fairy-tale fashion first presents herself to him as an aged crone to test his kindness of heart. Before the final triumph of love and wisdom in the Masonic key of E flat with which the overture began, the music reverts to the C minor of Tamino's first encounter with the serpent—we know thereby who sent the serpent—and the Queen of the Night, the three ladies and Monostatos in unholy and desperate alliance make an attempt on the temple itself, to be thrust back to eternal night without the intervention of human hand. But every sentence of verbal description, even of the music, must increase the impression of an irredeemable gallimaufry. It seems as though every kind of theatre music which Mozart had ever used is present, and the full deployment of choral music as well. But this is not all. The journey to Leipzig also makes its mark in perhaps the most extraordinary musical ingredient of all. Just before Tamino is admitted to the trials he is met by two armed men who warn him but encourage him: if he can overcome the terror of death he will swing himself from earth to heaven. What the orchestra plays is a chorale prelude, no less, with the tune on the wind instruments supporting the armed men delivering it in octaves, whilst the strings surround it in wonderful counterpoints forming between them an incessant march of quavers. The usual words of the tune—as used by Bach, for example—are 'Ach Gott von Himmel sieh' darein' ('O God look down from heaven'). A Lutheran chorale in the temple of Isis and Osiris!

Untold thousands of words have been, and will be, expended over apparent loose ends in the plot, with some writers positing an all-embracing theology whilst others feel obliged to suggest some *volte-face* in the course of its construction. But at the end of the day the music makes all clear and bathes us in conviction. If the opera is about the power of love in its widest sense it is also about the power of music—of Papageno's bells setting the slaves and Monostatos a-dancing and Tamino's flute bringing all sorts of wild beasts to listen. (In this connection the nineteenth-century poet and dramatist Grillparzer tells in his autobiography how his nurse had the unforgettable experience of being an ape at the first performance.) Mozart believed in the message of *Die Zauberflöte*, and what pleased him most was the *silent approval*, as he expressed it to his wife. But the fact of the matter is that we write about it because Mozart wrote the music.

The opera, significantly called by one journal 'the new comedy with machines', rapidly became a success. There must have been some twenty performances in October, for Count Zinzendorf's diary says that on 6 November he attended the 24th performance. 'The music and the designs are pretty, the rest an incredible farce. A huge audience.' We do not know what Mozart received, but it would usually be a once-for-all payment. On 7 October Constanze went to resume her cure at Baden accompanied by her sister Sophie and presumably two-months-old Franz Xaver Wolfgang. Coming home the same evening from *Die Zauberflöte* the bereft Mozart immediately writes to Baden. 'Immediately after you left I played two games of billiards with Herr von Mozart, that chap who wrote the opera now running at Schikaneder's theatre: then I sold my pony for 14 ducats: then I told Joseph [probably the landlord of the neighbouring 'Golden Snake'] to get Primus [one of the waiters] to bring me some black coffee, with which I smoked an excellent pipe of tobacco; and then I orchestrated almost the whole of Stadler's rondo.' This is the last movement of Mozart's final concerto, that for clarinet, K.622. As with the clarinet quintet, the published version shows places where the lesser range of the ordinary clarinet has been accommodated, leaving no real doubt that Stadler's basset-clarinet was the instrument originally envisaged. In the first two movements there is an unmistakable likeness to some of the themes of the sister-work, the slow movement again giving full scope to the *cantabile* of the clarinet, but now from time to time surrounding it with the hymn-like solemnities of *Die Zauberflöte*. The outer movements show their later date not by any loss of freshness in the music, but by the invention of ever-new touches of counterpoint. 'Stadler's rondo' is as charming as any of its dance-like predecessors for piano in the same vein, and gives no hint that there could not be more to come.

Mozart's last completed work was catalogued under 15 November as 'a little Freemason cantata' (K.623). It was performed under his direction to mark the inauguration of a new temple of the 'New-Crowned Hope' lodge. There is a jubilant male-voice chorus in an easily-learnt style. The same conviction as in *Die Zauberflöte* shines through a tenor/bass duet; the shape, rhythm and key of the tenor's phrase for the 'dedication to concord' are a reminder of the self-dedicatory ensemble that precedes the trials. It is not possible to regard the music, and particularly the last few bars of recitative before the duet, as being other than a final statement of Mozart's belief in brotherly love. Two days later he took to his bed.

And so to the Requiem. Franz, Count von Walsegg zu Stuppach was an amateur musician who frequently employed professionals for home music. An innocent diversion of his was secretly to commission works from composers and copy their scores in his own hand, from which copyists would produce the parts for the performers. They had to guess the composer, and some were always courteous enough to suggest the Count. Fifty ducats were advanced, probably in early summer, as half the commission. Work on the score must have proceeded as health, two operas, a concerto and a cantata permitted. What Mozart composed was the whole Introitus (though without writing out the instrumental parts of the Kyrie fugue), and all the vocal parts, the bass and the leading instrumental parts of the 'Dies Irae' sequence up to the eighth bar of its last number, the 'Lacrimosa'. He probably left the 'Lacrimosa' at this point because he wanted to work out an 'Amen' fugue for this number, a sketch of which exists (though not nearly long enough for valid completion). Assuming he was too ill to proceed with this, he would then have turned to the 'Domine Jesu' and 'Hostias' which were in his head, so as to permit him to write out the vocal parts, the bass and a few lines for violin. How much of the remainder of the Requiem is by Mozart, and in what sense, is a question likely to remain unanswered. When her husband died Constanze, fearful of having to forgo the commission and return the advance, first gave the score to Joseph Eybler to complete. Mozart had in the previous year given him a testimonial for a Kapellmeister's post, and he was an assiduous attender during the final illness. Addressing himself to the completion of the orchestration of the 'Dies Irae' sequence Eybler produced respectable and acceptable work, filling in Mozart's empty staves, as far as 'Confutatis'; but then he gave up the task. He might indeed have been pressed for time, but it is significant that he gave up at the point where he would have to face the task of actual composing—the completion of the 'Lacrimosa' after Mozart's tremendous opening. There exist two bars of tune in his hand after 'homo reus'. Eybler turned out to be a successful and respected composer, but not capable of thinking Mozartean thoughts.

The work was then completed by the man who should have had it in the first place, Süssmayr. He was not only a pupil but a family friend. He had helped Mozart with the last two operas, doing such tasks as preparing a rehearsal score for *Die Zauberflöte* at Baden whilst looking after Constanze for Mozart. They called him, amongst other things, 'Snai', and a typical P.S. runs 'I send Süssmayr a few good *nose-pulls* and a proper *hair-yank*.' Perhaps a word or an action out of place with the overwrought widow delayed the obvious choice. The open question is how far Süssmayr knew Mozart's intentions. The Abbé Maximilian Stadler was called in by the widow to put Mozart's manuscripts into order. Writing 35 years after the death in his 'Defence of the Authenticity of Mozart's Requiem' (Vienna, 1826) he makes two important statements: 'The widow told me that there were some few leaves of music found on Mozart's writing-desk after his death which she had given to Herr Süssmayr. She did not know what they contained, nor what use Süssmayr made of them.' '. . . and Süssmayr did not have much more to do [in the completion] than most composers leave to their copyists.'

There seems no reason at all to doubt the statement of Constanze's sister Sophie Haibel, though not written till 1825 as a contribution to Nissen's biography: 'Sissmaier was there at M's bedside, and the famous Requiem lay on the bed-cover, and Mozart was explaining to him how he ought to finish it after his death.'

The authenticity of the completion is thus likely to remain for ever a matter of subjective conviction. For what it is worth, the present writer has come to regard the Benedictus and the Agnus Dei as being somewhere very near the truth.

The Introitus begins with the Masonic sound of basset-horns as the uppermost wind instruments, with their alto sound substituting for the treble, so to speak. Sober and dignified as their mourning may be, the violins add sighing palpitations of an increasingly urgent nature, as though the prayer for perpetual light has little hope of being answered. The plainsong *Tonus peregrinus* is led out by the soprano soloist with smoother lines of accompaniment, but as the chorus takes over the chant for 'unto Thee shall all flesh come' the accompaniment is more jagged still. The Kyrie fugue takes an archaic formula as the leading one of its twin subjects, but the music loses its Handelian flavour as it sweeps to a passionate chromatic climax. The 'Dies Irae' chorus continues at a frightening intensity, held for a moment at the trombone solo of 'Tuba mirum' before the soloists in succession turn the music from cosmic wrath to human pleading. So the alternations continue with the beautiful counterpoint of 'Recordare' being surrounded with the smell of sulphur. The end of 'Confutatis' contains truly unearthly harmonies as the soul's prayer sinks lower and lower, again with a palpitating accompaniment which seems to offer no hope. The 'Lacrimosa' in its eighth bar contains the last notes that Mozart ever wrote—a climatic cry on 'Homo reus' ('guilty man').

The terror-struck music, compared with the noble stoicism of the Masonic Funeral Music, seems to bespeak a state of mind quite out of the ordinary, which somehow accords with the notion (historically suspect though it may be) that Mozart had persuaded himself that he had been commissioned to write the Requiem for his own death.

Swelling limbs, high fever, paralysing pains in the joints, and severe headaches were the symptoms, treated by Dr Closset with cold compresses and unremitting bleeding. On 3 December he seemed to rally somewhat, and the next afternoon three friends helped him sing parts of the Requiem—Mozart the alto.

But just before one in the morning of Monday 5 December he died.

Post-Mortem

Much sentimentality and recrimination have been expended on Mozart's death and burial. Carl Bär in *Mozart: Krankheit—Tod—Begräbnis* (Salzburg, 1972) sets most of this to rest. After looking at such medical evidence as there is he feels that the only tenable description of the last illness is 'rheumatic fever'. Even the most eminent doctors of the time—and Dr Closset and Dr Sallaba who was called in for consultation can be reckoned among them—knew nothing of heart attacks, nor that an onset of rheumatic fever in childhood could weaken the heart. If anything were likely to kill a patient through overworking a heart it would be the practice of bleeding, which took out a dismaying proportion of the total.

If however the supposition previously made by some others that the cause of death was uraemia following a lengthy spell of kidney disease could be upheld it might make for an easier explanation of what a layman would call hallucinations, and might go further to explain the intermittently abnormal state of mind shown over the Requiem.

As to the burial the strict sanitary laws insisted on 'twice 24 hours' as being the minimum time between death and burial, there being a very real fear of burial alive. Thus a burial on 6 December which was a fine day would be at any rate illegal, and it is likely that it took place on 7 December. The 7th became a very wet windy day, as claimed by eye-witnesses, as evening drew on—and six p.m. was the earliest permitted hour for the bodies to be taken from the city to the cemeteries outside. A third-class funeral (not a pauper's funeral) was what the great majority of citizens had at that time. As for the 'common grave', the putting of bodies five or six at a time in the graves was the specified practice, space being at a premium. There were exceptions; for a Gluck there could be individual treatment. But who in Vienna had in 1791 any inkling that Mozart was in his class?

Main Sources

The Introduction explains why this source list is short. Pride of place must go to the monumental collection, not only of letters from and to the Mozarts, but of enormously detailed notes upon them, whose title is *Mozart: Briefe und Aufzeichnungen*, editors Wilhelm A. Bauer, Otto Erich Deutsch and Joseph Heinz Eibl, seven volumes (Bärenreiter, Kassel, 1962–75). The standard though incomplete collection of letters in English translation is Emily Anderson (with Cecil B. Oldman), *The Letters of Mozart and His Family* (London, 1938) in three volumes, with a second edition (Macmillan, London; St Martins Press, New York, 1966) in two volumes.

The non-letters documents, with a wealth of notes on them, are edited by Otto Erich Deutsch in *Mozart: Die Dokumente seines Lebens* (Neue Mozart-Ausgabe X/34, Bärenreiter, Kassel, 1961) of which the English edition is *Mozart: a documentary biography*, translated by Eric Blom, Peter Branscombe and Jeremy Noble (A. & C. Black, London; Collier Macmillan, New York, 1964).

The name of Deutsch occurs yet again as editor of the most complete collection of pictures relative to Mozart's life, on which the initial work was done by Maximilian Zenger, *Mozart und seine Welt in zeitgenössichen Bildern* (Neue Mozart-Ausgabe X/32, Bärenreiter, Kassel, 1961).

The current edition of Köchel's *Chronologisch-thematisches Verzeichnis ...* is the sixth, edited by Franz Giegling, Alexander Weinmann and Gerd Sievers (Breitkopf and Härtel, Wiesbaden, 1964).

A very useful résumé of the 1973 state of Mozart studies is in the 100th volume of Proceedings of the Royal Musical Association, by a notable Mozartean, Alec Hyatt King: *Some Aspects of Recent Mozart Research*, which pays tribute to, and gives references for, the remarkable recent studies of Wolfgang Plath, without which it would be folly to attempt attributions as between Leopold and Wolfgang.

Most, though not all, of the music has now (1979) appeared in Bärenreiter's Neue Mozart-Ausgabe (Kassel, 1955 ff.), whose prefaces and Kritische Berichte are a mine of information, historical and practical.

Although some of its battles may now be said to have been won, Edward Dent's *Mozart's Operas: a critical study* (3rd (current) edition, Oxford University

Press, London and New York, 1955) has left so obvious a mark on this book that it would be ungrateful and disingenuous not to single it out.

The *Mozart-Jahrbuch*, under the aegis of the Mozarteum at Salzburg, has since 1950 been an ever-flowing fountain-head.

Wolfgang Plath's major contributions in the handwriting field are both in the *Mozart-Jahrbuch* under the title 'Beiträge zur Mozart-Autographie'. The first part, in *MJ* 1960/61, pp. 82 f., is mainly concerned with the handwriting of Leopold and the consequences of its recognition. The second, in *MJ* 1976/77, pp. 131 f., became available just in time for this book to take account of the chronology for the decade 1770–80 based on Plath's very detailed and convincing analysis of the changes down the years in Wolfgang's own musical handwriting. This involved the reappraisal of the dates of literally dozens of works, perhaps the most notable being some of the piano sonatas previously reckoned as Parisian.

Notes on Sources by Chapters

Chapters 1 and 2

Volume IX/2 of the series *Denkmäler der Tonkunst in Bayern* contains a selection of Leopold's music sacred and secular. Its introduction, by Max Seiffert (Berlin, 1909) contains invaluable lists. First the complete Salzburg 'Kirchen- und Hofkalender' for 1757. Second, names, numbers and categories of the Salzburg musical establishment in the period 1743–86, including Leopold's perceptive and laconic comments on some of them. Third, a thematic catalogue of Leopold's works.

The artistic works of Leopold's forebears are described and in part illustrated in Adolf Layer, *Die Augsburger Künstlerfamilie Mozart* (Augsburg, 1970), and to Layer we also owe information on Leopold's upbringing, in *Eine Jugend in Augsburg. Leopold Mozart 1719–1737* (Augsburg, 1975).

The series *Denkmäler der Tonkunst in Österreich* contains in Volume LV Eberlin's oratorio *Der blutschwitzende Jesus* together with extracts from his school-drama *Sigismundus*, and more Eberlin appears in Volume LXXX which also shows the work of three other Salzburg church composers, K. Biber, Biechteler and Adlgasser.

An English edition of Leopold's *Violinschule* is *A Treatise on the Fundamental Principles of Violin Playing*, translated by Editha Knocker (2nd ed. Oxford University Press, London and New York, 1951).

Chapter 3

A standard work in English is C.S. Terry, *J.C. Bach* (Oxford University Press, London and New York, 1929), which also includes pictures of Vauxhall Gardens.

A thoroughgoing description of Bach's symphonic style with a good deal of musical illustration is in Fritz Tutenberg, *Die Sinfonik Johann Christian Bachs* (Wolfenbüttel, 1928). For details of the family's dealings with Frankfurt see A.R. Mohr, *Das Frankfurter Mozart-Buch* (Frankfurt on Main, 1968). The London stay is detailed in Pohl, *Mozart in London* (Vienna, 1867).

Chapter 4

Acknowledgement is made to the library of King's College, Cambridge for a photostat of the first movement of Raupach's Sonata in B flat, op. 1, no. 1, whereby a first-hand judgement could be made of its reworking in the pasticcio piano concerto K.39.

Leopold's *Litaniae de venerabili altaris Sacramento* is published in the Neue Mozart-Ausgabe Series X/28, Abteiling 3-5/1.

For an ampler technical critique of Wolfgang's Bologna test-piece 'Quaerite primum', K.86, see the very sympathetic but acute remarks of Hellmut Feder-hofer in his edition of the work for the NMA (Series 1, Werkgruppe 3). It is to Federhofer that we must turn on questions of authenticity in some of the church works; see his article in *MJ* 1958, pp. 97 f.: 'Probleme der Echtheits-bestimmung der kleineren kirchenmusikalischen Werke W.A. Mozarts' (continuation in *MJ* 1960/61, pp. 43 f.).

Chapter 5

Relevant beyond the bounds of this chapter is Nathan Broder, 'Mozart and the Clavier' in *Musical Quarterly* Volume XXVII, Number 4 (October 1941), pp. 422 f. More on the Mesmers in O.E. Deutsch, 'Die Mesmers und die Mozarts', in *MJ* 1954, pp. 54 f.

Chapter 6

There is an interesting symphony in B flat by Cannabich in *Denkmäler der Tonkunst in Bayern*, Volume VIII/2, and Holzbauer's opera *Günther von Schwarzburg* occupies Volumes VIII and IX of *Denkmäler deutscher Tonkunst*. Many details of the musical scene in Paris are to be found in Barry S. Brook, *La Symphonie française de la seconde moitié du XVIIIe siècle*, three volumes, but see especially Volume I (Paris, 1962).

Chapter 7

For more on *Idomeneo* see Daniel Heartz, 'The Genesis of Mozart's *Idomeneo*' in *MJ* 1967, pp. 150 f. For a comprehensive essay on the 13-instrument serenade see D.N. Leeson and D. Whitwell in *MJ* 1976/77 pp. 97 f.

Chapters 8, 9 and 10

The Vienna which became Wolfgang's home is described, as a political milieu as well as a city, in E. Wangermann, *The Austrian Achievement 1700–1800*

(Thames & Hudson, London; Harcourt Brace, New York, 1973). Other helpful general reading—since a general bibliography must here be out of the question—will be found in the seventh volume of the *New Oxford History of Music* entitled *The Age of Enlightenment 1745 to 1790*, edited by Egon Wellesz and Frederick Sternfeld (second edition, London and New York, 1974) containing chapters by specialists on individual genres. Illumination on many and varied works (but perhaps especially on the C major piano concerto K.503 and on *Don Giovanni*) comes from Charles Rosen's renowned book *The Classical Style, Haydn, Mozart, Beethoven* (Faber & Faber, London; Viking Press, New York, 1971).

Chapter 11

An interesting and well-argued view of *The Magic Flute* as an integrated plot involving no basic change of direction is advanced by Dorothy Koenigsberger in 'A New Metaphor for Mozart's *Magic Flute*', *European Studies Review*, Volume V, Number 3, July 1975, pp. 229 f.

My surmises as to why Constanze did not immediately entrust Süssmayr with the completion of the Requiem will seem pale indeed before the suggestion made in *MJ* 1976/77 by Dieter Schickling that Süssmayr might be—amongst other things—the father of Franz Xaver Wolfgang Mozart. The article is 'Einige ungeklärte Fragen zur Geschichte der Requiem-Vollendung', pp. 265 f. But it is immediately followed by a robust rejoinder from the man mainly responsible for many currently-accepted facts of Mozartiana, Joseph Heinz Eibl: 'Süssmayr und Constanze', pp. 277 f.

Index of Names

This index excludes references to Wolfgang, his father (except his works), his mother, sister, wife and children, Salzburg and Vienna.

Index of Mozart's works mentioned in this book

*denotes a work partly or wholly in Leopold's hand, or in which there are grounds for presuming his participation.

Index of Mozart's works mentioned in this book